C000205339

The Forgotten Battle of 1066

FULFORD

The Forgotten Battle
of
1066
FULFORD

CHARLES JONES

TEMPUS

This book is dedicated to my son Will Jones who has had to put up with so much. Thank you.

First published 2006

Tempus Publishing Limited
The Mill, Brimscombe Port,
Stroud, Gloucestershire, GL5 2QG
www.tempus-publishing.com

British Library Cataloguing in Publication Data.
A catalogue record for this book is available from the British Library.

ISBN 0 7524 3810 7

Typesetting and origination by Tempus Publishing Limited
Printed in Great Britain

Contents

Foreword

The ongoing investigative work at the muddy ford, south of York, now enables a detailed discussion of the events of 20 September 1066 at Fulford. This book draws together the evidence, written, physical and deducible, of the events leading to the first of three battles in the autumn of 1066.

It is remarkable how many ancient documents report the events of eleventh-century England. This book rests on the pillars of recent scholarship, which has identified, compared and reported the many sources covering these events. These works are identified along with a discussion of the treatments of source material later. The book would have been impossible without them.

This work tries to explain what led to this first battle of 1066, why it took place at Fulford, what actually happened on the battlefield and what were the consequences. The possibility that there was a greater strategic plan behind the invasions of 1066 is also explored, together with the effect that military overstretch had on Anglo-Saxon England.

Battles do not happen in a political, dynastic, economic or social vacuum. This book therefore delves into the period's dynastic complexities, not just to understand the pragmatic politics that emerged during the generation preceding these events but to provide the context and motivations for the curtain-raiser of 1066. This is a magnificent human drama.

I have attempted to tell a remarkable story of some impressive people. As fiction, an editor would demand that this plot was simplified and made more credible. Hollywood could not cope with such a cast of characters or unlikely sequence of events.

Two young warriors, Edwin and Morcar, grandsons of the remarkable Lady Godiva, faced not only the greatest warrior of the age but also his ally, Earl Tostig. Tostig was the brother of the recently selected, one could almost say elected, King Harold II of England. Tostig had been ousted in a coup the year before by those he was now facing at Fulford.

Tostig's plots and plans posed strategic problems for England. His marriage had made William of Normandy his kin. His opponents, Edwin and Morcar, were also his brothers-in-law and, when their sister bore twins to King Harold, were uncles to an heir to the throne of England. Sadly, this is not Hollywood and there is an unhappy ending for all these good people. I do, however, try to end on a happy note in the closing words of the book.

I am very grateful to the many friends in York who have supported me in this enterprise and encouraged me to write this book. Special thanks go to Val Parker, who has not only got her hands dirty exploring the battle site but has undertaken the editorial work for the book.

I encourage readers to look at the short section explaining how the literary sources have been used and reconciled with the available physical evidence. The battlefield is like a thousand-year-old crime-scene investigation; I attempt to explain how the gaps and inevitable conflicts in evidence have been handled.

It is unclear why so little attention has hitherto been paid to this important battle of 1066. I hope this book will begin to redress this neglect.

Charles Jones
Oxford 2005

Prelude to the
Events of 1066

As Harold Godwinson, King Harold II of England for almost 250 days, stood on the shores of the Isle of Wight in early September 1066 he might have felt a sense of accomplishment. He could hardly have expected to find himself in his exalted, and now seemingly secure, position.

Harold was the second son of a great warlord, Godwin. Like his father, he was accustomed to serving kings rather than wearing the crown. His father's political skills enabled the family to survive the rule of six kings of England. This feat was remarkable because four of the six accessions had been disputed. Choosing the wrong side had proved disastrous the lives and fortunes of much of the old Anglo-Saxon nobility during the closing decades of the first millennium.

The twenty-four-year reign of Edward, which ended as 1066 dawned, had seen many crises resolved peacefully. One confrontation had seen Harold, along with the entire Godwin family, banished abroad. The restoration of Earl Godwin's fortunes after barely a year in exile demonstrated a mastery of the power politics that had kept the borders secure and the country free from civil strife for over a generation.

This was a time of change. England, like its continental neighbours, was beginning to act as a nation. In the surrounding lands, warring factions were being forged into nations. The strife in the Nordic lands had produced what we might now interpret as a sense of national identity. The territories of Norway, Sweden and Denmark were being defined.

Further south, the unity provided by Charlemagne at the start of the ninth century had proved elusive, but the nascent state of France can be traced back to his military and intellectual domination of western Europe. The great dream of a new Roman Empire, under the spiritual guidance of the Church of Rome and the military protection of the German emperor, would last for many centuries.

In England the warlords and an independent clergy had developed a way of talking rather than fighting. Although Harold had no royal blood, he was the choice of powerful men to lead their land. A strong king was the best guarantee of peace at home and abroad. The only candidate from the ancient bloodline of King Alfred was thirteen-year-old Edgar, who remained under the protection of Harold's elder sister, the widowed queen, Edith.

The rise to pre-eminence of Wessex within the territory we now call England began with the departure of the Romans during the fifth century. We can only speculate about the transformation of the Celtic societies during the succeeding centuries. The story resumes during the seventh century when lowland Britain was occupied by what we call the Anglo-Saxons, migrants from the Germanic tribes. They arrived as hired protectors but soon settled and integrated.

Warfare was endemic among the modest kingdoms where warrior-chiefs strove to extend or defend their territory. By the start of the ninth century, we can define four regional kingdoms to which the local leaders were subject. The names attached to these southern kingdoms suggest an ethnic basis for these areas. East Anglia was the smallest, named after the East Angles, and Wessex was the western Saxon lands. The limit of Anglo-Saxon territory is defined in the name Mercia, which meant boundary, while the area north of the river Humber was Northumbria. The rivers Humber and Mersey (Mercia) divided the land.

One unifying factor among these territories was their use of the Germanic tongue, which we call Old English. It did not completely replace Celtic, which remained in use in areas where the population had been driven to margins, such as Cornwall. Although the accepted story relates that the monk Augustine brought Christianity to the island, in fact it had been arriving with travellers, brides, monks and hermits from the time of the Romans. Some of these missionaries were recorded by the monk Bede in his *Historia Ecclesiastica Gentis Anglorum*.

The extent to which the stable social structure had evolved from the Celtic customs has yet to be explored. But the Anglo-Saxon overlords also came from a Celtic culture and took responsibility for the welfare of their people, and this was recognised as their supreme duty among the Celts.

Stability brought prosperity and prosperity attracted predators. English coins were currency on the European trade routes. The choice of monasteries as soft targets to plunder ensured that the early raids were recorded and probably exaggerated in the surviving literature. England, Ireland and Francia were all targets for the seamen from Denmark.

First the Vikings raided. Then these raids turned into expeditions. Sixty years after the first recorded attack, the Norsemen had settled. The rulers of Northumbria and East Anglia were defeated and Mercia submitted. Only Wessex held out against the expanding Danelaw. This was the time of Alfred.

When King Alfred died in 899, his territory of Wessex was established as the only area to survive Norse conquest. Alfred's children – the remarkable Ethelflaed, Lady of the Mercians, and Edward – founded a dynasty that would last until the accession of Harold in 1066. It would take two generations for the rulers of Wessex to bring the land we recognise as England under their control. Fortified strong points and a defensive army plus a naval levy restored some stability to the country. However, control did not bring peace to England.

Alfred had come to appreciate the benefit of laws and administration during his time as a monk. At intervals, set initially at six years, silver pennies were collected and re-minted by licensed moneyers. A stable currency was essential for trade and provided a way to tax the land and enrich the king. He began the recording of property upon which the Domesday survey would build.

This extension of control did not go unchallenged. In 937, Olaf, the king from Dublin, Constantine, King of the Scots and Owen, King of Strathclyde allied against King Athelstan. The decisive victory of the united English at the battle of Brunanburgh can be recognised with hindsight as securing the leadership of the kings from Wessex over the English land.

Civil strife was not over. The exiled Norwegian, Eric 'Bloodaxe', managed to hold York for a few years from 950, and King Sweyn and his son Cnut would impose their Danish rule once again on England as the new millennium dawned. But after Cnut, Wessex once again provided the royal line in England.

The events of 1066 would soon prove that the era of military legitimacy was not yet at an end, even though King Edward did not have his own army. Disputes that could have led on a number of occasions during Edward's long reign to a coup or civil war had been avoided. The rules of national governance were still ill-defined, but resolving disputes without bloodshed had preserved the Godwinson family.

Harold, like his father Earl Godwin, had recognised that government in England was changing. The complex business of politics had served both well. Harold's actions in 1065 when he allowed his brother, Tostig, to be exiled had in effect emancipated the north of the kingdom and suggested that the dominance of Wessex was about to evolve into a united kingdom.

The turmoil of the year 1066 had so far been limited to the travels and coastal raids of Tostig, but these had stopped in the late summer. Harold could well understand the grievance his younger brother harboured. But the politics of peace had its victims and Tostig had been a loser on this occasion.

Every career had its setbacks, and such belligerent posturing was an accepted prelude to comebacks. The Godwinson family and the earl of Mercia had both been exiled but both were restored to their fortunes within the year. Harold had campaigned with Tostig just three years before in Wales so he knew to respect his brother's military judgement. Their attempt at a sophisticated pincer movement had not worked, partly because Tostig had not mastered the new techniques of mounted warfare. The recent silence from his exiled brother justified a feeling of unease, but it was harvest time.

From traders, and other agents abroad, Harold knew in some detail about the preparations of William and his invasion plans from Normandy. And news of the six-month preparations for summoning the Norwegian fleet would also have been spread from the Norse lands by summer traders. Continental communications were good, with trips to Rome on most nobles' itineraries.

Dared King Harold hope that these threats would now pass, just as others had passed before here in England?

I

The England of King Harold Godwinson

As King Harold II prepared to dismiss the army that had loyally stayed beyond their allotted time, he recognised that he was the leader of a land that was enjoying the benefits of unity. The young earls who held the great northern lands of Mercia and Northumbria stood ready to confront the expected northern attack. His recent marriage to the sister of these two brother-earls provided a bond of kinship that was recognised as a guarantee of unity.

The military force King Harold had summoned, using the ancient system of fyrd, had stayed on the Isle of Wight beyond its obligation. We believe that the period of service with the fyrd lasted two months, and men would have arrived with the necessary coin or provisions to supply their needs. Maintaining an army on an island must have imposed some logistics problems. The story that the army had run out of provisions is not altogether credible, however, as soldiers are very resourceful at finding food.

Harold's army had gathered no later than July. This was still the 'hungry-gap' when winter stocks of food were running low and the fields held the promise of future food but there was surprisingly little to be gathered during the summer. The crops planted in spring, and tended during the early summer, would be growing to fruition ready for harvesting in the autumn. It was nearly time to gather and celebrate the harvest. The ordinary men of the levy could return to their homes, where their able bodies would be welcomed as the work to gather the harvest went on.

The gamble that Harold was about to take was to try to guess the English weather and also predict the mind of his adversary, Duke William. William had not sailed from Normandy – although his fleet had been blessed by the papal representative it had sat ready for over a month. Chroniclers would later record that the failure of the prevailing westerly winds had kept William's fleet in port throughout July and August and into September. This is hard to credit, as August is the month chosen for the great sailing festival in this part of the Channel at Cowes. Perhaps William was extremely unlucky. But he might have been playing a waiting game.

If William knew the time that the fyrd had assembled, he could have worked out when they would disperse. It made a great deal of sense to wait. There are also some tantalising clues that Harold's 'navy' was also picketing the crossing. A heavily laden invasion fleet would be no match for English warships. The evidence that such a clash did indeed take place is discussed later.

Just as Norman sources record the capture, and release, of English spies, so William must have been aware of the trap that the English had prepared for the invaders. The English army was assembled, with their ships, on the Isle of Wight, so they could have confronted William's army within a day of landing. If that happened, there would be no time for the invaders to construct the bailey they had brought with them to maintain a foothold. William chose to wait.

Harold's adversary had certainly kept him guessing in this game of brinkmanship. Persuading the English army to hang on until the omens of autumnal weather were manifest put all the pressure on the waiting William, who had to keep his coalition together. This was a clever game being played by two experts.

Dispersing was the risk that King Harold had to take. There was no custom or law of war that prevented an invasion sailing in the autumn, but it was unusual. The winds in September become less reliable and would deteriorate through the winter. Harold had made the Channel crossing many times. He had also led at least three seaborne expeditions, so understood this element of warfare. In Scandinavia during this era, sea-battles were almost as common as clashes on land. Harold probably recognised that the conditions would eventually be right for William's fleet to cross. Perhaps he felt he had done enough to force William to put his invasion on hold for a year.

There is doubtless some substance in the story that rations were low, but an army can always find food. One cannot rule out the possibility that King Harold hoped to tempt William out of his haven for a battle at sea by so publicly releasing his army, using low rations as the ruse. These were sophisticated strategists. Aware of the risk he was taking, Harold might also have ordered another army to muster. The summons could have gone into the shires with the dispersing fyrd. As events would show, King Harold was right to be confident that several thousand fresh soldiers could be summoned. He would need two more armies within weeks.

So withdrawing from the Isle of Wight was a gamble for Harold. None of the chronicles suggests that Duke William was playing a waiting game, but subsequent events strongly suggest that his month-long delay was strategic. King Harold's troops were conveyed back to the mainland starting on 8 September. Having deposited the army, the English fleet apparently did not set sail until 12 September. This delay is not explained. 12 September is the day William's fleet left the mouth of the river Dives heading for England.

A few days later Harold heard the news he had hoped for. William's fleet had been caught at sea and destroyed. The destruction was started by the English navy and completed by a great storm. The storm had scattered both fleets and the reports reaching England must have been confused and, it would transpire, exaggerated.

Harold would have been elated. He was spared the knowledge of the events that would unfold during the next five weeks. Three great battles would be fought, with each protagonist winning just one of these great clashes. The final victory would not be his and the land that he had ruled since January would not follow the route he now anticipated. Instead it would follow a path dictated by the person he had prepared this southern army to meet, William of Normandy.

PATH TO LEADERSHIP

The narrative of the events that promoted Harold to the throne of England in 1066 is complex but important, as they provoked the various invasions of 1066. The challenge to Harold's legitimacy was central to the claims made by William when mustering support for

his invasion from Normandy, and William's defamations have sur-
vived remarkably unchallenged during the intervening millennium.
The challenge from the north, which would lead to the battle at
Fulford, was just as complex.

King Harold's path to the throne was unique. No commoner in
the preceding centuries had assumed the throne of England. The
very special circumstances that brought about Harold's accession are
rooted in the tribal traditions of the Anglo-Saxons. Tacitus, writing
during the first century in his book *Germania,* recorded the details of
the barbarian tribes that were threatening the European dominance
of the Roman Empire. He sets out how the leaders were chosen:

> They choose their kings for their noble birth, their leaders for their
> valour. The power even of the kings is not absolute or arbitrary. As for
> the leaders, it is their example rather than their authority that wins
> them special admiration – for their energy, their distinction, or their
> presence in the van of fight... Chiefs are courted by embassies and
> complimented by gifts, and they often virtually decide wars by the
> mere weight of their reputation.

The royal line, stretching back to the time of Alfred, had produced
nine kings. There were some young candidates who were genetically
qualified for kingship, although their numbers were diminishing. For
example, Count Walter and his wife died in mysterious circumstances
while in Norman custody. Walter of Mantes, the Count of Maine, was
a sixth-generation descendant of Alfred. The late King Edward's queen,
Edith, had been nurturing another leading survivor of the bloodline
of Alfred, the son of Edward the Exile, who was about thirteen in
1066 but a strong future candidate for the throne of England.

England's succession had been achieved by selecting suitable kings
from among those qualified by birth. But events can be an unkind
critic of fixed formats, and the chosen one did not always deliver.
The accession of the boy king, Ethelred, who reigned for almost
forty years, would expose the weakness of the heredity principle,
especially when a degree of 'selection' was invoked by his murder-
ous mother.

The respect and legitimacy noted by Tacitus had temporarily been
lost by the kings of England. The direct result was several Danish
invasions plus factional fighting, which produced two generations of

instability during the long reign of Ethelred. It was the influence of the powerful earls promoted by the Danish King Cnut, and especially Earl Godwin of Wessex, that restored stability under the benign reign of King Edward the Confessor.

The old English word *cyning* means 'of the kin'. King Edward had been married to Harold's sister. Harold's mother had King Cnut as a brother-in-law. The powerful people in England were persuaded that Harold was indeed kin and some royalty had 'rubbed off' on the family. Apart from Edgar, who was under the Godwinson family protection, there were no kingly candidates. The lack of royal blood was a relatively small problem when selecting a credible leader following Edward's death.

Harold could certainly fulfil most of the other criteria listed by Tacitus. He had leadership qualities and had demonstrated his valour not only when fighting but also in his preparedness to confront problems. The pragmatic political institution, the Witan, which had evolved rapidly during the reign of the late King Edward, chose a man of energy and distinction as its new king.

We know little about the operation of the Witenagemot, or Witan, apart from some of its decisions. This prototype House of Lords exercised substantial power. During the reign of Edward it allowed the king to test the support he enjoyed for proposed actions without the risks attached to actually testing it on the battlefield. In 1051 the Witan had sanctioned the exile of the Godwinson family and their restoration the following year.

This was not consensual government, but it gave the powerful factions in the land a meaningful voice. The assembly of nobles would undoubtedly have been vulnerable to political and other pressures. People in power seek to preserve their positions and will form and break expedient alliances. This was an embryonic political forum. The Witan had backed the exile of several earls, so it is evident that they had some power and possibly a degree of independence. Harold was their choice for king.

Harold was the inheritor of a legacy whose faltering development had provided the foundations of a sound national military, administrative and legal system. The accession of Harold might have been the start of representative governance. It is worth examining the events that created these conditions as they offer an explanation of why England fought as a united country in 1066.

THE EVOLUTION OF ENGLAND

The Kingdom of England that Harold would lead in 1066 was forged in the fires of Viking raids of the ninth century. Writing as the raids reached their height, Bede, living on the front line in Jarrow, records the battles between local kings in his moralistic history about the coming of Christianity to England. The habit of tribal warfare in Britain could not match the mobility and leadership shown by the Norse attackers. Alfred was able to do just enough to prevent the complete conquest of Anglo-Saxon England and earned the title 'Great', which makes him unique among English kings. His children, and especially his daughter Ethelflaed, continued his work and recovered the lands lost in the Danelaw, creating an entity where local wars became uncommon, if we trust the records of the chroniclers.

Another powerful woman came to lead the new nation of England after the death of King Edgar in 975. Elfrida, King Edgar's second wife, always claimed special privileges for herself because she had been anointed by the Church as queen of England. She was crowned queen alongside her husband at Bath Abbey on 11 May 973 using the coronation ceremony that survives to this day. Her key demand was that her son Ethelred, rather than Edgar's other son Edward, should succeed his father, who died in July 975. Queen Elfrida was overruled and Edward became king – but not for long.

Edward met a mysterious death at Corfe Castle in Dorset, when visiting the dowager queen Elfrida and his half-brother, Ethelred. There was tension in England, caused partly by famine, but there was known to be a faction of landowners who were set on recovering land they regarded as their own which had been given to the Church, a move which King Edward resisted. Edward's body lay undiscovered for a year. Henry of Huntingdon was clear who was to blame:

> [Edward] was treasonably slain by his own family... it is reported that his stepmother, that is the mother of king Ethelred, stabbed him with a dagger while she was in the act of offering him a cup to drink.

No study exists of quite how popular titles or nicknames attached themselves to the rulers of that era. However, they might be interpreted as representative of the popular voice. The murdered Edward became know as 'the Martyr'. Nobody was punished for this regicide, but Elfrida must be considered a prime suspect.

Elfrida is implicated in the murder of her first husband, Ethelbald, Earl of East Anglia. King Edgar is alleged to have slain the earl with Elfrida's help in order to marry the widow around 967. This allegation is hard to reconcile with Edgar's nickname, which was 'the Peaceful'.

So in 978, Ethelred became king following the murder of his half-brother, Edward. Ethelred was perhaps ten years old, so the effective power was wielded by his mother who acted as regent.

Disastrous results flowed from the promotion of a child to lead the kingdom. The memory of this would have been recalled by the wise men of 1066, who wanted to avoid repeating this mistake and placing another boy on the throne.

The maternal assertiveness of Elfrida did not serve the country well, and in 985, with Ethelred in his early twenties, his mother was 'sent away'. Elfrida now founded a Benedictine Priory at Wherwell in Hampshire to atone for the murder of her stepson and first husband. Whether this was a filial falling-out, a domestic dispute between two queens or perhaps the adult king now preferring to assert himself, we do not know. All are credible. King Ethelred promptly chose new councillors, to judge from those witnessing his charters.

Unfortunately, the new advisers were self-servers. The growing power of the Church and ecclesiastical land were their prime targets. For the Church, the disasters that befell the kingdom of England during King Ethelred's reign were a clear punishment for the attacks on the monastic property. Even the return of the reformed dowager Elfrida to power did not improve matters.

This period of bad governance would open the final chapter in the line of kings that stretched back to Alfred. Ethelred and his overlooked first wife, Aelfgyva, produced eleven children, among them five sons. These sons would find themselves effectively dispossessed when another powerful queen and mother arrived on the scene. Only the second son of this first marriage, Edmund, in his very short reign, would demonstrate the ability to rally the English and confront invaders just as his the great-great-great-grandfather Alfred had done.

A decade of poor weather is blamed for forcing those on the agricultural fringe of northern Europe to resume their raiding and migration. If it was not possible to grow enough food, at least the means of purchasing supplies had to be obtained to sustain the population. The Viking raids in the south began in 990, led by Olaf Trygvasson. As a child, Godwin might have witnessed the raids along the south coast.

This phase of Viking attack has given us the finest surviving description of a battle. It is in the very best tradition of the gallant English loser. When the force of Brythnoth, a leading earl in East Anglia, effectively isolated the invaders, the latter asked if they could come across the causeway and fight 'on a more even place'. The request was granted and the trapped Vikings triumphed after a hard fight.

The battle of Maldon took place in 990. Earl Brythnoth demonstrated the thinking that would lead Earl Morcar to confront a superior force at Fulford in 1066. Just south of modern Maldon, near Blackwater, the raiders had found an island that could only be reached along the causeways that emerged at low tide. In 1066, King Harald of Norway would choose a similar base at Riccall.

Earl Brythnoth could have simply blockaded the Vikings but the invaders could have boarded their longships and rowed away to continue their raiding elsewhere. His mission was to destroy the attackers so the earl would have wanted the Vikings to come to dry land to do battle.

Three generations later at Fulford, Earl Morcar would also have to take the battle to the invaders. In taking his action, Morcar would have been well aware of the events of Maldon that were told in ballads, just one of which has come down to us. The battle was also recorded in an embroidered wall-hanging by Brythnoth's widow, which sadly has not survived.

These Viking raiders wanted money. Danegeld was a national tax imposed to pay this ransom. It raised £36,000 of silver in 1007. In 1012, £48,000 was needed to persuade the attackers to leave. A context for these amounts can be appreciated by examining the values listed in the Domesday surveys. One comparison might be with the value of landholding as measured in terms of their annual agricultural earning potential. In Frank Barlow's book on the Godwins, he assesses the value yielded by Harold Godwinson's landholdings in 1066 as £7,000. The Viking harvest was therefore extremely good. Danegeld was extracting more than the annual product of England so it is fortunate that the Vikings did not return every year.

King Ethelred managed to drive a wedge between the Danes and the victor of Maldon, Olaf Trygvasson from Norway. In 994 Ethelred is reported to have been present when Olaf Trygvasson was baptised, following his conversion on the Isles of Scilly by the local Christian hermit who appeared to foretell the future. In 995 he returned to Norway, where he was recognised as king. King Olaf I began the unification of Norway but leapt to his death from his longship when his army faced annihilation by the combined Norse armies opposed to central government. Sixty years later, a unified Norway would send an army to meet the English at Fulford.

From 1000 the Danes were able to conduct their raiding using the harbours in Normandy for shelter. King Ethelred's response was to marry for a second time. His new bride was Emma, the daughter of Richard I, Count of Normandy, and granddaughter of a Viking raider, Rollo. This Viking enclave in Frankish territory had been traded to buy off the Norse attacks, effectively a piece of Danelaw across the Channel. In a deal that puts the Danegeld being paid by the English king into perspective, the overlord of the Frankish lands had actually ceded the land in exchange for an oath that the raids into Frankish lands by the Norse would stop.

The treaty of Saint Clair-sur-Epte agreed to cede the region of the lower Seine on condition that the incomers were baptised and accepted that they were subjects of the French king. The deal that created Normandy appears to have been successful in achieving its aim of preventing raids deep into French territory along the great rivers of northern France, unlike the payment of a ransom adopted in England.

Emma arrived as Ethelred's second wife in 1002. This political alliance gave King Ethelred the confidence to move against the Danes. Perhaps King Ethelred hoped via this marriage to enlist Viking to oppose Viking or at least deny the use of Normandy as a base for the raiders.

The new queen, Emma, was fortunate in that the powerful dowager queen, Elfrida, died in 1002. Emma replaced both the existing wife and the queen mother, insisting that she too must be anointed by the Church in her role as queen. Emma, as we shall soon see, was another frontline politician. Queen Emma, after a short delay, seems to have performed her motherly duty and provided three children, Edward, Alfred and Godgifu, during the early years of the relationship with Ethelred.

The dowager, Elfrida, cannot be wholly blamed for the title of 'bad counsel' (*Unred*) that was attaching itself to King Ethelred. In the absence of a strong leader, the great magnates began feuding among themselves. Many noble names vanish from the witnesses to royal charters after 1005, which has led Frank Barlow to talk of a 'palace revolution'. The name of the Mercian, Eadric, and his family appears regularly. His nickname was 'Sterona' (the Acquisitor). Analysis of those adding their signatures to surviving royal charters provides some clues as to the people who were the power in the land. Thus Eadric the Acquisitor seems to have achieved pre-eminence in the kingdom as the earl of Mercia. We can speculate about the advancement of Eadric but it might not be unconnected with the changes surrounding the arrival of Queen Emma at the court of King Ethelred.

There is also scope for more speculation about the arrival of Emma and the timing of what we know as the St Bryce's Day massacre of 13 November 1002. Queen Emma is known to have given birth to at least one of her children, Edward, at Islip, just north of Oxford, between 1003 and 1005 (this was not a protracted labour but reflects inconsistencies in ancient record keeping). This suggests that Oxford was the base for the new wife.

Coincidentally perhaps, it was the church of Saint Frideswide, the minster church of Oxford's foundress and on the site now occupied by Christ Church Cathedral, that was burnt down on St Bryce's Day. Many seeking sanctuary inside were killed. It is said that King Sweyn Forkbeard's sister Gunnhilde and her children were among those who are believed to have died. There is no evidence that Danish families in other parts of England suffered during this genocidal outburst.

This extract from the charter for the rebuilding of the church provides a clear insight into the deluded style of governance being practised by King Ethelred:

> For it is fully agreed that to all dwelling in this country it will be
> well known that, since a decree was sent out by me with the counsel
> of my leading men and magnates, to the effect that all the Danes
> who had sprung up in this island, sprouting like cockle amongst the
> wheat, were to be destroyed by a most just extermination, and thus
> this decree was to be put into effect even as far as death, those Danes
> who dwelt in the afore-mentioned town, striving to escape death,

entered this sanctuary of Christ, having broken by force the doors
and bolts, and resolved to make refuge and defense for themselves
therein against the people of the town and the suburbs; but when all
the people in pursuit strove, forced by necessity, to drive them out,
and could not, they set fire to the planks and burnt, as it seems, this
church with its ornaments and its books. Afterwards, with God's aid,
it was renewed by me.

The St Bryce's Day massacre is one of the more infamous events in
England's history. The social and psychological motives that foster
genocide are perhaps better understood today. Weak government,
insecurity, economic decline and high taxation were the ingredients
which conspired to promote the hunt for a scapegoat.

This attempt at ethnic cleansing made matters worse. Early Viking
raids were followed by the more serious incursions from 1009 and
culminated in the invasion by King Sweyn Forkbeard of Denmark,
Cnut's father, in 1013. Previous raids had collected provisions and
loot but this was a raid of conquest. The motive might have been
the perceived weakness of this affluent land but revenge for the St
Bryce's Day massacre of November 1002 was another motive. If
revenge was on Sweyn's menu then it was a dish that was taken when
it was eleven years cold.

The formerly united England was becoming a nation divided.
The ancient division of Danelaw re-emerged, the chronicler at
Peterborough tells us.

> Before the month of August came king Sweyn with his fleet to
> Sandwich. He went very quickly about East Anglia into the Humber's
> mouth, and so upward along the Trent till he came to Gainsborough.
> Earl Uhtred and all Northumbria quickly bowed to him, as did all
> the folk of Lindsey, then the folk of the Five Boroughs.

Sweyn was given the customary hostages. He organised an army
before heading south 'in full force' leaving his ships and the hostages
with his young son Cnut.

After he came over Watling Street, they worked the most evil
that a force might do. They went to Oxford, and the town-dwellers
soon bowed to him, and gave hostages. From there they went to
Winchester, and did the same, then eastward to London.

The Londoners put up some effective resistance and it is possible that king Ethelred was still in the city with his family at that stage. Sweyn initially decided to bypass the city. He 'crossed the Thames at Wallingford on his way to Bath', and stayed there with his troops; ealdorman Aethelmaer came, and the western thanes with him. They all bowed to Sweyn and gave hostages.

In late 1013 a group of notable thanes pledged allegiance to King Sweyn of Denmark at Bath, according to the English chroniclers. The invader was preferable to the king of England. As was the custom, hostages were exchanged between the two factions as a guarantee of good conduct. Several scholars have suggested that Godwin's father and grandfather were among those given as hostages. If that were the case, the young Godwin might also have been a likely candidate as one of the hostages. Fortunately he was not chosen.

London was isolated and finally surrendered at the end of the year after Ethelred had fled to Normandy. The Witan declared Sweyn 'full king' on Christmas Day 1013.

Sweyn died in Gainsborough on 3 February 1014, having ruled England for scarely five weeks. He was succeeded as king of Denmark by his eldest son, Harold II. However, the Danish fleet proclaimed the younger son Cnut king of England. The chronicle talks specifically of the fleet rather than the army. It appears that the eighteen-year-old Cnut did not have an effective army because Sweyn's troops planned to take their dead king home to Denmark. For the moment, England was without a king.

The balance of power swung in favour of their hereditary king and Ethelred was once again king of England. The Witan, as representative of the powers in the land, called on Edmund, the eldest son of King Ethelred, to lead them. It looked like another coup, but Edmund immediately dispatched his younger brother to Normandy, where the royal family had gone into exile the year before.

According to Snorri's history, Edmund was supported in his attempt to retake London by Cnut's old enemy Olaf Trygvasson. The bridge over the Thames was 'so broad that two wagons could pass each other upon it' and had forts at either end. Olaf's men roofed their ships, rowed up to the bridge, and, under a barrage of missiles, 'laid their cables around the piles which supported it, and then rowed off with all the ships as hard as they could down the stream'.

London Bridge came tumbling down. The fort at the south end was taken, and the forces in the north surrendered. Ethelred 'was proclaimed king'. Queen Emma might be the lady who would bring the Norman stonemasons to build London Bridge 'up again', in gratitude to the London citizens, although a proper stone bridge was not started for another century.

Outmanoeuvred by those who had weeks before encouraged the Danish takeover, Cnut felt betrayed. Cnut had the hands, noses and ears of the noble hostages cut off before retreating to Denmark, perhaps to gather a force of his own to invade England.

Back in power, King Ethelred had many scores to settle. His agent was, as usual, Earl Eadric of Mercia. The chroniclers of 1015 record the treacherous murder of Sigeferth and Morcar, two leading men in the Midlands.

In spite of loyally helping to restore his father to the throne, it is clear that Edmund, Ethelred's eldest son at about twenty-two years old, also harboured ambitions. He recognised that simply being the eldest son from the first marriage was not enough. He needed an army. He acted swiftly during 1015. His first act was to get married to Morcar's widow, Ealdgyth. This was far from straightforward, as she was being 'detained at Malmesbury'. Whether Edmund's intentions were romantic or political the language and events of the time fail to inform us.

Ealdgyth had been widowed when Morcar was murdered earlier in the year. There can be little doubt that the murder of her husband, and her own detention, had been ordered by the recently returned King Ethelred, Edmund's father. His agent had doubtless been Earl Eadric.

Ealdgyth was herself kin to many of the noble lines of the north and Edmund was therefore tied by marriage to many of the most powerful families in Northumbria. It was precisely this network which provoked King Ethelred to imprison her. The north was still not under control or governed in a manner that the men of Wessex approved of. There was still too much tribal loyalty and independent action, which to outsiders translated into lawless behaviour. The leading nobleman in Northumbria was now Earl Uthred, who already enjoyed some royal protection as he had recently married for the third time, to one of the daughters of King Ethelred.

Edmund married Ealdgyth and so was now a part of the northern network. Edmund quickly took possession of the estates that had been confiscated by the Crown after the assassination of Ealdgyth's husband and which had not yet been reassigned. He now had the powerbase that came with a substantial landholding. These preemptive actions were vital for Edmund if he was to compete for the crown and win the support of the Witan in the power struggle that would follow the death of his father. Queen Emma would have tried to ensure that Edmund was deprived of any significant force. She did not want him to challenge the offspring of her own union with his father, if one is able to judge from her future pattern of behaviour in protecting and promoting her own children.

This marriage between Edmund and Ealdgyth was therefore an act of treachery and rebellion against the plans of Queen Emma. It also looked like the first step of a coup against his recently restored king and father, Ethelred. No immediate consequences of this potentially explosive action are recorded and events quickly moved on. However, Edmund had definitely promoted himself to Aetheling, throneworthy status. The challenge to Edmund was not domestic but came from the Danes.

With the support of his brother, King Harald of Denmark, Cnut raised an invasion force. Among the army was a large contingent of Polish soldiers. The reason that these soldiers were recruited is interesting. There is some doubt about the identity of the mother of Harald and Cnut. There are some suggestions that she was a Slav, while other suggestions point to her being the daughter of the king of the Poles. Evidently, the brothers made a journey to bring their mother back to Denmark from Poland and such a journey would have provided an opportunity to ask for the use of a Polish force to assist Cnut. Harald still needed his own army to secure Denmark.

Another key ally for Denmark in this renewed invasion was Erik, who had held the territory that would soon become the southern part of Norway. The invasion of England had already diverted resources away from Norway, allowing Olaf, son of Harald Fairhair, to occupy the upland part of Norway. Erik's departure to join Cnut's fleet would allow Olaf to make himself king of Norway for a while and build the foundations for a nation that his half-brother, Harald, would be able to mobilise to invade England half a century later.

The sources have numbered Cnut's fleet between 200 and 1,000 ships. The lowest estimate comes from the earliest source. This suggests an invasion force of at least 8,000 men. The invasion force landed in Wessex during the summer of 1015. This strategic timing would have a profound effect upon the fortunes of a leading man of Wessex, Godwin.

The south might have been chosen for the landing because Cnut's earlier abandonment of the country had alienated the people in the old Danelaw. But Earl Uthred was now son-in-law to King Ethelred and Uthred's subsequent murder by Cnut shows that the bond between the north and the Danes had been ruptured. It is also likely that Cnut would have been made aware that Edmund was in the north raising an army. Since Edmund had provided the rallying point for resistance after the sudden death of King Sweyn, Cnut was wise to expect a hostile reception.

When Cnut landed, he was quickly joined by Earl Eadric the Aquisitor and soon the earls and thanes were once again submitting to him. Cnut and his impressive force of Poles, Norwegians and men of Wessex and Mercia moved through the land, but this time progressing from south to north.

Nowhere in any of these expeditions do we find reports of delays caused by the weather, such as would later be reported by chroniclers of the Norman invasion. Even travelling against the prevailing wind and late in the year, Cnut's substantial fleet was able to cross a wide stretch of water and choose a distant landing place in Wessex. William could certainly have crossed the Channel with his fleet fifty years later if it had been strategically sensible to do so.

1015 was an unusually long campaigning year. Cnut had an expensive army on loan and, with so many from Poland, they were possibly used to much harsher conditions during winter. He therefore continued his campaign to establish his control of England during the winter, heading north around Christmas. Ahead of him, Prince Edmund and the premier earl of Northumbria, Uthred, now Edmund's brother-in-law, had already devastated the lands controlled by Earl Eadric of Mercia.

As was customary, the northern leaders would have released their thanes, allowing each one to take their men back to their homelands before winter. With communications made difficult by the Northumbrian terrain and the limited infrastructure, it would be the spring before they would meet again. The business of getting through the winter months would dominate most ordinary lives. The territory north of the mighty river Humber and across the Pennine hills and into the Cheviot mountains had always provided a significant mountain fortress.

We do not know how Cnut penetrated Northumbria. An approach by land would be difficult because of the time of year plus the limited number of entry points, all of which could be guarded. So it is probable that he arrived by sea. Cnut had outmanoeuvred Uthred.

Uthred would be without an effective army or the possibility of recalling his men from their remote hamlets until the spring. So there would have been little he could do to resist Cnut's army when it appeared after Christmas.

Cnut was able to reach the Northumbrian territory, and 'out of necessity' Earl Uthred accepted the inevitable and prepared to submit to him. We know that Cnut set out at Christmas and the submission did not take place until March, so Cnut's army had been in the north for a month or more. Evidently Cnut was in control and Earl Uthred must have realised he would not be able to muster effective resistance even in the spring. In the context of the events of 1066, the reaction of Uthred offers two important indicators.

First, Uthred did not offer battle. The size of the opposing army is likely to have been superior to anything Uthred could muster. Cnut would have left a significant force in the south but that still provided him with an army of perhaps 4,000. Earl Uthred might have mustered a thousand men so he could have fought only if the enemy could be caught off balance, just as Edmund would do against Cnut in the following year. Evidently leaders could submit if the odds were completely stacked against them. From this it might be safe to assume that when Earl Morcar was confronting the invasion at Fulford in 1066, he must have believed he had a chance of winning.

Second, the foremost duty of a leader was to provide his people with security. The alternative to submission would unleash in Northumbria the fury of a tribe of men whose land and rules were almost unknown to the English. They were faced with a foe who would fight through winter. A generation of relative peace in the north meant that its people now had much to lose. In order to avoid the destruction of the homesteads and fresh harvest, Uthred would have to submit.

Fifty years later, more Norsemen would try to outmanoeuvre the natives. At Fulford the earls would find a location that would prevent the invaders making progress and force them to give battle. But it is what happened next in 1015 which would help determine who would be leading the Northumbrians at Fulford. An assassination was about to take place that would unleash a blood feud which would last beyond the Conquest.

Earl Uthred was to make his submission at a place called Wiheal, probably the modern Wighill, a village north of Tadcaster. Wighill is situated near the junction of several Roman roads, and the nearby river Wharfe would allow boats to be strategically located. Tadcaster was the place where, in 1066, Earl Edwin of Mercia positioned his army and fleet to block that route to the invaders.

As was the custom, Earl Uthred was entitled to bring a substantial armed escort to the meeting. The protection of dignitaries is now conducted by men in raincoats, who talk into their sleeves, but the modern ceremonial for greeting a head of state is still dominated by the Guard of Honour. Warships fire their cannon in salute to prove that they are not primed for action. The etiquette surrounding those who command military might when they meet is the formalisation of centuries of sensible precautions.

Weapons and armour would be left at the door in the care of either the royal servants or a few of their own company. The perceived danger was when approaching and leaving the location. There were some 'health and safety' guidelines about wearing weapons at feasts to avert those little accidents that happen when debate gets heated. We must assume that Earl Uthred's men would have checked that all looked right. Was Cnut in the hall and were his retainers unarmed? Satisfied, his bodyguard of housecarls would have disarmed and led the man whose life they were oath-bound to die for into the gloomy hall.

Concealed within the gloom of the room was a minor noble and old enemy, Thurbrand. One must imagine what happened next, for we only know that the entire party of visitors was soon dead. When Thurbrand gave the signal, Cnut's own men would have closed round him to ensure he could come to no harm in the chaotic gloom. Probably armed with little more than seaxes (daggers), the assassins fell on the visitors before their eyes had a chance to adjust to the dark of the hall's interior.

In a superb piece of historical detective work, Professor Richard Fletcher has made a detailed study of the few references to piece together the bloody consequences of this massacre in his book *Bloodfeud*. With the deed done, Cnut installed his brother-in-law, Erik, and prepared to head south to complete his reconquest of the England that his father had given to him. These events took place in

March, so spring was now approaching. In London, King Ethelred still held out.

This act of brutality did not bode well. However, unlike the pattern of so many rulers before and since, Cnut developed from a ruthless young warrior into a penitential statesman who saw his royal role as providing justice to his people. Cnut divided the country into four districts with military governors in each district. Eadric Sterona was already restored to his former land and title in Mercia and Erik controlled Northumbria. Another Danish councillor, Thorkell, was put in charge of East Anglia, while Cnut himself kept the prize of Wessex.

What follows illustrates the complex motivations driving the reactions to the threat of invasion and the behaviour of those who exercised power in England. Those who survived would provide the leadership for the events of 1066.

Cnut already had control of most of the territory of England, and when he brought his fleet up the Thames to besiege London in April of 1016, the ailing king died. Edmund was immediately declared king by the people of London, who now felt able to make such a claim of legitimacy. The subsequent events demonstrate that their view was shared by a significant minority of the power-brokers of the land. In spite of his large army, Cnut was not in control.

EDMUND IRONSIDE

1016 was a seminal year in the history of England. The indecisive rule of King Ethelred, which had lasted almost forty years, came to an end. Edmund, the one son of his first wife to make his mark, succeeded him. Edmund, whom history would call 'Ironside', would have a brief but brilliant career as a military leader contesting for the title of 'king of all England' with Cnut.

Edmund managed to move outside London before the siege was closed in the spring of 1016. He collected an army and defeated the Danes in several skirmishes. The outlook for the Danes must have seemed dark as the devious Earl Eadric of Mercia now deserted Cnut and joined Edmund's forces.

In October, Edmund's army was finally caught by the Danes at Ashingdon in Essex. The treacherous Earl Eadric deserted Edmund and the English were decisively defeated. Edmund, however, survived and fled to Gloucestershire.

The skill, support and effective leadership demonstrated by Edmund during his six-month campaign persuaded Cnut to agree terms. Times were changing and a struggle that would destroy the people and prosperity of England was an option the two leaders and the Witan were unwilling to risk. Cnut had an army to pay, Edmund had limited military means and the merchants wanted the restoration of security and prosperity.

For Cnut this was a pragmatic solution. A conquest of England looked elusive because of the general resistance. He could win all the battles but recognised that he might not win the country. He had learnt this lesson after his father's death. England was, at that stage, the only potential power base for the second son of a king. It was not everything he had hoped for but the part of England he held was a substantial prize.

Edmund would rule in the south and Cnut in the north of England. The Witan also agreed that Cnut's soldiers were to be paid a staggering £72,000, with an additional £10,500 for Cnut to create a treasury for himself in his new kingdom. The last sum was a charge that fell exclusively on London and indicates the important position the port had now attained as the hub of the island's prosperity. The records show that these sums were collected and paid by 1018.

The limited economic evidence suggests that the currency was stable. There is no evidence of general inflation, which suggests that national prosperity was growing fast enough to support the increasing Danegeld payment. A crude estimate, based on Danegeld payments, indicates that the country's income was growing at slightly over 3 per cent per year.

Edmund was given control of Wessex while Cnut received all of the country north of the Thames. It was another 'Danelaw division' of the country, although Watling Street, which connected Chester with London, seems to have been the boundary marker. The potential for renewed hostilities was removed when Edmund died on 30 November 1016. Such a sudden and unexplained death of a young man should have been the subject of much speculation, but the chroniclers are silent on the subject. It is worth noting that Cnut was unquestionably a ruthless man, who had already arranged for two earls to be murdered and would later have his brother-in-law killed. The next fifty years would see three more kings die before their time, including Cnut himself.

There remained several other claimants to succeed Edmund. Edmund had two brothers, but we hear nothing of them. Emma also had her two young sons, Alfred and Edward, from her marriage to Ethelred, plus a daughter, Godgifu. They were living in Normandy, their mother's native land. Emma would soon be a queen of England again, before either of her sons achieved maturity.

Edmund Ironside also had a son, born during the year his father was king of southern England. He would be known to history as Edward the Exile. Anxious to extinguish that royal lineage, Cnut sent the baby Edward to Denmark, where it is alleged the plan was to dispose of the child. However, in what could have provided a fairytale finish and a completely different plot to our tale of 1066, the baby was brought up as a prince in Kiev and married his princess. Had events been marginally different, Shakespeare could have written a sequel to 'The Prince of Denmark' but this time with a happy ending. Twenty-five years on, news reached King Edward that he had a nephew married to a Hungarian princess. Not until 1041 did the exiled Edward return. It is hardly surprising that he was a reluctant returnee. Tragically, he became another victim of an untimely death. He never even met his uncle. Edward the Exile's son Edgar was called 'the sworn king' and brought up at court by the childless royal couple. As a young boy, Edgar would be a witness to the events of 1066 and the early focus of English resistance.

However, in 1016 Cnut was accepted by the English as their king and nobody recorded their suspicions about the convenient death of King Edmund Ironside. Cnut took possession of England as king of a unified, if not united, kingdom. During Cnut's first year as king, several important Anglo-Saxon nobles were executed, including Eadric, whose execution seems to have been popular with the English people, as indicated by the comment in the Anglo-Saxon Chronicle that records he was killed 'very rightly'.

Evidence for purges among the minor nobility does not exist. Instead, the king ceased to rely upon them. The support of complex family bonds and obligations was not the way this foreign ruler intended to govern. Instead he called up a few trusted nobles to witness, and therefore enforce, his charters. With the notable exception of the murder of Uthred, rather than 'abolishing' the traditional loyalties, it seems that he simply ignored them and imposed a new order.

For the purposes of our narrative, we must condense the events of King Cnut's seventeen-year reign. Prosperity, backed by security and spirituality, was to be his method of governing his adopted country. He did not establish England as a new Danelaw. Nor did he establish it as a province, since, in the normal course of events, this would be his only domain. After a consultation at Oxford, he had Archbishop Wulfstan codify the laws based on those of King Edgar, Ethelred's father.

In 1018 there had been one incursion by Malcolm III across the northern border. England felt secure and the Danish fleet was paid off, although Cnut retained forty ships. The £72,000 of silver Danegeld collected from throughout the country in 1018 was probably not in the normal format of 'hack silver' but minted coins, to judge by the distribution of rare finds throughout Europe. The English monetary system was well organised prior to Cnut's reign, and he would extend the coin as the reliable unit of currency throughout the Norse lands he would shortly come to dominate.

The sudden death of his older brother, King Harald II, in late 1018 required Cnut to return and secure his succession in Denmark. Cnut evidently felt able to leave England. Thorkell the Tall, Earl of East Anglia, acted as regent during his absence, which lasted almost two years. Cnut was accompanied by some of the powerful, and therefore potentially dangerous, English nobility, among them the future Earl Godwin, who returned from his time in Denmark with a Danish wife and family.

Earl Thorkell was outlawed in 1021 when Cnut returned to England, although the king and his regent were reconciled by the time of Cnut's next trip to Denmark in 1023, when Thorkell was made regent for Cnut's very young son Harthacnut. The outlawing might therefore be seen more as an expression of Cnut's power than an indication of treachery or serious breach of trust. Olaf Haraldsson, who was now contending for control in Norway, had been Earl Thorkell's raiding partner during the 1009 raids along the English coast. Both had deserted King Sweyn and remained behind in England on a later raid, so Thorkell had 'form'.

The habit of ambitious treachery might have been temporarily suppressed in England, but it had not stopped in the Norse lands. In 1026 Cnut was once again in Denmark to face a threat from an alliance between King Onund-Jakob of Sweden and King Olaf

Denmark by Cnut. The allies this earned helped him in his campaign to subdue the nascent Norway.

In spite of the conflicts in the Nordic lands, diplomacy, rather than force, appeared to be Cnut's preferred foreign policy. When attending the coronation of Emperor Conrad II during his first pilgrimage to Rome in March 1027, he arranged the betrothal of his daughter Gunhild to Conrad's son. He attempted to maintain a good relationship with his warlike southern neighbour, Duke Robert the Devil of Normandy, by proposing his sister Estrith, who was recently widowed, in marriage. This offer was rejected, perhaps because of the age gap or Robert's local priorities.

However, Robert began to press Cnut to recognise the rights of Alfred and Edward, who were still exiles in his Normandy court. This was an unrealistic demand, since Robert's father, Richard, had given an undertaking at the time of Cnut's marriage to Emma that he would recognise the rights of their children. Cnut's defiance of Robert led to a break in friendly relations, although they were still kin as Cnut was married to Robert's aunt Emma. Robert and Cnut would both die in 1035, the former in Nicea on a pilgrimage to the Holy Land.

According to M.K. Lawson's study of Cnut, there are some hints in his charters that Robert may have collected an invasion fleet in 1033 to enforce the claim of his nephews, but that he used the assembled force against the Bretons. This might indicate that a claim to England was already lodged in the Norman psyche.

King Cnut died on 12 November 1035 at Shaftesbury and is buried in the minster at Winchester where his cask can be viewed to this day. Cnut was about forty when he died, and his death does not appear to have been anticipated. The succession was once again an issue, without any clear preparations for the government of his three kingdoms.

When Cnut died the eighteen-year-old Harthacnut was ruling Denmark for his absent father. There were two further sons of Cnut in contention but Emma was not their mother. Harold was twenty and living somewhere in England. Another son, Sweyn, had been ruling Norway with his mother's assistance. The competing claims of the two sons would again divide the northern and the southern earls.

The position of Earl Godwin was unenviable. The coming years would hone the political skills of the Godwinson family, who would need to survive the three regime changes that would precede the accession of Edward seven years later. England was in for another testing time. All Queen Emma's sons by her two regal husbands were now grown men, with Edward, her surviving son by King Ethelred, about thirty, while Harthacnut, her son by Cnut, was about eighteen.

But Cnut's love life had left two sets of heirs. The late king's first love, Aelfgyva, was born during the weak reign of King Ethelred. Her family were important landholders in modern Northamptonshire, possibly of Anglo-Danish stock. Suspicion bred violence, and in 1006 Aelfgyva's father, Aelthelm, was murdered while hunting with Earl Eadric. Around the same time her brothers Ufegeat and Wulfheah were blinded, apparently on King Ethelred's orders.

At some time before 1015, and perhaps as early as 1013, Cnut must have been introduced to Aelfgyva of Northampton and they became lovers. What we know of Aelfgyva indicates that she was probably a beautiful and certainly a politically astute young woman. One story, which may be fanciful, tells us that she was also a lover of Olaf Haraldasson during his time as a Norse raider or later as the hired defender of the east coast. The story goes on to say that Aelfgyva's affair with Cnut was a cause of some enmity between Cnut and Olaf. Olaf had certainly been hired to defend the English coast and it is not improbable that the two might have met, since Aelfgyva lived in the region where Olaf is understood to have been based.

Cnut and his lover produced two male children that we know about. Cnut appointed his younger son Sweyn as king of Norway after the defeat of Olaf in 1030. As the mother of Sweyn, Aelfgyva ruled as regent for her son, the king of Norway, between 1030 and 1035.

One motive for removing Aelfgyva and her offspring from England was that it would eliminate one contender for the throne. However, Sweyn was the second of Aelfgyva's sons. The logic would have been to send his elder son, Harold, later known as 'Harefoot' for his speed and skill at hunting, abroad. There are no clues about Harold's whereabouts prior to his father's death. There is good reason to suspect that he would not have been welcome at court. Queen Emma was adamant that her son Harthacnut was to inherit all his father's domains. Given what happened next, it is probable that Harold had been under the protection of Earl Leofric and his lady, Godiva. They had only one son and the couple had extensive landholdings extending into Harold's native land of East Anglia. Leofric was one of those promoted by Cnut, so would provide a safe house for his eldest son.

When Cnut died, the *Chronicle* describes a confrontation in which the northern thanes, led by Earl Leofric of Mercia, met the southern leaders at Oxford on the border between Wessex and Mercia. They 'chose Harold... for himself and his brother Harthacnut'. Harold was the man on the spot. This was another critical moment for Earl Godwin.

The *Chronicle* also notes that the chief men of Wessex opposed this as long as they could, doubtless encouraged by Queen Emma. Godwin maintained his support for the absent ruler. According to the *Chronicle*, the Witan and all the leading men of Wessex opposed the kingship of Harold Harefoot as long as they could, and in 1036 a compromise was reached.

The kingdom was divided. Harold ruled north of the Thames, leaving Earl Godwin as regent in the south. This situation could have lasted for only a matter of months, because in the same year two of the leading commentators of the time, William of Malmesbury and Henry of Huntingdon, concur in finding that Godwin had to submit to the *de facto* king and do his bidding.

The acceptance of the inevitable is the hallmark of Earl Godwin's actions throughout his long life. Faced with the overwhelming force of northern earls, it is not fanciful to imagine his role in the negotiations. He should perhaps take credit for what appears in the record. Harthacnut had assumed his father's crown in Denmark. His half-brother would act as his regent in England, where Harthacnut's portion was Wessex.

Once the compromise was agreed, King Harold Harefoot moved swiftly to Winchester to seize the royal treasury of Queen Emma, along with her dower lands. Emma was afforded the protection of Harold's household troops but was, in effect, detained. Emma evidently enjoyed little if any support. She would suffer the same indignity again but the next time it would be administered by her own son. According to the *Chronicle* she was 'driven out without any mercy to face the raging winter'. Emma was evidently not a lovable person.

A son of Aelfgyva had won the first round. Harold Harefoot ruled England while Emma's son ruled Denmark. Aelfgyva also suffered a setback in 1035. Olaf's son, Magnus, who was still a boy of ten, had returned from exile in Russia when Cnut died and, with the support of his Swedish stepmother, who sold her jewellery to help fund the mission, was proclaimed king of Norway.

Aelfgyva's son sought to rally support but felt:

> ...that we do not trust to these bondes; but let us rather go to the land where all the people are sure and true to us, and where we will obtain forces to conquer this country again.

So Sweyn left Norway and sailed to Denmark, where his half-brother King Harthacnut was not just happy to receive him but offered him a share of the kingdoms. With a son of Cnut to defend Denmark, especially one who had a grudge against King Magnus of Norway, Harthacnut could confidently leave Denmark to take his place as king of England. However, Sweyn died later in the year, putting Harthacnut's plan on hold again.

But Emma's ambitions were not satisfied. Both contenders for the throne had one essential ingredient in their contest for power, an ambitious and skilful mother. The power that these women could command would determine the succession.

In the *Encomium Emmae Reginae*, written during 1041, the author, who we assume was writing under instruction from Queen Emma herself, claims she made it a precondition of her marriage to Cnut that he would not set any sons from another wife to rule over their children. So according to Emma, her son Harthacnut was the rightful 'full' king of England and Denmark. She was doubtless incandescent at the prospect of both thrones being shared with Aelfgyva's sons.

This encomium (and the OED defines the word encomium as 'high-flown praise') was written after Cnut's death when the alleged oath sworn by Cnut had evidently been broken. Not for the first time would the Normans use alleged oath-breaking as a call for action and redress. It is a masterful work of self-justification but one that she might later rue, as events continued to take an unexpected direction.

Cnut appeared to have managed affairs rather well. The kingdom of England passed to Harold Harefoot, the first King Harold of England and son of Cnut by his lover, Aelfgyva. Aelfgyva had been appointed as regent of Norway in 1030 for her son, Sweyn, so she was well out of reach of the dangerous Queen Emma.

Sweyn's rule of Norway would not outlast his father, Cnut. The period of the regency of his mother is recalled unfavourably in a

Norwegian proverb. The Norsemen were evidently not ready for the southern English ways of administration. Exactly thirty years later, Tostig Godwinson would earn the displeasure of the northern folk when he attempted to impose laws and taxes to which they were unaccustomed. Aelfgyva is soon lost to us. Perhaps she accepted that she had lost out to Emma. Once her father, two brothers, her partner Cnut and finally her two sons were dead, this fascinating lady becomes invisible to recorded history.

Harold (it is not clear if we should call him king at this stage) was right to be alert to the threat posed by Emma. Her son, Harthacnut, was engaged in what was likely to be a long struggle to defend the ancestral home of his father. As was often the case, new rulers were quickly tested by their neighbours. Magnus, son of the sainted Olaf, threw off the Danish regency of Aelfgyva and the Nordic rivalry resumed.

In 1036 the opposing kings, one eleven and the other seventeen, announced that they would have a battle at the Gaut river. But wiser heads prevailed.

> The lendermen in the one army sent messengers to their connections and friends in the other; and it came to a proposal for a reconciliation between the two kings, especially as, from both kings being but young and childish... The peace was to be a brotherly union under oath to keep the peace towards each other to the end of their lives; and if one of them should die without leaving a son, the longest liver should succeed to the whole land and people.

An important provision of their treaty stated that should either king die without an heir, his kingdom would pass to the survivor. Magnus of Norway was therefore in line to inherit all the lands of Cnut. There is no talk of this right extending to any heirs and successors, as some have claimed in support of Harald's invasion of 1066. However, the love life of Cnut had linked the Nordic and English thrones by treaty.

Emma, perhaps tired of waiting for events in Denmark to resolve themselves, instead turned to her two sons in Normandy to support her.

> Emma, queen in name only, imparts motherly salutation to her sons Edward and Alfred. Now that our lord Cnut had died daily you are

deprived more and more of the kingdom, your inheritance, and I wonder what plan you are adopting... your procrastination is becoming from day to day a support to the usurper of your rule [Harold Harefoot]. For he goes around hamlets and cities ceaselessly, and makes the chief men his friends by gifts, threats, and prayers. But they would rather that one of you should rule over them... I entreat, therefore, that one of you come to me speedily and privately, to receive from me wholesome counsel, and to know in what manner this matter, which I desire, must be brought to pass. Send back word what you are going to do about these matters by the present messenger whoever he may be. Farewell beloved ones of my heart.

Early in 1037 Edward launched an exploratory raid with forty ships and landed in Southampton Water. Militarily it achieved little and Edward returned to Normandy with some booty from the people of Wessex. As his modest force made its way towards Winchester, they were opposed and withdrew. The other son, Alfred, adopted a different approach. It appears that he first went to Flanders to gather a suitable force, possibly arranged by his mother. With connections of kinship, she could expect some support. They probably attempted to sail down the Thames but were intercepted and captured by Earl Godwin.

'He detained Alfred, when he was hastening towards London to confer with King Harold as he had commanded, and placed him in strait custody', John of Worcester records. The torture and death of 600 followers of Alfred at Guildford is blamed on Godwin, following which:

> ...the Aethling Alfred was led most tightly bound in chains to the island of Ely, but as soon as the ship touched land his eye were most bloodily plucked out and he was thus led to the monastery, and handed over to the custody of the monks.

This was inside Mercian territory and out of Earl Godwin's territory. Alfred died, presumably of his wounds.

Earl Godwin's part in this outrage would provide the basis for two further crises in his rise to pre-eminence. However, Emma in her *Encomium* puts all the blame for the atrocities and murder of her son on Harold Harefoot. The short-term effect of these invasions was to unite the country behind Harold, who was declared full king of England in 1037. Evidently Earl Godwin had now abandoned Emma, who was expelled and headed not for Normandy but to Bruges in Flanders, where we assume she awaited the arrival of her son from Denmark with a force sufficient to restore both himself and her to power in England.

According to Emma, there was a meeting in Bruges with her son Edward, at which he disclaimed any interest in succeeding to the throne of England, although he would soon inherit the crown. There is no record of Edward participating in the military campaigns other than his one incursion to Southampton during his lengthy exile in Normandy. This contrasts with Harold Godwinson, who is depicted fighting for the Normans during his own short sojourn there. There would have been adequate opportunities for Edward to hone his martial skills had he wanted to, and it was unusual for a noble not to develop his skills as a soldier. Without an army or even a reputation as a leader in battle, he knew that he had no realistic prospect of dominating England. Events would prove him wrong.

In 1040 Harold Harefoot died, another unexplained death. The Witan, 'with general approval', selected Harthacnut to fill the English throne. Not until a treaty between Magnus and Harthacnut was arranged could the latter turn his attention to England.

Harthacnut was able to depart for Bruges with just ten ships to meet his mother in the autumn of 1039. He did not appear to be in a hurry. Perhaps it is coincidence that his potential opponent then died. King Harthacnut landed unopposed at Sandwich on 17 June 1040 with sixty-two ships and was well received.

Earl Godwin appreciated his unenviable position with the arrival of the new king and made a unique gesture. He presented a magnificent longboat, complete with a retinue of eighty armed retainers, to the returning king. Such a transfer of practical power appears to have blunted the instinct to exact revenge for any part Godwin played in the death of Harthacnut's half-brother, Alfred.

Earl Godwin was called to trial and he answered the summons. He put his case to the new king. He had been loyal to his father Cnut and then followed the orders of the successor recognised by the Witan and offered to take an oath to the new king. Godwin was able to swear an oath that he had no part in the murder. By the standards of the time it was a smooth and bloodless transition.

Because Harthacnut was childless and unmarried, he invited his half-brother Edward, still in Normandy, to England as heir presumptive to the English throne. Emma's sons were evidently not the marrying kind.

Edward's motives for leaving Normandy are unclear. There is no suggestion in Emma's *Encomium* that she supported the move. Certainly Edward's treatment of his mother after his accession in seizing her treasury and sending her to a convent does not suggest that he felt her support had been relied upon in the past, or could be in the future.

Edward would also have to meet Godwin, who had defeated the invasion by his brother. However, these two men, Godwin somewhat the senior, were able to establish a rapport. Both had survived an extraordinarily turbulent time that had seen six kings rule England. There might have been an understanding of the complexities of the current politics in which both had shown they were survivors.

The *Chronicles* tell us that before the funeral of Harthacnut the people of London had accepted Edward as their king. The *Vitae Edwardii (Life of Edward)*, written under the direction of Godwin's daughter Edith, reports that it was her father who championed Edward's claim to the throne, although the same work suggests that Edward had to be fetched as a reluctant traveller from Normandy. The fact that Edward accepted the eldest daughter of Godwin as his wife shows that the new king was willing to bind himself to Godwin.

Two events of note are recorded during Harthacnut's short reign. A revolt at Worcester broke out in 1041 against high taxes. Earl Godwin was sent into Mercia to crush the rebellion. He was ordered to punish the citizens of Worcester, who had killed the bailiffs sent to enforce the collection of a tax. The town was sacked but the citizens were given time to escape. The story about Lady Godiva, a prominent landowner in her own right, riding naked through the streets of Coventry to mitigate the level of taxes comes from the reign of Harthacnut.

A year later, on 8 June, Harthacnut died while drinking wine at a wedding feast. Yet another suspicious death of a young man. William of Poitiers, writing after 1066, suggests that Harthacnut was already suffering from some illness. This might account for the invitation that all chroniclers agree was issued to Edward to come to England during 1041. So Edward had been the king-in-waiting, and had been based in England for a year.

However, it was not until Easter Sunday, 3 April 1043, that Edward was consecrated king by Archbishop Eadsige at Winchester. He was evidently not a man in a hurry. Edward had already learned to be a cautious king if he wanted to survive.

One can forgive Edward for making the dispossession of his mother one of his first acts. He might have justified it on the grounds of filial revenge. The more statesmanlike motive might have been to ensure that he was not compromised like his father, Ethelred, who had been under the control of the queen mother, Elfrida. Edward would soon have another powerful woman at his side, Harold's sister Edith.

On 23 January 1045, over two years after being declared king, he married the eldest daughter of Earl Godwin. Edith was twenty-five, Edward forty. The age difference of fifteen years made this an improbable marriage. Earl Godwin could anticipate becoming the grandfather of a king, thereby assuring the continued pre-eminence of the family whose fortunes he had spectacularly advanced. But both were past their prime. The marriage was barren and there were later claims that it was unconsummated by the saintly Edward.

The succession issue was one that must have occupied King Edward's attention. His first attempt was to look towards a Norman takeover, which we shall explore in detail later. The Godwinsons had a different strategy to find a legitimate heir to the throne. There is also evidence from the various embassies sent abroad that there was a search under way to locate an 'English' successor. In the summer of 1054 Edward sent Bishop Ealdred of Worcester to Emperor Henry III, but he returned without contacting Edmund Ironside's son, also called Edward, who had narrowly cheated death as an infant when Cnut took England in 1016.

In late 1056, we discover that Harold Godwinson was witness to a charter for his brother-in-law Count Baldwin V in St Omer. Henry III had died the previous month and delegations were heading towards Cologne for the coronation of Henry IV.

Edith's story of this time, set out in *Vitae Edwardii*, records that her brother Harold visited Rome and returned with holy relics for his abbey foundation at Waltham. We cannot be certain, but by piecing together the diary of Harold's journey we can see it is possible that he took time to encourage Edward, a sixth-generation descendant of King Alfred, to return from exile. He reluctantly returned with his young family in 1057.

Sadly this attempt to establish an English lineage was defeated by the untimely death of Edward the Exile soon after arriving in London, 'to the misfortune of this poor realm', as the *Chronicle* records. He died on 19 April and was buried in St Paul's. Edward's son was awarded the title 'Aetheling', which recognised his eligibility to take the throne.

A line in *Vitae Edwardii* talks of how Edith showered her motherly love on those 'who were said to be of royal stock'. Did the childless royal couple in effect adopt the exiles?

EDWARD'S DEATH

The royal court at Westminster would have attracted the powerful people of the land at Christmas 1065. The dedication of Edward's minster provided the context for the gathering but news of the king's failing health would have spread, although the sources make no mention of the state of his health. The king was absent when his West Minster was dedicated on 28 December. He was evidently a very sick man. It has been suggested that he had been suffering the many side effects of diabetes.

The last words of Edward are also reported.

> May God be gracious to this my wife for the zealous solicitude of her service for certainly she has served me devotedly and always stood close by my side like a beloved daughter. May the forgiving God grant her the reward of eternal happiness.

The next passage which we take to be addressed to Harold goes on:

> I commend this woman with all the kingdom to your protection. Serve and honour her with faithful obedience as your lady and sister, which she is, and do not despoil her as long as she lives of any of the honour got from me.

This record of Edward's last will was written down under the instructions of the dowager queen. The words are tantalisingly ambiguous.

If this is an accurate report, and there would have been numerous witnesses, so it is probably close to what was said, it is hardly a clear expression passing the crown to Harold. It is plausible that Edward was expressing a wish that Queen Edith should maintain the rule in his kingdom. She was still young and had at court an Aetheling, Edgar, who might one day continue the royal line of Alfred. Each generation had produced a powerful lady who had acted as regent in all but name. The mother of Ethelred, Elfrida, had guided the country during his youth. Emma, wife to two kings, had played an active role in their fate, if not the governance of the country. King Alfred's daughter Ethelflaed, widowed early, had come close to reuniting all of the Danelaw under Mercian control. Handing the country to the care of Edward's wife would seem to have been a viable option with adequate precedent.

King Edward lay dying for a week. There was plenty of time for consultation among the powerful in the land and probably a number of audiences with the dying king for a proper leave-taking. A regency under Queen Edith does not appear to have been an option the powerful gathering subsequently considered. The claims of Edgar Aetheling are not mentioned in any of the sources surrounding the death or succession.

Harold, on the other hand, had experience, influence and power. The other sources indicate that the words quoted by the dying king were not his last on the subject of his succession. We cannot know if the king had to be persuaded to nominate Harold. The dying words of a person were accorded considerable authority, especially by the Church, so there can be little doubt that the king did nominate Harold, although it still leaves open the possibility that he envisaged the role as one of the queen's champion.

Any ambiguity was removed by the Witan, which offered the crown to Harold. Because no dissent is recorded, and none is evident in the events of 1066, it is reasonable to say that there was no opposition to the selection of Harold. His speedy marriage to the sister of the earls Edwin and Morcar brought the bond of kinship and offered the prospect that the houses of Wessex and Mercia would establish a new royal dynasty. Like any good political solution it seemed to offer everybody a prize.

How mindful the assembly was of the tentative claims of William of Normandy or Sweyn of Denmark we cannot tell. Both claims had 'time-expired' and been overtaken by events. Unity was their best defence.

Edward died on 4 or 5 January 1066 of what we believe was a stroke, possibly brought on by a diabetic condition. He was buried by the high altar of his new church on the feast of the Epiphany, 6 January 1066. The same day, Harold was consecrated by one or both of the archbishops from Canterbury and York.

There was nothing sinister or unseemly in this haste. Custom dictated that coronations should take place during the Church festivals. The Church authorities might have seen this as auspicious, but for the secular authorities these traditional festivals were when people gathered together. The feast of the Epiphany fell on 6 January and marked the last day of the Christmas festival.

It is hard to see in any of the actions by members of the Godwin family much evidence of naked ambition. Rather, the opposite is demonstrated by their willingness to find and foster other potential claimants to the throne.

The Witan was made up of a group of about sixty lords and bishops and they considered the merits of the two candidates, Harold Godwinson and Edgar Aetheling. The debate could not have lasted long. By 6 January 1066, the Witan decided that Harold was to be the next king of England.

It is tempting to imagine that Edward's reign was an experiment in new government. A monarch had ruled by right of inheritance, after he had received the tacit support of the people as represented in the Witan, with military support provided by a people's army. It was, however, a set of unique circumstances that promoted the situation. But the outcome had provided stable government through a difficult reign. This might not have been a comfortable situation for the king. Kings could normally enforce their will but Edward was obliged to act through his earls. The experiment had been surprisingly successful but it would be many centuries before this balance of power was tried again.

2

King Harald of Norway

VICTOR OF THE BATTLE AT FULFORD

There are two questions that seek answers when examining the life of the victor at Fulford, Harald Sigurdson. What made this fifty-year-old warrior such a formidable opponent? Why was King Harald of Norway invading England? The answer to both questions can be found by examining the complex northern societies where the Vikings were evolving into nations.

Those brought up with the stories bequeathed by the Anglo-Saxon tradition should be grateful to their ancestors. By comparison, the history of the Nordic nations is unfathomable. Those in the British Isles might perhaps imagine how the history of these islands might have evolved if the nations had been more evenly matched geographically. In the place of one dominant territory, imagine having three who routinely made and broke an 'Act of Union'. Those in North America could instead imagine a land with flexible borders extending from the Antarctic to what remains of the northern ice cap. Then add fifty wars of independence, wars of conquest and civil wars to convey some idea of the Nordic Sagas that have defined three modern nations, one with a great sense of fun, another whose social conscience masks a visceral conservatism and another that has learned to enjoy nature's bounty.

Therefore Harald's tale as told here cannot capture the complexities of Norse history in the same way that a study of the rulers of England can provide a picture of the evolution of the institution of government.

Harald was born in the year 1015, son of Sigurd Syr. His father was a sub-king who appears to have enjoyed the produce of his farming, to judge by his nickname, which translated means 'Sow'. He was not alone in having a sartorial epithet attached to his name. King Olaf II, his maternal half-brother, was known as Olaf the Stout, a handle he would lose only when he was beatified and became Saint Olaf.

Olaf II was Harald's older half-brother, who was the son of Harald Grenske, great-grandchild of Harald I of Norway, known as Fairhair. There was a twenty-year gap between Harald and his big brother. King Harald Fairhair played a key part in the process that would establish national identities among the Vikings. The bloody process would prove even more tortuous than that concurrently starting in the British islands. Harald, son of Sigurd, therefore had only very dilute royal blood flowing in his veins. He was royal by association rather than birth, rather like Harold Godwinson.

Olaf had spent some years in England fighting for King Ethelred against the Danish raids. But in 1015 when the raids became a full invasion led by King Sweyn Forkbeard, Olaf seized the opportunity and returned to Norway, where he declared himself king as a descendant of the Harald Fairhair family line. Harald Fairhair could claim to have laid the foundation of Norway, not least because he left twenty-one sons, including such fratricidal kings as Eric Bloodaxe.

Two generations later, in 1016, with the support of some 'kings' from the Uplands, Olaf defeated Earl Sweyn, who was the effective overlord in Norway, at the sea-battle known as Nesje. Within a few years Olaf had won control of more territory than had been enjoyed by any of his predecessors in Norway.

While King Cnut was reorganising the governance of England, sweeping away the old warlords and putting the minor nobility in its place, Olaf was annihilating the petty kings in Norway to create a similar, king-centred governance. Christianity had been actively promoted by his namesake Olaf I, twenty years before. This was Olaf Trygvasson, not to be confused with Olaf son of Harald or Haraldsson. Olaf I was a moderniser, who probably imported an

English moneyer, as the name GODPINEM-ONO appears on some of Olaf's coins, doubtless minted from the English Danegeld. Olaf II now enforced the practice of Christianity throughout his kingdom, suppressing all practices associated with pagan worship.

King Olaf II was able to pursue his policies as he was temporarily freed from the need to secure his frontiers. Cnut was occupied securing and organising his English land and then, following the death of his elder brother, was forced to spend two years securing his unexpected inheritance to the throne of Denmark.

The northern coast of Scotland and the island chains that stretch north-east from John O'Groats provided a refuge for families threatened by Olaf's brutal reorganisation. These Norse settlements were attacked by Olaf, providing the recently discovered Iceland with a new wave of settlers.

The Shetland and Orkney Islands, which provided several safe havens for Nordic mariners, were brought under the control of a resurgent Norway. These islands would provide a stopping place, a source of troops and a base for Harald's family in 1066, on his way to Fulford.

The childhood of Harald might therefore have been a relatively peaceful time under the protection of his half-brother. We can assume that the child was schooled in the arts of warfare from an early age, as we find several examples of royal sons leading troops as soon as they reached their teens. Childhood had to be hurried at a time when forty was considered a ripe old age and grey hairs merited respect. Harald was in his ninth year when Olaf's ambitions led him to contemplate foreign military affairs. As this decade of relative Norse tranquillity drew to a close, King Olaf produced a son and heir, Magnus, displacing Harald as the likely choice as heir to Olaf's throne.

In 1026 King Olaf, in alliance with King Onund-Jakob of Sweden, challenged Cnut. In the ensuing sea-battle Cnut's fleet was driven off but he nevertheless retained command of the sea. Olaf was therefore obliged to return to Norway overland, leaving his ships to overwinter in Sweden.

As Olaf made his way west, Cnut was heading south on a pilgrimage to Rome, leaving Earl Hakon to buy the loyalty of southern Norwegian nobility with offers of money. When Cnut returned with a fleet of fifty ships, directly from England in 1028, his overlordship was accepted without the need for a battle. Olaf could not muster an army from among those he had rather brutally reorganised and was forced to go into exile in Russia. Young Harald might have joined him but we have no record.

Cnut then summoned an assembly of Nordic nobles at Trondheim in Norway, where his twelve-year-old son Harthacnut was affirmed as king of Denmark with the respected Earl Hakon as governor of Norway. However, Earl Hakon perished by drowning a few years later. This was the set of circumstances that promoted a noble lady from Northampton to be regent in Norway.

One story, mentioned earlier, tells us that Aelfgyva was also a lover of Olaf, afterwards the king and saint of Norway, during one of his imputed stints as a defender of England's coast against attack from Danish raiders. Aelfgyva and Cnut's children were now at risk because England had a new mistress, Queen Emma. The appointment of Aelfgyva is perhaps the ironic gesture you might expect from Cnut, a ruler who we are told tried to demonstrate the limits of his power by failing to turn the tide. It was a wonderfully ambiguous appointment.

Olaf had introduced a number of English churchmen into Norway who continued their work while he was in exile. While their spirituality might have proved acceptable, the centralised authority and tithes that came with the adoption of the ways of the Church were not popular in Norway. It is possible that the regency of Aelfgyva for her younger son Sweyn suffered by association. The 'English ways' of taxation and central organisation that Aelfgyva tried to introduce would eventually prove unacceptable.

It is notable that surviving records make no mention of King Sweyn of Norway, except in Denmark where his half-brother was ruling. Sweyn must have been about twenty and perhaps their father, Cnut, felt his two boys should consolidate the family hold in Denmark, leaving Aelfgyva the task of governing the northern reaches of Norway.

The effect of the uncertainty caused by the transitions in 1029 was that some of the lords in northern Norway returned their loyalty to Olaf. It would have taken some weeks for news of Hakon's accident to reach Cnut and for the new arrangements to be made. But this was a sufficient loosening of control to encourage Olaf to return from exile for a final, fatal meeting with Cnut.

At the battle of Stiklestad in 1030, King Olaf was killed and the land of Norway came under control of the king of Denmark. Harald was fifteen years old when he was wounded and escaped.

The life of a nomadic adventurer followed. King Harald would be 'fifty years old when he was killed fighting on English soil in 1066', according to the summary of his life provided by one saga. The details are rather more interesting, informative and relevant to Harald's actions in 1066.

Olaf's defeat was absolute, even though he exhorted his small army to mark their helmets with the sign of the cross. The battle went to the opposing Christian king and his big battalions. King Cnut now took direct family control of Norway, exploiting the central authority of Church and state that Olaf had helped extend, possibly to his own personal cost. Before following young Harald's wanderings in exile, it is worth exploring the extraordinary events following the death of Olaf.

Strange happenings were reported which would nurture the weak shoots of nationalism that Olaf had sowed in Norway. The man who had forced his spear through King Olaf, who history records as one Tore Hund, returned to the battlefield to locate the body of the king. He reported that the king's face was just as full of colour as when he was alive. One drop of the king's blood miraculously healed a wound Tore had received in the battle. A farmer and his son then retrieved the corpse, wrapped it in linen and laid it in an outhouse.

A blind man came to the farmer asking for shelter and was directed to stay in their outhouse. When he came in contact with the dead body of Olaf, the blind man regained his sight. The farmer also reported a strange light from the outhouse and became worried that the body would be discovered. Tradition tells us that they cunningly constructed two coffins, one for the king and the other loaded with rocks and dirt.

Their ruse was not altogether successful, as the coffin with the body was eventually seized and sunk in the fjord of Trondheim, where it wound up on a sandbank. But miraculous stories about the late King Olaf began to circulate among a population that was already growing disenchanted with their Danish and English overlords. The seeds of a national identity had germinated throughout the land.

Along with the taxes, which had been the downfall of earlier would-be rulers of Norway, nobody was now allowed to leave the country without the king's consent. Then the crops failed and food prices soared. A little coastal raiding was out of the question. The farmer Torgils and his son Grim now went to the bishop Grimkell and told their story of Olaf's miraculous powers. King Sweyn, and probably his mother Aelfgyva, was asked for permission to unearth the corpse and the request was granted.

Tradition says that one year and five days had passed since Olaf had been killed. The coffin was recovered from the sand and when opened smelled fresh, with the body of the king undecayed. Aelfgyva was apparently present as an observer of these events and was a more sceptical spectator. She is quoted as saying 'Late rots the corpse that lies in sand. It wouldn't have been that way if they had buried the king in the earth.'

The bishop trimmed Olaf's hair and beard to demonstrate how much they had grown. Aelfgyva remained sceptical and suggested that a realistic test of holiness might be to see if these hair trimmings could survive fire, which of course they did when the bishop conducted the experiment and placed them on a fire.

The holiness of Olaf was accepted by the Church and his body was buried in a fine ceremony above the high altar in the Klemenschurch at Nidaros, which Olaf himself had founded. Nationalism now had an icon and place of pilgrimage.

A fresh spring suddenly appeared where the coffin had been found on the sandbank and its water had miraculous curative, to add to its proven preservative, powers. Pilgrims now travelled to Nidaros. When Adam of Bremen wrote his great work about the history of the archdiocese of Hamburg-Bremen in the 1070s, the pilgrimages to Nidaros were already attracting local people as well as those from the wider continent.

Olaf's case was helped by Bishop Grimkell, whom he brought with him from England to help impose Christian practices throughout Norway. Olaf's beatification was doutless helped by Bishop Grimkell, who, under canon law of the time, was able to beatify Olaf as early as August 1031. Grimkell eventually returned to England and was appointed bishop of Selsey in the south-east of England from 1039 until 1047.

Olaf was not given his sainthood by the Pope. At this time, it was not required. The affirmation of the local bishop was enough. It was not until the latter part of the twelfth century that the decision to centralise the business of canonisation was taken in Rome.

These events ensured that Harald would in time have a united land to return to. In the intervening fifteen years his journey would take him a long way from Norway. Peasants concealed Harald after the battle until his wounds had healed. Making his way east along the forest paths to avoid the common road, he met others from the defeated army. They remained in Norway until winter was over. The saga then takes up the story.

> The spring of 1031 Harald and Ragnvald got ships, and went east in summer to Russia to King Jarisleif, and were with him all the following winter. Harald remained several years in Russia, and travelled far and wide in the Eastern land. Then he began his expedition out to Greece, and had a great suite of men with him; and on he went to Constantinople. He presented himself to the empress, and went into her pay; and immediately, in autumn, went on board the galleys manned with troops which went out to the Greek sea.

Harald's leadership potential was evident because in 'a short time... all the Varings flocked to him, and they all joined together when there was a battle'. Harald soon earned his place as chief of the Varings.

The Varangian Guard were founded by Emperor Basil II in 988, with 6,000 Russian Viking warriors sent by the Varangian Tsar Vladimir of Russia. Their name comes from an old Norse word relating to sharers of an oath. The name Varangian evolved to mean any foreigner in the service of the Byzantine government. The oath-swearing and the loyalty of the hearth troops among the Norse and Anglo-Saxon troops made them ideal bodyguards where local tradition favoured intrigue. The Byzantine texts talk about the Varangian Guard in terms of distinctive nationalities, implying that a number of different national divisions composed the guard.

Interestingly, the Varangian Guard is not mentioned in the Byzantine sources until 1034, which is about the time that Harald reached Constantinople. Membership of the Varangian Guard was profitable and positions had to be purchased. However, a Norseman from Scandinavia or Russia would expect to return home a rich man. The fortune of Harald Sigurdson, the future king of Norway, was founded on his service with the guard.

Following the Muslim takeover of Sicily, North Africa and Spain, the 'Pax Romana that had pervaded the Mediterranean slowly and fitfully declined, and piratical infestation returned. Great empires thrived on trade, so piracy was a problem that had to be checked. One permanent job for this mercenary army of seafarers was to keep the pirates at bay. Along with Gyrger, who was a relation of the empress, they 'fought much against the corsairs' or pirates in the eastern Mediterranean.

One figure, often called Aralte (Harald?), is mentioned by Greek, Arab and Byzantine chroniclers at this time. It is reported that he fought in Sicily, Bulgaria, Athens, Venice and even Africa. Ironically, it was also Norsemen from Normandy who threatened Byzantine provinces in southern Italy at the beginning of the eleventh century.

The Normans had allied themselves with the Meles, on the Atlantic coast of France, where locals were in rebellion against their Byzantine overlords. The colonial legacy of the ancient superpowers was undergoing rationalisation as national and geographical identities began to emerge. The Varangians defeated the Normans and their allies, which allowed the Byzantine government to regain a foothold in territories it had lost to the Arabs.

In 1040, the Bulgarians revolted against the rule of Michael IV. The Varangian Guard, under the command of Harald, was part of the force assigned to subdue the revolt, where Harald's actions earned a commendation from Emperor Michael. Upon his return to Byzantium he and his followers were given a post in the palace guard. The Germanic tradition of unswerving loyalty to their leader must have endeared these foreigners to his services as lifeguard.

Michael IV was soon forced to abdicate due to the ill health from which he soon died. Michael V, his nephew, was appointed as a figurehead emperor while his uncles retained real power.

Harald's life as an exile sheds an interesting light on Norse engagement in politics. When Emperor Romanus III died, Harald and the guard had supported the widowed Empress Zoë. She married Michael IV and they co-ruled from 1034 to 1041. When husband number two died, the palace guards became embroiled in Byzantine infighting between the supporters of Empress Zoë and the supporters of the brothers of the late Michael IV. Unfortunately, the brothers did not trust the Varangian Guard and appointed eunuchs in their place as bodyguards. So it was back to field soldiering for Harald after a few years of palace life.

Harald was forceful as well as cunning, as this story reported by Thiolef shows:

There were many things they [Harald and his commander Gyrger] quarrelled about, but the end always was that Harald got his own way. It came thus to an arbitration between them, at which the best and most sagacious men should give their judgment in the case. At this arbitration it was determined, with the consent of all parties, that lots should be thrown into a box, and the Greeks and Varings should draw which was first to ride, or to row, or to take place in a harbour, or to choose tent ground; and each side should be satisfied with what the drawing of the lots gave them.

Accordingly the lots were made and marked. Harald said to Gyrger, 'Let me see what mark thou hast put upon thy lot, that we may not both mark our lots in the same way.' He did so. Then Harald marked his lot, and put it into the box along with the other. The man who was to draw out the lots then took up one of the lots between his fingers, held it up in the air, and said, 'This lot shall be the first to ride, and to row, and to take place in harbour and on the tent field.' Harald seized his hand, snatched the die, and threw it into the sea, and called out, 'That was our lot!' Gyrger said, 'Why did you not let other people see it?' Harald replies, 'Look at the one remaining in the box, there you see your own mark upon it.' Accordingly the lot which was left behind was examined, and all men saw that Gyrger's mark was upon it, and accordingly the judgment was given that the Varings had gained the first choice in all they had been quarrelling about.

A war leader of that time needed courage and cunning. The leader had to be at the centre of an affray but he also had to be a winner. There was probably no shortage of courageous men, but what made Harald so successful was his strategic and tactical cunning. A little of the background to his soldiering exploits may help explain where he developed the subtle strategy employed during his invasion in 1066.

The subtlety of Harald can be judged from two of his siege strategies. He allowed his troops to be taunted by the defenders and told them to make sport and play in front of the gates, but carefully out of bow-shot. Eventually, when the defenders were emboldened, they also began to make sport. This relaxed atmosphere continued for some time. One day, the ever-vigilant Harald noticed that the defenders were off guard and the gate plus the town were seized.

On another occasion he feigned his death, ensuring that spies carried news of his deteriorating condition to the besieged. His entourage at length announced his death and begged for a Christian burial inside consecrated ground. Eager for the wealth such an internee would bring, there was almost a race to receive the oversized coffin, which was wedged in the gate long enough for the Varangians to throw off their mourning attire and seize the town. Harald might have heard of the Trojan horse episode at Troy during his service at nearby Constantinople, which perhaps led him to innovate with the 'Trojan coffin' ploy.

Ever the opportunist, Harald would exploit any advantage he could find. When tasked to take a castle during the campaign for control of Sicily, the saga describes his novel approach. He made his bird-catchers catch the small birds which had their nests within the castle, but flew into the woods by day to get food for their young. He had small splinters of tarred wood bound upon the backs of the birds, smeared these over with wax and sulphur, and set fire to them.

> As soon as the birds were let loose they all flew at once to the castle to their young, and to their nests, which they had under the house roofs that were covered with reeds or straw. The fire from the birds seized upon the house roofs; and although each bird could only carry a small burden of fire, yet all at once there was a mighty flame, caused by so many birds carrying fire with them and spreading it widely among the house roofs.
>
> Thus one house after the other was set on fire, until the castle itself was in flames. Then the people came out of the castle and begged for mercy; the same men who for many days had set at defiance the Greek army and its leader. Harald granted life and safety to all who asked quarter, and made himself master of the place.

Harald's reputation as a soldier was well founded.

> It thus happened often that when he commanded the army he gained victories, while Gyrger could do nothing. The troops observed this, and insisted they would be more successful if Harald alone was chief of the whole army, and upbraided the general with never effecting anything, neither himself, nor his people.

On one occasion Harald deliberately hung back so that it would be clear what each commander could achieve. Harald always won victory and with it booty, plus a few defectors from Gyrger. This was the subtle, ruthless and experienced warrior whom the young earls would try to stop at Fulford

Harald's reputation alone allowed him to subjugate the land around the Jordan river without unsheathing his sword. He used the opportunity for a pilgrimage:

> He then went out to Jordan and bathed therein, according to the custom of other pilgrims. Harald gave great gifts to our Lord's grave, to the Holy Cross, and other holy relics in the land of Jerusalem. He also cleared the whole road all the way out to Jordan, by killing the robbers and other disturbers of the peace.

Sadly Sweyn, the eldest son of Earl Godwin, did not benefit from this clearing out of bandits, as he was killed returning from pilgrimage in 1052, by which time Harald was already undisputed king of Norway.

When Harald returned to Constantinople from Jerusalem he evidently was planning to return to his native land. Magnus, his brother's son, had become king of Norway in 1035 and had added Denmark to his kingdom in 1042. This inheritance had come to Magnus according to the terms of the treaty made during the disputed succession in England after the death of Cnut. Following the sudden death of Harthacnut in England, Magnus was king of two lands.

Harald, already approaching thirty, decided the time had come to give up his foreign service. His nephew, King Magnus, was still a teenager, so there appeared to be no realistic prospect of inheriting the throne of Norway. Magnus had also developed into an effective warrior. He could muster a fleet of seventy ships in 1042 when he went to take possession of Denmark.

The ship in which King Magnus sailed was a magnificent longboat with thirty benches for oars. The name given to this ship was *Bison* and the prow had a carving of the head of this North American beast, while the stern had the tail of a buffalo carved on it. The transatlantic adventurers had evidently discovered more than good fishing on their voyages towards the setting sun.

When news reached Empress Zoë that Harald was thinking of quitting her service, she was evidently displeased. Such a move would upset the balance of power within palace politics. In true Byzantine style, she raised an accusation against Harald to detain him. She claimed that he had misapplied the property of the Greek emperor which he had obtained on campaigns as commander of the army. There was also a romantic dimension. A young and beautiful girl called Maria, a niece of Empress Zoë, had perhaps been courted by Harald, although the empress had not approved and refused to countenance any relationship. The campaign to marginalise Harald's forceful influence was continued by Emperor Michael V. He equipped an expedition which included the Varangian Guard but let someone else lead them in place of Harald. Other insults followed. Michael finally had Harald imprisoned on charges of wrongfully appropriating wealth. His crime was not providing the proper tithe or proportion to the emperor from the spoils he gained in war.

Harald, along with Haldor and Ulf, was lowered into a dungeon. These two Icelandic companions in prison were evidently his soulmates as well as cellmates. It is perhaps one reason why we are so well informed by the sagas about the life of Harald, because Snorri Sturluson, who would become the most famous chronicler of these events as the author of *Heimskringla*, was a descendant of Haldor. This is how Snorri records the life of his ancestor:

> Haldor was very stout and strong, and remarkably handsome in appearance. King Harald gave him this testimony, that he, among all his men, cared least about doubtful circumstances, whether they betokened danger or pleasure; for, whatever turned up, he was never in higher nor in lower spirits, never slept less nor more on account of them, nor ate or drank but according to his custom. Haldor was not a man of many words, but short in conversation, told his opinion bluntly and was obstinate and hard; and this could not please the king, who had many clever people about him zealous in his service. Haldor remained a short time with the king; and then came to Iceland, where he took up his abode in Hjardarholt, and dwelt in that farm to a very advanced age. Ulf Uspakson stood in great esteem with King Harald; for he was a man of great understanding, clever in conversation, active and brave, and withal true and sincere. King Harald made Ulf his marshal.

Harald and his companions were lowered into a formidable dungeon with only one high window for access. This is how the tale of their escape is told much later:

Next night a lady of distinction with two servants came, by the help
of ladders, to the top of the tower, let down a rope into the prison
and hauled them up. Saint Olaf had formerly cured this lady of a
sickness and he had appeared to her in a vision and told her to deliver
his brother.

The Varangian Guard, who had sided with the empress, restored the
city temporarily to her control to facilitate their escape. Harald was
intent upon a speedy getaway. After a decade in the service of the
eastern empire, Harald knew not to tarry, as fortunes could ebb as
quickly as the tide. It appears that escape from prison and departure
from Constantinople were both the work of the same night.

Their escape was not without some considerable adventure. First,
they blinded the emperor who had imprisoned Harald. They took
two boats and had enough time to load their property, although
much of the accumulated wealth had been shipped to Russia in
previous years. The harbour lay between the east and west sides of
the city. To protect the imperial fleet, the entrance was blocked by a
chain which was stretched between the two banks.

To escape they would have to get past this obstacle. They evidently did
not possess the authority or perhaps lacked the time to order the chain to
be lowered. They cleared the chains that famously blocked access to the
city with another ingenious manoeuvre. As they approached the chain,
Harald ordered all those not rowing to take themselves and their luggage
to the rear of the galley. This would ensure that the bow mounted the
chain when they hit it. In what must be a perfectly timed move, the
human ballast would rush to the bow, tipping the boat over the chain
and allowing the momentum to carry it forward to freedom.

> The galleys thus ran up and lay on the iron chain. As soon as they
> stood fast on it, and would advance no farther, Harald ordered all the
> men to run forward into the bow. Then the galley, in which Harald
> was, balanced forwards and swung down over the chain...

The second boat tried to repeat this manoeuvre, 'but the other, which
remained fast athwart the chain, split in two, by which many men
were lost'. Perhaps the flexible longboats could have taken the strain
but the back of the second galley was broken. In the darkness, some
perished as they were carried away by the current.

Harald's one remaining ship was now into the Bosporus. Turning west, he made for the Mediterranean and the long journey home. The identity of the lady who had assisted in his escape is not given. The sagas report that Maria, whose relationship a jealous Empress Zoë had frustrated, was taken by Harald as they retreated. Could this have been to protect her from punishment for releasing them from prison? This provides an interesting romantic sideline which casts Harald as a chivalrous softie rather than a pillager, which is the customary view of this Viking warrior.

Whatever Harald's motive for taking Maria from Constantinople, she was put ashore with a message for Empress Zoë pointing out her impotence to regulate his comings and goings. Harald's heart, it appears, had already been captured by Elisabeth, daughter of the Russian king Jarisleif. With her military support gone, Empress Zoë was forced to become a nun and to give up her claim to the throne.

The long voyage home took Harald round the Mediterranean, the Iberian peninsula and up the Channel coast to his Baltic home. Along the way, Harald had plenty of time to compose sixteen poems about this 9,000km voyage, only one of which the chroniclers chose to record:

> Past Sicily's wide plains we flew,
> A dauntless, never-wearied crew;
> Our viking steed rushed through the sea,
> As viking-like fast, fast sailed we.
> Never, I think, along this shore
> Did Norsemen ever sail before;
> Yet to the Russian queen, I fear,
> My gold-adorned, I am not dear.

The journey home would have taken at least three months, given an average speed of 100km per day. But with some days added for rest, repair and restocking, plus the days lost when they took shelter from storms, the journey probably lasted longer. It is fanciful, but tempting, to imagine that the leader composed one topical poem per week to entertain his crew with his lovesick pinings. Sixteen weeks for the return trip would still make it an impressive circumnavigation of the seaboard of the European landmass.

He need not have worried about the object of his affections. Upon his return with wealth, a small army and a royal brother, King Jarisleif gave Harald his daughter Elisabeth (Ellisif), the Ruse princess, in marriage in the winter of 1045. Although another Norwegian wife would be introduced much later to provide a male heir, Harald's marriage to Elisabeth would survive until his death.

In the spring Harald began his journey from Novgorod. By the summer he had reached Sweden, where Elisabeth's uncle, Olaf, was king. This ensured the couple had a welcome among the Viking peoples, although it is unclear why he did not head straight back to Norway where his nephew had ruled for over a decade. Had he done so it would have avoided an awkward, if short-lived, alliance developing.

Norway was the current superpower in the Baltic and the other nations had just rebelled against its domination. King Magnus had appointed Earl Sweyn to rule over his second kingdom of Denmark. Sweyn was of Danish royal stock and his power and ambition grew until he had himself 'promoted' from earl to king. In several battles Sweyn was defeated by Magnus, but the former was not discouraged. In 1045 King Magnus decisively beat Sweyn at the sea-battle of Helganes. Sweyn had not been able to make it home and spent another winter in Sweden.

Harald and Sweyn apparently were kindred spirits. The problem was that Sweyn was currently Magnus' number one enemy. Nevertheless, Harald joined forces with Sweyn, who was also the Swedish king's nephew, to raid Denmark during the summer of 1046, although the territory was now firmly controlled by Norway. To redress any idea that Harald had gone soft, the following skald was composed after the sacking of the Danish port of Roskilde.

> Few were they of escape to tell,
> For, sorrow-worn, the people fell:
> The only captives from the fray
> Were lovely maidens led away.
> And in wild terror to the strand,
> Down to the ships, the linked band
> Of fair-haired girls is roughly driven,
> Their soft skins by the irons riven.

News of Harald's return and his prowess, wealth and connections must have reached King Magnus in Norway. Magnus must now have perceived his uncle as a serious threat and he was persuaded that negotiations were the best course. For Magnus the calculation was 'how long would it be before Harald's fleet landed in Norway to take the crown by force?' But it was Harald's party that made the first move.

> Those of Harald's men who were in his counsel said that it would be a great misfortune if relations like Harald and Magnus should fight and throw a death-spear against each other; and therefore many offered to attempt bringing about some agreement between them, and the kings, by their persuasion, agreed to it. Thereupon some men were sent off in a light boat, in which they sailed south in all haste to Denmark, and got some Danish men, who were proven friends of King Magnus, to propose this matter to Harald. This affair was conducted very secretly.

Security surrounding the negotiations was not as tight as the Norwegians might have wished, because the sagas record the words of Sweyn when he challenged Harald to explain himself:

> A little after this it happened that Harald and Sweyn one evening were sitting at table drinking and talking together, and Sweyn asked Harald what valuable piece of all his property he esteemed the most. He answered, it was his banner Land-waster. Sweyn asked what was there remarkable about it, that he valued it so highly.
>
> Harald replied, it was a common saying that he must gain the victory before whom that banner is borne, and it had turned out so ever since he had owned it.
>
> Sweyn responded, 'I will begin to believe there is such virtue in the banner when thou hast held three battles with thy relation Magnus, and hast gained them all.'
>
> Then answered Harald with an angry voice, 'I know my relationship to King Magnus, without thy reminding me of it; and although we are now going in arms against him, our meeting may be of a better sort.'
>
> Sweyn changed colour, and said, 'There are people, Harald, who say that thou hast done as much before as only to hold that part of an agreement which appears to suit thy own interest best.'
>
> Harald answers, 'It becomes thee ill to say that I have not stood by an agreement, when I know what king Magnus could tell of thy proceedings with him.'

We are lucky to have the recording of such a frank exchange between two warriors whose ambition gave them complete freedom in their private manoeuvres, while reprimanding rivals who exercised similar flexibility in their public loyalty.

The saga then records that each went his own way. Soon the allies were in open dispute. Harald survived an assassination attempt. Having anticipated what was likely to happen, Harald had left a log in his normal sleeping place to take the axe blow that fell that night. Another speedy departure was effected.

Harald and his men were made welcome in Norway. The Nordic sagas (as we saw earlier, and in contrast with the dry record made in the monastic chronicles around England) provide extensive detail about the welcome feasting, proclamations and gifts that were given. The following day, King Harald, as we must now call him, divided his wealth with King Magnus, who had made it clear that he, Magnus, took precedence and that his co-king's task was to expand the territory of Norway.

King Harald responded:

> Yesterday you gave us a large kingdom, which your hand won from your and our enemies, and took us in partnership with you, which was well done; and this has cost you much. Now we on our side have been in foreign parts, and oft in peril of life, to gather together the gold which you here see.
>
> Now, King Magnus, I will divide this with you. We shall both own this movable property, and each have his equal share of it, as each has his equal half share of Norway. I know that our dispositions are different, as thou art more liberal than I am; therefore let us divide this property equally between us, so that each may have his share free to do with as he will.

King Harald had a strong sense of history. He was not a man who forgot, and he seldom forgave. Even amid the exchanges and merriment, while Magnus confessed that his land had been impoverished by all the internal and external strife, Harald chose this moment to raise the matter of ownership of the gold ring which Magnus was wearing. King Magnus jokingly suggested that his ring represented all the gold remaining in Norway before the bounty which had just been donated by Harald. Magnus pointed out that it had been given to him by their father, 'Olaf the Saint', when they parted for the last time.

King Harald answered:

> It is true, king Magnus, what thou sayest. Thy father gave thee this ring, but he took the ring from my father for some trifling cause; and in truth it was not a good time for small kings in Norway when thy father was in full power.

Olaf had indeed persecuted the minor kings in his quest to establish control and Christianity in Norway and Harald evidently still nursed the injustice he had been told was done to his father by his new ally.

It was not going to be a comfortable relationship, although the chroniclers blame others for making mischief between the joint kings. But Harald clearly needed no help to generate discord. Soon he was up to his old trick of upstaging his overlord. When King Magnus prepared to drive Harald off the prime mooring by force, Harald backed down, saying that it was the custom for the wisest to give way.

During the winter of 1046, the kings made a trip north to Nidaros to inspect the tomb of Olaf, who was now credited with many miraculous cures. Olaf's influence went beyond providing medical relief. He was also a purveyor of political advice. One night Saint he appeared to King Magnus in a dream, asking 'Wilt thou choose, my son, to follow me, or to become a mighty king, and have long life, but to commit a crime which thou wilt never be able to expiate?' Magnus deferred to his father, who advised him to follow, and soon he fell sick and, after putting his affairs in order, died. Quite what great crime Olaf was predicting is unclear, but a clash with Harald was looming and the death of one of the co-kings appeared inevitable. This was a tidy, but intriguing, resolution of the power struggle between Magnus and Harald.

Soon Harald, too, was not having things his own way for once. Loyalty to the old king, Magnus, prevented Harald from exerting his authority over Denmark. Instead, much of the army wanted to take Magnus home to his final resting place near his father in Trondheim and Nidaros, where he was laid to rest late in 1048.

In 1048 King Harald was able to get his plan back on course, although by now King Sweyn had returned from his Swedish exile and was firmly in control of Denmark. A decade of attrition was the result.

To begin, the attacks to the south were no more than summer raids and Harald did not have it all his own way. Logistics were a problem. So King Harald had a trading place built called Oslo, where he could better launch his attacks on Denmark.

The showdown was slow in coming. King Sweyn's strategy seemed to be to avoid battle until he was confident in victory. The failure of the Danes to come out and fight caused Harald to let much of his levy go home. The Danes almost caught Harald off guard. Only by floating their booty on the surface to slow down their pursuers and eventually dumping their prisoners in the water did the Northmen escape, since a compassionate King Sweyn allowed his ships to recover these prisoners..

In 1063 the great sea-battle of Nisa should have decided affairs. It was another stunning victory against the odds for Harald but it still failed to subjugate the Danes. After two more years of hostility, a peace was agreed. King Harald was also busy at home enforcing his authority, and on one occasion only the intervention of friends prevented him coming to blows with his own son Magnus, now a stroppy teenager approaching sixteen years old and flushed with various military successes.

Magnus had led a fleet to restore Earl Aelfgar to his position in Mercia five years earlier, in 1058. Earl Ealfgar had, in the family tradition, held the earldom of East Anglia, as his father Earl Leofric had done before. It was during his father's tenure that his mother had ridden into legend with her naked trip on horseback into the marketplace at Coventry.

1057 saw the death of two of the great English earls. Leofric and Ralf both died in that year. Earl Siward of Northumbria had died two years before and Earl Godwin had only been dead for four years. The old order created by Cnut was being replaced by the next generation, which was introducing new rivalries in the kingdom of England.

The silence that surrounds the activities of Earl Leofric testifies to his loyal support not just for the king but also for a united England. He was another survivor of the purges of Cnut, in which intelligence and loyalty appeared to be the keys to survival. His only son, Aelfgar, possessed a different temperament.

No sooner had Earl Aelfgar taken over his father's land in Mercia than he was once again outlawed by King Edward. He had already

been outlawed in 1055 when he was earl of East Anglia, possibly at
the behest of the Godwin family, whose eldest son, Sweyn, had also
been outlawed for misdemeanours, which included over-familiar
dealings with the Welsh. Now Aelfgar was exiled on the suspicion
that he was too close to, and possibly conspiring with, Gruffydd
ap Llywelyn. The latter was now married to Aelfgar's daughter,
Ealdgyth, and they had produced one child, a daughter called Nest.
In the political language of the time, a marriage was synonymous
with political alliance.

The following year Earl Aelfgar was back. In 1058 he was supported by a fleet headed by Magnus, the elder son of King Harald.
Harald's Russian princess, Elisabeth, had only given him two daughters. Back in Norway, Harald took Thora as his 'kingly companion'.
She produced two boys, Magnus and Olaf. The eldest boy was probably ten or eleven when he led this expedition but evidently this
was an enlightened father, who sent the young Viking to see the
world. Magnus would have sailed the northern and western coasts
of Scotland and England. It is likely that he would have landed in
Dublin as well as the land of the foreigners, Wales.

The chroniclers are enigmatic about the settlement in England,
which was achieved without any fighting. 'It is tedious to relate fully
how things went' the *Anglo-Saxon Chronicle* (D) notes, concealing
from our view what might have been revealed. The censors were
already at work to ensure we heard the story of those in power.

To the English earls, the exile and restoration sent the message that
any hint of disloyalty would be punished but that it could be forgiven.
Presumably the hope was that the lesson would be learnt. However,
this was the earl's second offence so it is not clear why it was so quickly
overlooked. We do not have access to the 'tedious' details of the negotiations, presumably conducted by the king's enforcer, Earl Harold.

To the Norwegians and Welsh it sent a very different message.
Compromise and capitulation were signs of weakness. Young Magnus
doubtless carried this message back to Norway: the English were
unwilling to fight. This may have been true, but whether it was an act
of policy or a lack of preparedness we cannot judge. The expedition
had also shown King Harald what a powerful force could achieve,
especially if the spot was well chosen and the timing right.

Harald was now approaching fifty years of age. This was an outstand-
ing achievement for a warrior who had spent almost all of the last

thirty-five years on military campaigns. To have not only escaped death or any reported injury but also to have been consistently victorious in battle is truly remarkable. Just as all political careers are doomed to end in failure, so Harald must have expected that he would eventually die in battle.

The battle at Nisa in 1062 might have been the turning point of Harald's Nordic ambitions. As an experienced general, he now recognised that there was little prospect of a decisive victory over his southern neighbour. So in 1064 he made overtures of peace to which King Sweyn reacted with understandable suspicion. Harald's extraordinary cunning and stratagems were well known to his old adversary and erstwhile fighting companion. However, by 1065 prisoners were exchanged and both men undertook that they would never again fight each other.

It is possible to interpret this treaty with Denmark as preparing the way for the invasion of England, but there is no evidence to suggest that this was part of King Harald's plans at that stage. It might have been one of his options. However, the history of the next few centuries in England would illustrate that kings who did not occupy their belligerent lieutenants with warfare risked civil strife. Kings who tried to live in peace have gone down as 'weak'.

Perhaps King Harald appreciated that there were those among his people who were so much in the habit of warfare that inactivity threatened the civil peace. This was not the legacy he wanted to leave to his son. The expedition to England would allow him to remove this warrior element and others who might challenge the rule of his son, Magnus. This was less a stratagem, more the act of a statesman. But still we have no evidence that he was planning this in 1065 when he agreed terms with King Sweyn.

We certainly read of opposition within Norway to the proposed peace with Denmark. Perhaps it was his awareness of a bellicose party in Norway that made Harald receptive to the overtures from Earl Tostig when he arrived in 1066. We will explore later the circumstances that brought the brother of King Harold of England to Norway, seeking allies to invade his homeland later. King Harald of Norway was not the person to whom Tostig originally addressed his request for support. Tostig had naturally looked to the land of his mother to support his return to England.

It was a masterstroke by King Sweyn to pass Tostig's request on to his northern neighbour, King Harald. Did the Danish court counsellors sense the possibility another subtle stratagem worthy of King Harald? Did they suspect that the Norwegians would attack if Denmark lay open and their ships were engaged in an English adventure? One can imagine that there was considerable nervousness at the court of King Sweyn as their neighbours assembled another massive fleet in 1066, under the pretext of invading England.

HARALD'S MOTIVES FOR INVASION

Historians have focused on the legalities or diplomatic niceties of the two armies invading England in 1066. A Norwegian claim to the throne of England has its origins in the terms of the deal that ended the fighting in 1036 between Harthacnut of Denmark and Magnus of Norway. Under the terms of their truce, the surviving king would inherit the other's kingdom.

Frank Barlow, in his history of the Godwins, reports that between 1043 and 1047 King Magnus of Norway did indeed harbour plans to invade England. The sagas tell us that King Magnus sent ambassadors to King Edward in England with a letter. After the formalities, the letter got down to business.

> Ye must have heard of the agreement which I and Harthacnut made, that he of us two who survived the other should have all the land and people which the deceased had possessed. Now it has so turned out, as ye have no doubt heard, that I have taken the Danish dominions as my heritage after Harthacnut. But before he departed this life he had England as well as Denmark; therefore I consider myself now, in consequence of my rights by this agreement, to own England also. Now I will therefore that thou deliver to me the kingdom; otherwise I will seek to take it by arms, both from Denmark and Norway; and let him rule the land to whom fate gives the victory.

King Edward's reply is masterful, not because of the recital of the complex succession in England but for the last line of his long letter.

> It is known to all men in this country that King Ethelred, my father, was udal-born to this kingdom, both after the old and new law of inheritance. We were four sons after him; and when he by death left

the throne my brother Edmund took the government and kingdom; for he was the oldest of us brothers, and I was well satisfied that it was so. And after him my stepfather, Canute the Great, took the kingdom, and as long as he lived there was no access to it. After him my brother Harald was king as long as he lived; and after him my brother Harthacnut took the kingdoms both of Denmark and England; for he thought that a just brotherly division that he should have both England and Denmark, and that I should have no kingdom at all. Now he died, and then it was the resolution of all the people of the country to take me for king here in England. So long as I had no kingly title I served only superiors in all respects, like those who had no claims by birth to land or kingdom. Now, however, I have received the kingly title, and am consecrated king. I have established my royal dignity and authority, as my father before me; and while I live I will not renounce my title.

If King Magnus come here with an army, I will gather no army against him; but he shall only get the opportunity of taking England when he has taken my life.

King Magnus was probably surprised when his ambassadors returned with Edward's message. Magnus decided to let King Edward have his kingdom 'in peace for me'. The claim by Magnus was therefore acknowledged.

So Magnus, and in time his half-brother Harald, could therefore claim that the Danish truce terms of 1039 entitled Norway to claim the kingdom of England. However, agreements were very personal affairs and in the absence of any clause to the effect that it passed to the 'heirs and successors' it is reasonable to assume that the agreement lapsed with King Magnus in 1047. Snorri certainly reports of the treaty made between Harald and Sweyn that 'this peace should endure as long as they were kings'. The durability of such agreements was emphasised after Harald's death in England. King Sweyn let it be known that 'the peace between the Northmen and the Danes was at an end, and insisted that the league between Harald and Sweyn was not for longer time than their lives'.

King Magnus in effect recognised that his agreement was only valid for his lifetime by 'returning' Denmark to Sweyn, a grandson of King Sweyn Forkbeard and a nephew of both Cnut and Earl Godwin. When King Harald assumed full control of his kingdom, his struggle was with his southern neighbours, the Danes. Nowhere is there any reference to the enforcement of the 1039 treaty imply- ing that Harald considered that it had lapsed. Magnus did not renew the embassies to England or make any further claim. The terms had effectively expired or lapsed.

Battle had some clear 'constitutional' advantages in resolving disputes. The battle either eliminated one party to the dispute or destroyed the power of one side by defeating their army. When battles were between tens or hundreds of warriors the social cost was low. A century before, a king could muster a force that was measured in the hundreds. But as organisation and prosperity allowed ever larger armies to be deployed, and a second army could be mobilised if the first was destroyed, the cost became higher.

As we have seen in the complex events that followed the reign of King Ethelred, deals were done to avoid battle. This was an era when the personality of a leader and, more importantly, the power that he could project, were the key determinants in who emerged as king.

Therefore deals, truces and posturing were being tried as a better way to decide the outcome of disputes. Experienced war leaders understood that the outcome of battle was far from certain and it often made sense to settle the dispute by negotiation.

Beyond the legal case, many other motivations for Harald's invasion of England can be imagined. King Harald had not been successful in his attempts to dominate the Danes. Perhaps a motive was the desire to expand the Nordic empire. Maybe occupying the land of the man who had brought him long years of exile, Cnut, might have been attractive to the humour of the old warrior, Harald.

We will examine Harald's response to the request from Earl Tostig later. As a consummate political operator, King Harald saw that the balance of advantage outweighed the risks in deciding to take a fleet to England. A dozen fleets had been successful in taking possession of kingdoms during Harald's lifetime. With the massive fleet that he could muster, the case for this adventure must have been strong.

Magnus, Harald's son, was recognised as king of Norway in the summer before Harald's departure. Perhaps King Harald, who had spent his life using manoeuvre and the exercise of military might to achieve and hold power, appreciated the vulnerability of his son. By removing the veterans of his decade of warfare, Harald would give Magnus time to establish himself over the young Turks of the new generation of warriors. He certainly left for England having put his affairs of state thoroughly in order.

Harald had enjoyed a long and apparently happy relationship with his wife even though, once he was the sole ruler of Norway, he appears to have taken his duty to produce a male heir seriously. He stayed with Elisabeth, who would accompany him on his final journey as far as the Orkneys.

The royal saga reports on Harald's family life:

> The winter after King Magnus the Good died, King Harald took Thora, daughter of Thorberg Arnason, and they had two sons; the oldest called Magnus, and the other Olaf. King Harald and Queen Ellisif had two daughters; the one Maria, the other Ingegerd.

Harald was evidently a devoted father. Along with his wife, Harald also took his daughters and his younger son, Olaf, on the invasion of England. This is a strong indication that he intended to stay. All this amounts to an impressive act of statesmanship and not one immediately associated with a warrior just looking for another fight. Perhaps his motivation was to ensure the legacy for his family. Only Magnus and his mother Thora would be left in Norway when they set out for England in 1066.

Before King Harald left Norway he paid a visit to Nidaros and the shrine of Olaf. He performed the ritual of clipping the hair and nails but this time also threw the keys, his own and the duplicate set made for the old king, Magnus, into the water. This was another act of closure.

King Harald then sailed with his own ships to meet the fleet assembled at the Solunds, strategically opposite the Shetland Isles, just north of Bergen. The size of the fleet is recorded as 'nearly 200 ships' plus many supporting craft for provisions. The sagas now report three separate omens all predicting a bad outcome for the mission. These tales were recorded over a century later when the conclusion of this chapter was well known. They provide some drama to the narrative but also indicate that the pagan ways were not entirely lost. Clearly, the ominous note of all the dreams had no effect at all upon Harald's course of action.

At the Solund Isles a man called Gyrd, one of Harald's crew, had a dream:

He thought he was standing in the king's ship and saw a great witch-wife standing on the island, with a fork in one hand and a trough in the other. He thought also that he saw over all the fleet, and that a fowl was sitting upon every ship's stern, and that these fowls were all ravens and the witch sang this song:

From the east I'll 'tice the king,
To the west the king I'll bring;
Many a noble bone will be
Ravens o'er Giuke's ship are sitting,
Eyeing the prey they think most fitting.
Upon the stern I'll sail with them!
Upon the stern I'll sail with them!

The next omen is recorded by a man called Thord:

He dreamt one night that he saw King Harald's fleet coming to land, and he knew the land to be England. He saw a great battle-array on the land; and he thought both sides began to fight, and had many banners flapping in the air. And before the army of the people of the country was riding a huge witch-wife upon a wolf; and the wolf had a man's carcass in his mouth, and the blood was dropping from his jaws; and when he had eaten up one body she threw another into his mouth, and so one after another, and he swallowed them all.

   This was her song:

Skade's eagle eyes
The king's ill luck espies:
Though glancing shields
Hide the green fields,
The king's ill luck she spies.
To bode the doom of this great king,
The flesh of bleeding men I fling
To hairy jaw and hungry maw!
To hairy jaw and hungry maw!

King Harald also had a dream about meeting his brother, King Olaf, who sang him this verse:

In many a fight
My name was bright;
Men weep, and tell
How Olaf fell.
Thy death is near;
Thy corpse, I fear,
The crow will feed,
The witch-wife's steed.

These are the dispositions of a man facing his fate. The kingdom was in safe hands and his long-suffering wife and much-loved daughters would go with him to face what fate had in store.

The Nordic sagas are candid in their appraisals of their leaders' faults and virtues. This is how Snorri sets down history's judgement on Harald:

> King Harald was most greedy of power, and of all distinction and honour. He was bountiful to the friends who suited him.
>
> King Harald never fled from battle, but often tried cunning ways to escape when he had to do with great superiority of forces. All the men who followed King Harald in battle or skirmish said that when he stood in great danger, or anything came suddenly upon him, he always took that course which all afterwards saw gave the best hope of a fortunate issue.
>
> King Harald was very proud, and his pride increased after he was established in the country; and it came so far that at last it was not good to speak against him, or to propose anything different from what he desired.

He would be called 'Hardrade', which can be interpreted as 'severe counsellor', 'tyrant' or 'ruthless', but as the writer appraises in his judgement, it was not good to speak against him. So it is unlikely that he ever heard himself addressed as 'Hardrade'.

This was the experienced warrior whom the young earls would try to stop at Fulford.

3

Defence of the Kingdom in 1066

The new King Harold of England was forced to adopt a sophisticated plan to defend his kingdom in 1066.

In the north, he faced possible attack from the Danes or the Norwegians. He could be reasonably confident that the present enmity between these Nordic powers would prevent both of them attacking together. With luck, the mutual suspicion between the northern neighbours might keep both of them at bay for fear that the other might take advantage of the distraction.

The domestic struggle for power and influence during the long reign of Edward might so easily have seen the defence of the north and east coasts in the capable custody of his brother Tostig. Instead, his brother was conspiring and advising England's enemies. The defence in the north was entrusted to the younger son of Earl Aelfgar of Mercia, Earl Morcar. Harold had been engaged in a very personal power struggle with Morcar's late father, but the relationship had been repaired.

In the centre of the kingdom, the threat from his exiled brother would depend on the support he could muster in Flanders. Edward's mother, Emma, had built a base there and Harold's brother, Tostig, had married into the family. When the new king had wanted to assist the Germanic emperor in punishing the count of Flanders for the support he had offered rebellious neighbours, Earl Godwin was a reluctant participant.

However, Flanders now appeared content to remain under the notional control of a weak and distant Frankish king, recognising that its own ambitions needed to be limited. It would be 150 years before Flanders was subjugated by France. In the meantime it would serve as neutral trading territory, a place where the Godwin family and many others could take refuge, a medieval incarnation of Switzerland.

The success of Flanders was as a trading place. Its real struggle was with the sea and the many rivers that crossed its territory. The inhabitants of the Low Countries would later boast that while God had made the world, they had made their own land by wresting it from the sea. King Harold would not have assessed the risk from just across the Channel as significant, even though the late Earl Godwin was held responsible for the murder of the men of Flanders who escorted Emma's son Alfred on his disastrous mission to England, and Earl Tostig was brother-in-law to the count.

In the south, Harold knew that he faced a powerful adversary across the water. The threat came from William of Normandy, who was probably born in September 1027, making him the same age as Harold. William's mother, Herleva Arlette, was the daughter of a tanner, who might also have served as the local undertaker, both hard and smelly occupations. Nevertheless, from this household, a beauty that would captivate a duke was produced.

The romantic myth that has surrounded the courting of William's mother tells us that Robert, the younger brother of the reigning duke of Normandy, was smitten by the beauty of Herleva as she washed linen at the river's edge. He had some difficulty persuading her father, Fulbert, to give his permission for a meeting and she, in turn, refused to come to Robert in secret.

The scene was set for one of history's great trysts if even the modest version of what was evidently a passionate meeting is to be believed. Herleva rode proudly into the castle on horseback. During subsequent romantic activity she reported feeling the very moment of conception and she later reported a vision of a tree that grew so large the whole of Normandy was in its shade.

Robert's actions and intentions were honourable, certainly measured by the standards of the day. Recognising that he might need to make a political marriage, Robert found a suitable husband for

Herleva among his vassals, one Herluin de Conteville. Herleva had at least two more children with her husband, among them Odo, later the warrior bishop of Bayeux.

THE FIRST NORMAN INVASION

There can be no doubt that the Normans had hopes of absorbing England. Was the landing in 1066 the second coming of the Normans? King Edward was a Norman by upbringing and half his blood was from his Norman mother. A very good case can be made that when Edward began to consider his succession the duke of Normandy was an early choice. The tale of this attempted takeover is one of intrigue and power struggle that any modern student of politics will recognise. The attempted palace coup was the first act in the drama that would climax with the invasions of 1066.

For the first years of his reign King Edward pursued a prudent policy. Edward had little alternative but to rely on Earl Godwin as his prime councillor. Edward did not arrive with a recognisable set of his own Norman courtiers and he did not have any powerful connections in England. He might not even have mastered the English language. King Edward was therefore a stranger at court, lacking friends and influence.

This cannot have been a comfortable position for the new monarch, who had been brought up in a land where power came from the military force one could deploy. King Edward's power lay in the unity his weak military position provided. This gave him a vital role as it allowed him to play power-broker between the various earls. As Edward had demonstrated in his reply to the challenge from King Magnus, he had no intention or ambition to raise an army and rule under its authority. Edward had his own plans, as Earl Godwin would soon discover.

One is entitled to wonder just how much real communication passed between the king and his pre-eminent earl and protector, Godwin. The word 'currency' is employed as a synonym for money because it incorporates the most important feature of any token of exchange, its current acceptability as a measure of value. Money enjoys value as a means of exchange simply because people accept it as such. A very similar pragmatic approach attaches itself to the development of units of measure and language in early England.

Norman French, as a sub-language with Romance, Germanic and Norse origins, would not have been wholly unintelligible to many in England where a similar patchwork of languages, dialects and accents existed. Norman French is certainly not the language we know today as French. It was only in the fifteenth century that the French language was imposed as the official language within France. However, the majority of the population in France continued to use their local language until the upheaval of the Great War. Many scholars now believe that the existence of different languages in England was the motive for a new language that was rich in words but poor in grammatical rules. Therefore Edward and his chief minister might have struggled to make themselves understood along with everybody else.

It is notable that there is no reference to interpreters or communications problems in any texts. They were presumably just a part of life and therefore not worthy of comment. Merchants and others who moved around would become adept at making themselves understood and tuning their ear to the language spoken by those who mattered.

Godwin's sons, Sweyn and Harold, were made earls after the family had supported King Edward, when the dowager Emma was again deprived of her treasury and exiled in 1043 by another of her regal sons. The new king was testing the loyalty of all his premier earls with this mission. Leofric of Mercia and Siward of Northumbria were both in attendance, perhaps to ensure Earl Godwin would do the bidding of the new king rather than obey his mother, to whom Godwin had been allied from time to time during the uneasy transitions after the death of Cnut. Emma would now conclude her struggle for power by commissioning a history to be written to justify her maternal interference.

The motive for this pre-emptive move against Emma might have been a suspicion that she would support the cause of King Magnus of Norway. In the defensive dispositions of the new king, Earl Godwin would be called on to maintain a fleet at Sandwich, until the untimely death of Magnus and accession of King Harald as sole king in Norway allowed the fleet to be stood down after 1045. The chroniclers note that King Sweyn's 'contention in Denmark hindered his coming here'.

While Godwin guarded the south, Earl Siward was occupied maintaining the northern frontier of England. Macbeth, King of

Moray, was elected king of Scotland in place of Duncan's young sons in 1040. Malcolm, the elder of these sons, took refuge with his 'uncle', Siward. This created an 'English party' where attachments of kinship would contest control of Scotland until the time of the Stewarts and union with England. King Macbeth would haunt the dealings in Northumbria for the next decade and ultimately determine who would lead the resistance at Fulford.

Old Earl Leofric of Mercia had the task of maintaining the border with the Welsh princes and the Viking community based around Dublin, which was a prosperous centre and popular haven for exiles and raiders. Unlike Godwin, he and his wife Godiva had just the single son, Aelfgar. All of the ageing earls must have already sensed that the six sons of Godwin were well placed to inherit leadership over much of the kingdom. The shires given to the new earls, Sweyn and Harold Godwinson, had been part of traditional Mercian territory. Harold now held the earldom of East Anglia, which had belonged to Earl Leofric in former times. Sweyn received Oxfordshire, Gloucestershire and Herefordshire from the king, along with two shires from Godwin's land.

These holdings were entirely in the king's gift and had to be renewed by royal charter with each new monarch. The control and disposition of these titles, plus the income that the estates could generate for their earls, was one way the new king could exercise control and ensure he obtained military backing when he required it.

With the earls and their eligible sons occupied in the defence of the frontiers, King Edward could attend to his own affairs. The other area of influence open to Edward was in ecclesiastical appointments, where he soon began to introduce Norman abbots and bishops. From 1045 the names of Normans begin to appear in documents, as Edward felt confident enough to introduce some of those with whom he had grown up in exile into his English court circle. For five years, this influence grew.

On 23 January 1045, the forty-year-old King Edward married the eldest daughter of Earl Godwin. This was not a contract entered into in a rush. Thirty months had passed since Edward had become king. We are told nothing of the negotiations or drama surrounding this match. There do not appear to have been any eligible daughters among the leading earls but the record is notorious for omitting mention of those who do not feature in some incident. It is probable that Edward cast about carefully before deciding to accept a marriage to Edith.

The marriage swung the balance of power among the earls strongly in favour of the Godwinsons. The close bond that was forming with the premier family makes the events that unfolded over the next few years rather puzzling. It is possible that the marriage upset the domestic balance of power among England's earls. Could this have been Edward's intention?

Queen Edith was evidently intent upon bridging any culture and language gap and employed a Norman chambermaid, Matilda, as her constant companion. With a wife who was able to assist with everyday communication, independent life for the king must have improved after the marriage.

The problems for the Godwinsons began with the eldest son. Earl Sweyn attempted to master the perennial Welsh border situation by making a compact with one side to contain the other. This certainly looked like the Godwinson political way of working. In 1046 Sweyn joined with Gruffydd ap Llywelyn. By destabilising the Welsh kings, Sweyn might have planned to exert an effective controlling influence over this troublesome area and source of raiders. However, dealing with this traditional enemy looked suspect. It did not help that relations with the Welsh had been handled by the earls of Mercia in recent times. In the struggle to maintain the influence of his family, Earl Leofric of Mercia might have seen this as an opportunity to make mischief.

However, Earl Sweyn made life easy for his detractors as this was not his only offence. This renegade son would do much to craft his own fall from power. Not only did he claim that Cnut was his real father and therefore that he was a rightful candidate to the throne, but he 'ordered the abbess of Leominster to be brought to him, and kept her as long as it suited him, and then let her go home'. Although, like most of the near-contemporary English records on which we rely, this note was made by the Church, some serious act of impropriety probably did take place.

Sweyn's troubles were compounded by emissaries from Wales. Welshmen, presumably those whom Earl Sweyn had not allied with, got to King Edward first 'and accused the earls [Godwin, Sweyn and Harold] so that they might not come within his eyesight'. The Welshmen claimed 'they were coming thither in order to betray the king'.

The king evidently did not believe there was enough evidence against Godwin and Harold, but the alliance with Gruffydd was not denied. So the king outlawed Sweyn, dividing his holding between his brother Harold and his cousin Beorn. The Mercians might have hoped that they would benefit from the fall of Sweyn, but their influence was not yet being felt. Sweyn spent some time in Bruges before moving north to join another cousin, whose fifteen-year struggle with Harald of Norway was about to begin.

The winter of 1046 was also memorable for the weather:

> And in the same year, after Candlemas, came the strong winter, with frost and with snow, and with all kinds of bad weather; so that there was no man then alive who could remember so severe a winter as this was, both through loss of men and through loss of cattle; yea, fowls and fishes through much cold and hunger perished.

The following year, 1047, also began badly, with a raid on England's naval harbour at Sandwich. This appears to be a return to the old pattern of Viking coastal raiding. Both the king and the earl of Wessex are reported by the chronicles as being active in pursuing the raiders but, as usual, the initiative lay with the attackers. The signs were ominous.

The year also brought an earthquake in May of such magnitude that it was recorded from Worcester to Wick, after which there was a 'very great loss by disease of men and of cattle over all England', as is often the case after the debilitating effects of a harsh winter.

Yet in the space of a few years the situation would change dramatically, so that in 1050 King Edward

> ...abolished the Danegeld which king Ethelred imposed. That was in the thirty-ninth year after it had begun. That tribute harassed all the people of England;... and it was always paid before other imposts, which were levied indiscriminately, and vexed men variously.

The key events that would allow this tax to be relieved were taking place in Norway and Denmark, where two new rulers were establishing themselves and bringing their land and its residents under an unprecedented degree of control. The Church might take some credit for this with the education, administration and centralisation it brought. But the same year, William of Normandy had married Matilda and Pope Leo had gathered his cardinals together at Rheims for the dedication of the new cathedral. With so many important people preoccupied, a degree of tranquillity attended political affairs in England. The following year, 1050, was declared a jubilee and many around Europe took advantage of this opportunity to journey to Rome. England, a small player among the continental powers, was absent. There was trouble near the top.

1049 saw two events that would further weaken the Godwinsons. Emperor Henry III wanted to launch a punitive expedition against Baldwin in Flanders. To ensure that reinforcements could not be summoned in the form of Viking mercenaries, but also to prevent Baldwin's escape, Edward was asked to provide naval support. Godwin had enjoyed good relationships with Baldwin but he was forced to provide this blockade. However, it appears that Earl Godwin was not forced by the circumstances to attack Flanders. The king was evidently gaining control of Earl Godwin.

The second event of 1049 that would deeply upset, as well as damage the standing of, Godwin was the return of his outlawed son Sweyn. The chroniclers imply that he was no longer welcome in Denmark as he had 'ruined himself'. By mid-summer there had been a reconciliation with Baldwin and the blockade was stood down. Godwin and his nephew, Beorn, were taking their ships back along the south coast to their bases.

Sweyn Godwinson asked the king for a pardon and offered to swear oaths of loyalty. He also attempted to persuade Harold and Beorn to restore the land that had been his earl-lands. Perhaps he prevailed on Beorn to promise something that he could not deliver, because what happened next was shocking. Beorn was evidently very cautious about getting too close to his cousin Sweyn but eventually was kidnapped and Sweyn sailed away. Beorn seems to have been snatched at the Godwin family base of Bosham. The role of Beorn, an heir to the throne of Denmark, is never made clear. It is likely that he was a hostage. Hostages were routinely exchanged as a guarantee of a treaty. Hostages were not restrained but often given employment by those to whom they were assigned. As such many hostages might be seen slightly more in the role of ambassadors. They were certainly not prisoners and it was very rare for them to come to any harm even if the terms of an agreement were breached.

But Beorn was taken west to the mouth of either the river Dart or Axe, where he was murdered and buried. Now Sweyn was not simply outlawed but declared a *nithing* by all. This was not simply regal condemnation, but popular disapproval.

The first Godwin scion was removed from the scene permanently the following year, when he died at Constantinople returning from pilgrimage to the Holy Land. Earl Harold was now the eldest son in a family whose collective fortunes seemed to be failing. Edward was doubtless aware of the internal tensions about the succession, but with Earl Godwin's power diminished the king might have felt it was now a suitable time to promote closer ties with Normandy. In 1051, matters came to a head and Earl Godwin and his powerful clan were wrong-footed.

King Edward is often characterised in the rather simple terms familiar to readers of medieval history. *1066 and All That* reduces the human story to a few simple rules. Edward was a 'good king' who didn't seem to do very much. The flesh-and-blood man was more complex. In the events that climaxed during 1051, King Edward is revealed as a ruler working cautiously towards a new regime. He is not a weak man, manipulated by others, but rather a good manager who is working to bring about the changes he wants by the careful exercise of his limited power.

After six years of marriage, the failure to produce any children must have reawakened the matter of succession. The cause of the couple's infertility cannot be known. Edward has no recorded bastards, which is not unknown at this time but is unusual. He and Edith came from apparently fertile families (although, interestingly, not one of Queen Emma's sons produced any children). Edith was one of ten children, while Edward's father had over ten children and his mother had now provided England with three kings. There are some clues surrounding the deathbed scenes that Edward might have been suffering from diabetes. One in four men suffering from this disease also suffer from impotence. Since childlessness was held to be a woman's problem, Edith was doubtless content to go along with the story that celibacy was the cause and the saintly Edward's choice.

With the prospect of a natural heir receding, all the old plots, plans and ambitions could, realistically, be revived, having been put on hold after Edward's marriage. The two northern earls were apprehensive seeing the progress made by the Godwin scions. So Edward could rely on them for support.

After a decade on the throne, Edward was now in control of the affairs of state and made his move. The episode is easy to interpret as a well-planned manoeuvre by the Normans at court, working with the support of Edward, although no master plan exists or is even hinted at in surviving documents. However, the sequence of events and the way they are dealt with suggests some sophisticated political forethought.

The problems began with the arrival of visiting nobles who were to attend the court of the childless Edward. There was an incident at Dover which cost the lives of some locals and several of the retainers accompanying the visitors. This seemingly trivial event precipitated the downfall of the Godwin family.

The count of Boulogne, Eustace, visited Edward. Eustace was married to Edward's sister Godgifu. He was therefore close family. After his visit, Eustace returned to Dover to take a ship for home. His retainers tried to take over a suitable dwelling without the consent of its owner. A fracas developed. The householder was wounded and he then killed one of Eustace's men, who in their turn responded by taking a mounted entourage round to kill the householder.

Things now turned ugly as the townsfolk joined in. Soon Count Eustace was fleeing for his life as his followers were cut down. The chronicles say both sides lost about twenty killed. The tale that Eustace told when he returned to the sanctuary of Edward's court is not recorded. It is easy to imagine that he would have portrayed it as a treacherous ambush. There is no proof that this was premeditated. However, it came at the end of Eustace's mission: he did not continue his journey home but instead chose to return to Edward, perhaps scenting an opportunity. One chronicler also notes that Eustace 'put on his breastplate' along with all the other men in preparation for the encounter in Dover, implying that he was preparing for action.

It is much to Earl Godwin's credit that he 'perceived that one ought not to pronounce a verdict after hearing the charges of one side only', according to William of Malmesbury. He argued that Eustace's account was not accurate. However, the version reported to King Edward by his guests led the king to demand that Earl Godwin perform the same service he had carried out some years before at Worcester and punish those who disturbed the king's peace. Earl Godwin had doubtless heard the other side of the story by now from the folk of Dover, as it was a part of his domain of Wessex. These were his people. Their version portrayed the attack as one of unprovoked aggression.

Not for the first time, the cultural divide might have been at the root of the problem. Visitors could expect hospitality. But they had no right to demand it in England. It was a part of the Celtic culture that the Saxons had not displaced. The duty of hospitality came before any other. Continental society had evolved subtly different rules regarding social obligations. The roots of this distinction lie in the way societies had evolved as the European nations were formed.

The English owed various duties to their lord, in exactly the same way as their continental counterparts. However, in England the lord respected a tradition where the leader owed a reciprocal duty of care to those who were bound to him. If someone fell on hard times they would place their fate quite literally in the hands of their lord. Impoverished families, widows and orphans could place their head into the cupped hands of their local liege, who had to accept the obligation to maintain them as their loaf-giver.

This is probably an idealised formulation of the interlocking obligations of master and servant, but this early form of Saxon social security certainly extended care beyond the family or tribe, and created a complex web of obligations on both master and servant.

The critical point, however, was in the power it implied for the individual to make a personal choice. This sense of personal power had already promoted the Witan as a body empowered to make decisions affecting the most powerful in the land. The survival of these attitudes can also be seen in the Magna Carta, still some 150 years in the future.

Those brought up at one of the continental courts would not have recognised that popular consent played any part in their affairs. The peasantry was theirs to command. This concept of duty owed by the subject to their ruler would gradually be extended until monarchs were claiming nothing less than divine rights as God's anointed, thus provoking England's civil war. But the execution of Charles I was six centuries into the future.

Earl Godwin perceived his vulnerability and collected a force before he went to answer the king's summons. He might not have intended this as anything other than a sensible precaution but it could easily be interpreted as an act of rebellion by those at court. Godwin, with his son Harold, already had his army assembled to fight the Welsh who had launched a serious raid on Hereford. In the power politics of the time, the combined army of the Godwin family would be well understood by all. A countervailing force had to be mustered quickly.

The importance of this manoeuvre was not lost on the northern earls, Leofric of Mercia and Siward of Northumbria. These were mature and powerful warlords who recognised that the time had come to confront the rising power of the Godwinsons. They brought their armies to Gloucester to support King Edward. Again, there is no evidence that this was pre-planned, but those at court would have appreciated that the northern earls were free of other border engagements at this time, while Earl Godwin was distracted by the marriage of his son, Tostig, to the daughter of Count Baldwin in Flanders.

The northern earls were ready, but probably not really willing, to fight if it could be avoided. The best interpretation is that this was primarily gesture politics using the one language that was understood by all: military might. The Witan assembled and the situation appeared to have been defused. Edward granted peace to all and the forces dispersed, but Godwin was summoned to answer the charges relating to Dover in London later in the year.

King Edward now gathered a force of his own under Norman control. The source of the troops is unknown. Were they drawn from the Normans or did the northern earls perhaps lend some of the thanes who owed them loyalty in order to bolster the king's army? In the power play of the time, such support would have suited the northern earls as it would redress the balance between the three leading earls without bringing them into direct conflict.

The confrontation at Dover had therefore escalated way beyond a lethal street fight. Backed and encouraged by the Norman party at court, King Edward moved decisively. For the first time, Edward had his own military force. He summoned the Witan ahead of the meeting that had been scheduled with Earl Godwin for London.

The Witan then summoned Godwin and Harold to answer the various charges. They sensibly demanded hostages as a guarantee of safe conduct before they came to put their case. Hostages were refused, although the Godwinsons handed over their youngest member, Wulfnof, and the outlawed Sweyn's son, Hakon, to King Edward. These young hostages would soon be taken to Normandy and play their part in a later drama.

The various recordings of this affair give the impression that Earl Godwin recognised that his military position was too weak to allow any prospect of success. Furthermore, it is unclear what a military victory might have achieved. Had Godwin confronted the king's makeshift army, he might have won but the king would remain. There is little chance King Edward would have taken to the field himself and the death of the king would, in these circumstances, have provoked a war for the succession. The destruction of the English earls in a civil war might have been what the Norman party hoped to provoke.

Godwin and Harold did not appear in London to answer the charges and they were given five days safe conduct to leave the country in October 1051. Their destination was just over the Channel in Flanders, where the family of Earl Tostig's wife was based. Godwin collected his treasury from Bosham before the journey to Flanders. We learn that Harold and a younger brother, Leofwine, instead crossed over to Dublin and the protection of the lord of Leinster, probably taking their outlawed brother Sweyn's ships.

Since Godwin had fled instead of standing trial, he and his family were outlawed with lands and titles forfeit. Earl Aelfgar would now receive the earldom of East Anglia that had traditionally been the preserve of the Mercian nobility, but his tenure would be short. King Edward kept most of the confiscated lands in his own hands, perhaps indicating the start of a new role as king-militant. Godwin's downfall did not benefit the northern earls.

Edward's queen, Edith Godwinson, did not escape banishment. Archbishop Robert of Jumièges, installed in 1048 at Canterbury, urged divorce. However, Edith was probably sent to the abbey at Wherwell where a half-sister of Edward may have been the abbess. This Benedictine priory had been founded by King Ethelred's mother as a penance for her evil earthly deeds. The annals of the priory are incomplete, but the monk known as Florence of Worcester reports that the convent attached to the abbey was also used to confine Queen Emma at some point.

Removing his queen from court made two points. The first was the unambiguous message it sent about the future role of the Godwinsons. It also removed the prospect of a natural heir. Both messages needed to be sent if Edward was to introduce a Norman succession. Once again, we can speculate that this was his plan, but the chroniclers have left us no proof. Had the king wanted to keep Godwin, he could have done so. He seems to have had other plans.

As 1051 drew to a close, King Edward appeared to have established a regime that reflected his own upbringing in Normandy. He had perhaps also avenged the death of his brother Alfred, in which Godwin was implicated, and vanquished the Danish party in his court. A series of appointments put the Normans increasingly in control.

For Earl Godwin, this looked like the eclipse of a remarkable career. Godwin was probably born of a Danish mother around 993, which would make him no more than a year or two older then the late King Cnut. He appears to have inherited his family lands in Wessex in early manhood, so he was free to make his own choices in the complex and dangerous politics of the time.

It was probably the support of those like Godwin's father, who had defected to King Sweyn of Denmark back in 1013, that had secured the eventual succession for Cnut. Godwin's fortunes had risen along with Cnut's, who took him to Denmark when he went to secure the Danish throne after the death of his brother.

We know little of Godwin's martial exploits. Possibly they were few. The *Vitae Edwardii Regis* speaks of him as a wise counsellor rather than a mighty warrior. Perhaps it was his skill in negotiation and willingness to find workable compromises that brought him respect and advancement. Such political skills were an innovation. But they would continue to serve the Godwinson family well.

After awarding Godwin the title of earl in 1018, King Cnut apparently restored the extensive family holdings in Wessex. The following year Godwin married Gytha, the sister-in-law of Cnut. The marriage must have had the consent of Cnut, so binding Godwin to the king.

Cnut's sister Estrith had married Earl Ulf. Their union would produce the future King Sweyn, who would rule Denmark for a quarter of a century, half of it spent battling with King Harald of Norway before that threat was removed in 1066 by Harald's death at Stamford Bridge. Their second son, Earl Beorn, played a brief but tragic part in our story, when he was murdered by his cousin, Sweyn Godwinson. Gytha, Godwin's wife, was Earl Ulf's younger sister.

The following year Godwin was created earl of Wessex. Again according to *Vita Edwardii Regis,* Godwin was made 'office-bearer to almost all the kingdom', making him effectively the regent for the king during his regular absences from his English kingdom.

Godwin was therefore an experienced governor of the kingdom when Edward came to the throne. The same source notes that 'what he wrote all decreed should be written and what erased, erased'.

Gytha produced six sons and four daughters with Earl Godwin. One can read into the naming of the children the state of politics of the time. The first five children have Danish names. The last five, probably born after the death of Cnut, have Anglo-Saxon names.

Frank Barlow, in his study of the Godwin family, sums it up:

> He was of course an opportunist with a good eye for the winner, and through timely support securing victory for his candidate, a deed which earned him rewards. All the English nobles were involved in these high-risk operations. The prudent Godwin just did it better than the rest.

Edward was now able to return the hospitality he had enjoyed during his twenty-seven years of exile and invite William to visit him. There is no evidence that Edward and William were in any sense kindred spirits. But he was familiar with Norman ways and, with his queen now in a convent, no natural successor to Edward was in prospect. The succession must have been a topic that the king and duke discussed. It is entirely feasible that Edward might have recognised William as a potential successor. Indeed, it would have been remarkable if the latter had not actually suggested it.

Only one chronicle records a visit from William to England soon after Godwin's downfall:

> Then, soon, came William, the earl [of Normandy], from beyond seas with a great band of Frenchmen; and the king received him, and as many of his companions as it pleased him; and let him away again.

This was probably no more than a courtesy call, and there is no evidence or suggestion that any agreement was entered into.

At this point, the new Norman party must have been happy that they had won effective control of England. However, they had failed to take account of the power that resided with the earldoms beyond Wessex and the military weakness of the central authority was soon revealed. These manoeuvres had been subtle, with each party playing their hand well, but it was King Edward who had achieved the most in 1051.

The northern earls had arguably strengthened their positions by conniving at the downfall of Earl Godwin at a time when all the earls were ageing and contemplating their own, as well as the regal, succession. They had succession issues of their own pending. The Norman advisors seemed to have removed the warlord from the southern territories that formed the power base and wealth of the Godwinsons. William, back in Normandy, could anticipate a time when he would bring the wealthy and well-ordered territory of England under his control.

However, the success of the Norman party was short-lived. Gruffydd, King of the Welsh, took advantage of the incomers' inexperience and raided into the border territory. John of Worcester notes that many Normans were killed. These Normans, possibly ones who had been brought over by William, had been granted the border territory formerly occupied by Godwin's eldest son, Sweyn. The chronicles record that the Normans had already introduced their strategy of castle-building, but it did not save them.

In the same year, Harold and Leofwine raided the coast of the West Country from Ireland. Earl Godwin led his fleet back from Flanders and was able to sail along the coast; although the king did take steps to intercept him they were not successful, and Godwin returned to Flanders.

One can speculate that these raids were rather more than a rude awakening. The attack in Herefordshire might well have removed a significant element of the limited Norman military might in England. The vulnerability of the coastline had also been demonstrated. However, this tells only a part of the tale. Edward could have ordered a full military response to the threat of invasion. Instead, he relied upon the force that he now held as effectively the new earl of Wessex.

Prior to Godwin's flight, many of his followers had felt that their oath to the king forced them to defect. In all likelihood, Godwin would have released them because he had no way to transport, pay or lodge his army overseas. It was unthinkable to make them all outlaws. Their backing of the king, along with a desire to avoid bloodshed, are cited as two reasons for Godwin's flight. So King Edward was now reliant upon an army whose members had served Earl Godwin for a generation. Godwin might have confided to some of his thanes that he expected to return soon.

A year after he had gone into exile, rather than present himself for trial, Godwin was back in London. 'And Godwin stationed himself continually before London with his fleet, till he came to Southwark; where he abode some time, until the flood came up.' He had taken up a very similar position to the location he had abandoned some months earlier. Godwin must have intended to send the message that now he was ready to address the charges made against him.

Godwin then persuaded the burgesses of the city to support him, after which his ships 'weighed anchor and steered through the bridge by the south side'. His army crossed the bridge and 'arranged themselves by the Strand', effectively surrounding the king's ships. The purpose of Godwin's earlier trip along the south coast appears to have been to pick up an army from his ancestral earldom. The king's army and seamen

> were most of them loth to fight with their own kinsmen for there was little else of any great importance but Englishmen on either side; and they were also unwilling that this land should be the more exposed to outlandish people, because they destroyed each other.

They appreciated that a weak England would be a vulnerable land that would be open to invasion from many directions. Common sense was keeping civil war at bay.

There is no mention of the whereabouts of Edward when these events were taking place. Given the speed with which the Norman party leaves the country, it is probable that they already appreciated that their position was untenable. Word would have reached King Edward that Godwin was assembling an army. There would have been time either to summon the northern earls or to march his small army north, but Edward did neither. The army and the business community had voted with their feet in favour of peace and this meant the restoration of Godwin.

> Then it was determined that wise men should be sent between them, who should settle peace on either side. Godwin went up, and Harold his son, and their navy, as many as they then thought proper. Then advanced Bishop Stigand with God's assistance, and the wise men both within the town and without; who determined that hostages should be given on either side. And so they did.

King Edward is not known to have been present. He had moved his royal residences away from Oxford or Winchester to near the minster he was building beside the river Thames, just 7km to the west of the city of London. The seat of national government he established at his West Minster survives to this day.

Other Normans were inside the city: 'When Archbishop Robert and the Frenchmen knew that, they took horse.' An interesting footnote to this flight is that all the chroniclers of this event agree that the Normans departed on 'a crazy ship'.

There was still a legal charge hanging over Earl Godwin which had to be properly discharged.

> Then was proclaimed a general council without London; and all the earls and the best men in the land were at the council. There took up Earl Godwin his burthen, and cleared himself there before his lord King Edward, and before all the nation; proving that he was innocent of the crime laid to his charge, and to his son Harold and all his children. And the king gave the earl and his children, and all the men that were with him, his full friendship, and the full earldom, and all that he possessed before; and he gave the lady all that she had before.

The council also outlawed Archbishop Robert 'with all the Frenchmen'. The Norman party were held to be chiefly responsible for the 'discord between Earl Godwin and the king'. They also stood accused of instituting 'bad laws, and judged unrighteous judgment, and brought bad counsels into this land'. The chronicles imply that the council, which is synonymous with the Witan, would in future exercise some control over those who counselled the king.

To judge from the evidence of his future actions when dealing with the earls, King Edward does not appear dismayed by the loss of his courtiers or the apparent curtailing of his own influence. The opposite seems to be the case. The council was called together for all of the major changes, although the summary justice it dispensed indicated that it was a political rather than a judicial court.

This was not only a resounding defeat for the first attempted takeover by the Normans but established a community of purpose among the English, who recognised that the threat to them all came from the national identities developing beyond England's shores. These events therefore ensured that England would be able to defend itself in 1066.

There is also a strong sense in these events that something else had been created by the respect shown to the legal process and the resolution of the dispute by discussion among the leaders in the land.

The military message for Edward must have been clear, as Earl Godwin's return was not opposed. The northern earls did not rally to the king. These venerable earls might have recognised that Edward was introducing an outside influence that would confuse the succession. They did not want to become subjects of the Normans. The incomers had shown themselves incapable of performing their key duty to the country of maintaining secure borders.

But this was not a defeat for the king. The country he ruled was now stronger and more united. His policy had been defeated but he was still the head of state. The popular Archbishop Stigand was reinstated in Canterbury. However, the Normans had the ear of the papacy, especially with all of the abbey- and cathedral-building that was going on. Stigand would be denied the sanction of the Roman Church in his appointment.

About six months after his restoration, Earl Godwin collapsed while dining with the king the day after they had celebrated Easter. From the description, it sounds like a stroke. The earl lingered on for three days without showing any signs of recovery. The fact that he was buried alongside the recent kings in Winchester removes any doubt that Godwin was the king's prime minister. The earl was probably about to celebrate his sixtieth birthday when he died.

Across the sea in northern France the events would doubtless have been interpreted differently. Edward, effectively a son of Normandy, had invited the rulers to govern and eventually rule England. Only the military might of the Godwinsons, the treachery of the other earls and lack of military might among the Normans had disrupted the groundwork for a smooth transition of power. With the prospect of a peaceful takeover gone, William must have begun to contemplate the alternatives fourteen years before his eventual invasion in 1066.

Duke William had inherited extensive lands with many subordinate, or more often insubordinate, nobles along the northern coastal province, part of the Frankish empire. The duchy of Normandy had been extended from Flanders in the east to the Breton border in the west. Being some distance from the weak French court, Normandy enjoyed considerable autonomy.

It was shortly after the death of his brother, Duke Richard III, in 1026 that Robert became the duke of Normandy. Some histories hint at poisoning and even name Robert as the poisoner of his brother. Sudden and untimely death was remarkably common among kings around this time. Perhaps it was common among the general population. Certainly Cnut died unexpectedly, as had three of his immediate predecessors.

William inherited the ducal title at the age of seven in July 1035 when his natural father died at Nicaea, in modern Turkey, returning from a pilgrimage to the Holy Land. Before his death, Duke Robert demanded from his subjects an oath of loyalty to his son William, who was both illegitimate and of 'low birth'.

William's youth was surrounded by dangers which he was fortunate to survive. First his tutor Gilbert de Brionne was assassinated. Next to be killed was Turold, his preceptor, and finally the seneschal or steward of his household, Osbern de Crépon, had his throat cut, apparently while William slept nearby.

The limited protection that he did enjoy does not appear to have come from the powerful clique of nobility, and one is tempted to ascribe his survival to the intervention of his mother. His maternal uncle once had to smuggle the boy out of the castle and conceal him among the poor. His relatively low profile during his early childhood probably served him well, allowing the aristocracy to compete among themselves.

One spectator to these events was Edward, the surviving son of King Ethelred, who had been a refugee in Normandy from 1013. In 1036, Edward might have turned to the family of his cousin, Duke Robert, for support when he launched his brief invasion in support of his mother's efforts to secure the throne of England for her youngest son, Harthacnut. Edward, however, returned to England in 1041 and probably saw little or nothing of the young William.

William survived, and he laid the foundations for one of the most powerful territories inside the kingdom that was becoming France during the eleventh century. In 1042 he began his comeback when he besieged his own fortress at Falaise. Aged eighteen or nineteen, William had narrowly escaped another plot to kill him during a hunting expedition. Forewarned, he escaped alone on horseback to Falaise.

Now he asked his overlord Henry I, the king of France, for support. The showdown for William came in 1047 at Val-ès-Dunes near Caen. Aided by a key defection, William and Henry I easily won the day, quickly pardoning or exiling most of the rebels. With border wars part of power politics of the time, these clashes are remarkable for the lack of bloodshed, which contrasts with England, where the human cost of war, it might be argued, was gradually leading to posturing, negotiation and compromise as an alternative to combat.

This unsettled era in Normandy also saw the development of modest castles as strong points and a way of holding territory with a limited force. The Normandy inherited by Duke William was a productive agricultural land. Prosperity posed problems, as the growing population needed space. The various institutions of the Church could absorb many of these dispossessed and there was a good supply of workers and soldiers.

While William was consolidating his position as duke in Normandy, events in England were, by comparison, tranquil. However, the death of the three great earls of England would determine who would be ready to face the attacks of 1066.

Two years after the death of Godwin, Earl Siward died. The old earl had 'at the king's behest' led a land and naval expedition against King Macbeth in the previous year, 1054. The armies had met at Dunsinnan: the Scots lost 3,000 men, and the Saxons 1,500. Among the casualties were Osbeorn, the only son of Earl Siward. Macbeth retired to the north, defeated but not destroyed.

The battle was a tragedy for Earl Siward, however. His only son and his nephew were both dead. There was no obvious successor in Northumbria, especially as the blood feud begun at the time of Cnut had disrupted the succession. Shakespeare has Earl Siward accept the news of his son Osbeorn's death with these heroic if callous words.

> Why then, God's soldier be he! Had I as many sons as I have hairs, I would not wish them to a fairer death: And so, his knell is knoll'd'.

Siward had another son but he was too young to be considered. A caretaker would be required. A great royal council met during March 1055. The summons for the powerful of the land to meet was sent out at almost the time Earl Siward died and it is probable that this event provoked the need for a gathering.

One is entitled to speculate that the various parties arrived with their candidates. All their hands were trumped when Earl Aelfgar was exiled. This was possibly a simple act of revenge by Earl Harold for the Mercian involvement in the downfall of his brother Sweyn. Others have speculated that Aelfgar had greater ambitions, which included incorporating Northumbria into Mercia as a rival to Wessex.

The person playing the trump card was undoubtedly Earl Harold, who had the support of the king. It has also been suggested that the restored Queen Edith was taking a more active part in influencing affairs. Subsequent events certainly hint that she was an advocate for her brother Tostig.

The chroniclers are divided on the subject of Aelfgar's guilt. The charge was that he was consorting with the king's enemies in Wales. Only one version of the *Chronicles* suggests any admission on the part of Aelfgar and that might simply have been an angry outburst when he realised that he was to be marginalised. Earl Aelfgar could have justified his dealings with the Welsh by recalling the precedent set by the late Earl Sweyn. He could also point out that the cross-border raids had ceased. Had he been able to look into the future, he could have predicted that the border would remain peaceful for six years, until 1062.

There were few eligible candidates to take over Northumbria, especially with Aelfgar exiled, but it must have seemed like a Godwin takeover when the king's council appointed Tostig to be the new earl.

Aelfgar then pursued the route taken by Harold during his short exile and went to Ireland. Exile was an occupational hazard experienced by many nobles. It seems quite extraordinary that organising revolt and invasion should have become the recognised way to earn a pardon, but most recently Earl Harold had reconfirmed this precedent. A demonstration of power rather than any penitential acts achieved results in eleventh-century northern Europe.

Aelfgar lost no time in assembling a force of eighteen 'pirate' ships in Ireland and added to the force in Wales, where Gruffydd, who had earlier benefited from his alliance with Harold's Earl Sweyn to dominate the land of Wales, joined an expedition into Hereford with the normal looting and destruction.

Earl Harold was sent with an army to restore the situation but, when the attackers retreated, offered to negotiate, and a peace was agreed at Billingsley. The records imply that King Edward attended and the king of Wales was impressed with his counterpart's wisdom. Three important events flow from this meeting.

First, Earl Aelfgar was restored. Second, there is evidence of some innovation, as cavalry tactics had been employed and a fortification ditch, reminiscent of the burgh constructed after Alfred the Great, was built round Hereford. Third, Earl Harold was getting a chance to organise and lead an army, although one observes that he still chose the path of negotiation.

Aelfgar returned in time to be there when his father, Earl Leofric, died in autumn 1056. Aelfgar took over as the new earl and we soon find that his daughter was married to the king of Wales. This liaison was enough to have him banished again in 1058. The Mercians might have seen the hand of Harold behind this renewed act of banishment. However, at the king's court, the possibility of an alliance between a hostile Gruffydd ap Llywelyn and a powerful English earl was an unmistakable threat.

We noted earlier that the earl of Mercia was speedily restored to his land and titles without any formal ceremony, with the assistance this time of a Norwegian expedition under the young son of King Harald of Norway, Magnus. We do not find any records of armies being mobilised to repel any raids associated with this 'invasion'. So it is possible that this was another forceful demonstration which allowed the original evidence of the exile to be 'reviewed' and the exile to be rescinded.

We cannot be certain, but Earl Aelfgar may have died in 1062. Certainly Frank Barlow suggests that the death of Llywelyn's ally would bring their peace treaty to an end and account for the new Welsh raid. The forceful reaction of the Godwinson family in attacking Wales in the winter of 1062 suggests that they felt some need to respond quickly, as this was not the accustomed time for warring. Perhaps the Godwinson family wanted to make a pre-emptive strike to ensure that Wales would not become an effective ally of Mercia. Such a partnership would have to be destroyed before Aelfgar's son, Edwin, established himself within Mercia. We do not see any record of Edwin being noted as earl of Mercia until 1065.

In a little over a decade, a new set of earls had taken control in England. The transition had been complex but had been managed by Earl Harold without any civil strife so far. But the matter of the regal succession still remained unresolved and Tostig's position would prove to be precarious.

There can be little doubt that the English succession was now the subject of much debate. Two events occur in 1064 which indicate that this matter was receiving the attention of Earl Harold and Duke William.

In 1064 William of Normandy invaded the territory of Maine. The precise pretext for the attack is unknown and, in the affairs of Normandy, possibly had only a marginal significance. But what happened has significance for any ambitions that William harboured about taking the English throne. He captured Count Walter and his wife and made them prisoners. It was customary at the time to release nobles, holding a close relative as hostage. However, the couple died in mysterious circumstances while in his custody.

This death eliminated a strong claimant to the throne of England. Walter was the son of Godgifu, King Edward's sister. So Godgifu's parents were Emma of Normandy and King Ethelred. Walter was therefore the nephew of the king of England and had a good claim on the English throne, with a straight line back to King Alfred.

The second event of 1064 is the infamous visit to Normandy by Earl Harold. The visit is only reported in Norman sources but probably did take place, although most of the details reported by Norman commentators are suspect. This appears to be a straightforward visit, but the Norman chroniclers have spun a series of stories to justify William's invasion.

The idea that Harold was blown off course is weak. One does find records of ships being destroyed but such incidents are invariably associated with an enforced departure after a raid. On the other hand, one hears of innumerable voyages which appear to reach a satisfactory conclusion. The idea that Godwin was heading for Flanders from Bosham and landed in Ponthieu by mistake is not really credible. The route to Flanders would pass along the south coast of England, before crossing the Channel when the tide and the wind were both right.

It is perfectly possible that the sailors were blown away from their intended landing point, but this was not unusual when crossing a stretch of water with a strong current and sailing at right angles to the prevailing wind. The port of St Valéry-sur-Somme would be an obvious landing point and was the place where William would reassemble his force after their first attempt to cross the water in September 1066. The procedure would be to wait near or on the shore until conditions allowed the intended destination to be reached. Earl Harold might well have felt there was no need to wait and instead decided to land and ride to his destination.

Harold would have been well aware of the political situation across the Channel with family connections in Flanders including an earlier association with the count of Boulogne. Harold's home base was across the water, and with traders passing through he would have been well informed.

All of this amounts to a complete rejection of the fiction woven into the Bayeux Tapestry. It makes a good story which gives credit to the 'rescuers' and allows the duke of Normandy to be shown exercising his power over Earl Harold.

The purpose of the trip remains a matter of speculation. There are four contenders. First, had Harold gone to offer the throne to William? Because the chroniclers tend to report after events have taken place, we should not expect to find them inscribing an abortive plan in the chronicles. There are suggestions that King Edward was against the trip. The Bayeux Tapestry appears to show Edward admonishing Harold upon his return. Furthermore, Edward can have been in no doubt that the throne was not in his gift after the various events of his long reign. Perhaps Harold was going to discourage the duke from his oft-repeated claim that he would be king of England one day.

Second, was Harold going to negotiate the release of the family hostages? The Bayeux Tapestry certainly shows a Saxon character at the first meeting with William. There were two hostages being held in Normandy. The first was Wulfnoth, the youngest of the Godwinsons. The second is believed to be Hakon, the son of the late Earl Sweyn Godwinson. This mission does not appear to have been successful if it was indeed the plan. Wulfnoth would remain a hostage all of his life but would outlast all of the key actors.

A third possibility that is mentioned by Nordic sources is marriage, or rather marriages. William and Harold both had extensive families which would provide scope for some negotiation. More intriguing and teasing is the Nordic version. Describing Queen Matilda as 'one of the most beautiful women that could be seen', the saga continues:

> They often talked together for amusement at the drinking-table; and the earl [Duke William] went generally to bed, but Harald and the earl's wife sat long in the evenings talking together, and so it went on for a great part of the winter. In one of their conversations she said

to Harald, 'The earl has asked me what it is we have to talk about so much, for he is angry at it.' Harald replies, 'We shall then at once let him know all our conversation.' The following day, Harald asked the earl to a conference, and they went together into the conference-chamber; where also the queen was, and some of the councillors. Then Harald began thus: 'I have to inform you, earl, that there lies more in my visit here than I have let you know. I would ask your daughter in marriage, and have often spoke over this matter with her mother, and she has promised to support my suit with you.' As soon as Harald had made known this proposal of his, it was well received by all who were present. They explained the case to the earl; and at last it came so far that the earl was contracted to Harald, but as she was very young, it was resolved that the wedding should be deferred for some years.

A fourth possible motive was simply that of an ambassador hoping to deal with a range of issues, including some or all of the above. Harold might have been hedging his bets. If William was planning a takeover of England from Normandy it made sense for the leading earl of the land to make contact. Harold would also have been able to assess the military potential available. In this context, getting involved in some military activity, as shown in the Tapestry, was sensible.

It was not unusual for visits to last some weeks. The saga gives us a unique commentary on the winter weather in the Channel. It tells us that Harold's return was delayed by the weather. 'Harald remained there late in harvest, and was hospitably entertained; for the stormy weather continued, and there was no getting to sea, and this continued until winter set in; so the earl and Harald agreed that he should remain there all winter.'

We noted earlier that October can produce strong northerly winds that would carry unwary seagoers off into the Atlantic. Had Harold been away so long, some reference might have been spotted in some document or charter, so one is entitled to be suspicious that the saga is mistaken and is reporting the Norman excuse normally attached to the delayed departure of 1066. The same writer has Harold being brought up by King Edward 'like a son', so its reliability at this point in the narrative is questionable.

One point is clear: at some stage William obliged Harold to swear some sort of oath, presumably one binding him in some way to serve

William. The Bayeux Tapestry is designed to be ambiguous about the oath-swearing. The tapestry was the work of English hands and clearly demonstrates that there was a difference of view about the significance of the oath.

In the chronicle we read this obituary of William:

> He was gentle to the good men who loved God, and stern beyond measure to those people who resisted his will... Also, he was a very stern and violent man, so that no one dared to do anything contrary to his will.

Harold might well have felt forced into taking some sort of pledge and it would prove a costly mistake. The breach of this oath is contained in most post-Conquest documents. The single fact that Harold was an oath-breaker was taken as a sufficient condition to overthrow him and negate all of his charters. The contents of the oath appear unimportant. The claim that it was made on holy relics is interpreted as much more important. This single charge apparently provided the motive for the Pope to turn the duke's ambition into a crusade.

Students of modern politics will recognise this strategy, which attempts to focus everybody's attention on a single misdeed or ill-judged remark. The world of subtle compromise practised by the Godwinsons had encountered the crude realities of Norman politics, and lost.

4

Earl Tostig

THE CHOREOGRAPHER OF ENGLAND'S DEMISE

Tostig was perhaps the most significant choreographer of the events of 1066. The written record forces us to guess at his strategy but the events leading up to the three battles shed some light on these speculations and help us to piece together his plan. Was Earl Tostig a traitor to his country and family or a master strategist who might have opened a very different chapter of European history?

Tostig was probably born about 1029, the third son of Earl Godwin and his Danish wife Gytha. His name honours the Danish family connection and Godwin's overlord and patron, Cnut, who was king of Denmark and Norway as well as England at the time.

Tostig is first mentioned in the *Anglo-Saxon Chronicle* when he commanded one of the ships sent to aid Emperor Henry III against his future father-in-law, Count Baldwin V of Flanders. Two ships were actually sent out, one commanded by Harold, the other by Tostig, while the others of the fleet remained in Sandwich. It was a token gesture, fit for a twenty-year-old younger son of the leading earl of England. It was an opportunity for the young man to develop the leadership skills he would require to supplement his training as a warrior.

As far as we can discern from the record, there were few jobs and no vacant earldoms to allow Tostig to learn much about the art of government. Tostig is known to have been close to his sister and was probably in his early teens when she married King Edward. As Tostig was a regular hunting companion of the king, people have speculated that the young man might have spent much of his youth close to the court of King Edward, who would treat Tostig as his protégé.

MARRIAGE

In 1051 Tostig made a good marriage to Judith, half-sister of Count Baldwin V of Flanders. This was the same year that he shared the short exile with the rest of the family. It might be ascribing too much subtlety to the king's plans for the Norman takeover in England to suggest that Edward had ensured that his young friend would not lose everything when his family were dispossessed of the English land. There is no doubt that the Norman party that was in the ascendancy at the court of King Edward would have enjoyed discomfiting two powerful families, neither of which it counted among its allies.

Judith, also known as Fausta of Flanders, was born in 1030, the daughter of Baldwin IV. Her connections were impressive. Through her mother, Eleanor of Normandy, she was a cousin once removed of both King Edward of England and Duke William of Normandy. This was a good match for a third son of an earl who as yet held only minor lands around England.

The bride was probably twenty at the time of the marriage. By the standards of the time, this was rather old for a woman to be marrying. Her late marriage might help account for Judith's marrying a little below her status.

There would have appeared to be no age difference between Tostig and Judith. Snorri in his saga suggests that Tostig had two sons old enough to accompany him in 1066, who survived the battle at Stamford Bridge and returned to Norway with the few survivors. These would scarcely have been old enough to have been the product of this union so the speculation is that he fathered them before his marriage to Judith. After the marriage, Tostig is reported to have been faithful to his wife.

The evidence suggests that this was, or at least became, a loving relationship. The *Vita Edwardii* reports that the union produced children, although there is no record of the number, their gender or their fate. This is rather typical of the limited information available about Tostig, and about the key role he is about to play in our drama. We know that Judith died on 5 March 1094 in Bavaria.

Perhaps the patriarch of the Godwinson family saw a future for his son among the continental nobility. It is not quite so clear what Judith's half-brother, the count, could see as the likely benefits, as he sought to maintain his land against the growing power of the Franks. If the marriage was promoted by King Edward, the benefits to Count Baldwin are easier to understand.

Judith's half-brother, Baldwin, was emerging as a key player in the struggles for supremacy that would, over the next century, define the borders of France. This would help to ensure that King Edward could not so easily deploy the English power on the side of the Normans because his loyalty was divided.

Tostig also became a 'brother-in-law' to Duke William, as the latter had married Matilda, the daughter of Baldwin V and Judith's niece. This latter match was initially opposed by the Pope when it was proposed in 1049. Both partners descended from Rollo, the Norse founder of Normandy. The couple were very distant cousins at a time when the rules of consanguinity still extended to six generations. The Pope excommunicated William, but this was lifted when the pious couple agreed to build adjacent abbeys. The experience of negotiating with the Church in Rome would prove useful in 1066.

The evidence of 1066 suggests that the match with Judith did not dilute Tostig's ambition in England. His eldest brother, Sweyn, was by now out of the picures and the misfortunes of war could easily see Tostig as the head of the Godwinson family if his brother Harold were to be killed or lose favour. The marriage would also help 'promote' his claim to a senior earldom in England. For Tostig and the Godwinsons this was an excellent strategic match.

The nature of the moving sand bars, the prevailing winds and the strong currents through the Channel that separated England from continental Europe made the harbours of Flanders the first port of call. Flanders had provided a refuge for English regal exiles, the most recent being Queen Emma as she waited for her son Harthacnut to meet her in 1037.

Any sense of celebration after the marriage party did not last long for the Godwinson family. In their absence, Edward had introduced some Normans to his court. When Earl Godwin failed to redress the alleged insult to one continental visitor, the old earl and his younger children found themselves back in Flanders at the court of Baldwin.

There is no record of Tostig accompanying his father when he assembled the other members of his family for their return in the summer of 1052. Perhaps he stayed in Flanders to maintain the family base but this might also have been part of the political judgement that would keep at least one member of the family in favour with the Norman party. As noted earlier, the exile did not last long and the Godwinson family were now very firmly in power, having routed the Normans around King Edward. Tostig's prospect of promotion to the next vacant earldom was good.

The death of Earl Siward of Northumbria in March 1055 does not appear to have been wholly unexpected. The loss of his son in the battle with Macbeth the previous year must have come as a blow. The old earl appreciated that this was not an easy land to hold. There was a long lawless border in the north which required the sort of expedition that had cost his son's life.

Geography had made the land north of the river Humber a rather isolated region. This massive river and its many major tributaries limit access from the south. A ferry from Barton-on-Humber on the Lincolnshire bank to Brough in the north was the reliable communication route that the Romans had established to reach York. The modern A1 road provides the 'dry' route into Yorkshire. This has to cross a network of rivers as it makes its way north.

The Trent, Don, Aire and Wharfe each provide a barrier to communication and in the days before flood management the time and place of crossing had to be chosen carefully. Names such as Castleford and Doncaster attest to their role when the Romans first provided a national road transport system. The western side of ancient Northumbria is protected by England's backbone, the Pennines, and the hills of the Lake District. To the north the Cheviots and the barren hills of the Borders make this a hard land to transit.

One can argue that this relative inaccessibility meant that central control over this region was rather looser than that exercised over the other regions of England. The conflicts with Wales and Scotland support the argument that remoteness bred independent spirits. William of Malmesbury, the eleventh-century commentator, noted the effect of this divide in breeding independent natives. He also recorded the tendency of England's leaders not to include Northumbria on their routine itineraries.

With Siward's potential heir, Osbeorn, dead, there were a limited number of candidates to replace the dead earl. The Danish blood in Tostig's veins might have endeared his candidature to the nobility of Northumbria, where strong ties with the Norse were still recognised. The old earl is even referred to as 'Siward the Dane' in several texts.

The shortage of suitable candidates flowed from the incident described earlier. In 1016, Cnut had recognised that government of the north was different and meted out the treatment employed in Denmark. Earl Uhtred of Northumbria was to submit to Cnut, but when he entered the hall with his forty house troops the party was ambushed and massacred. Richard Fletcher in his wonderful book, *Bloodfeud*, summarises the sequence of events as described in one source:

> In outline, the story that the Durham anonymous had to tell was straightforward. Earl Uhtred's son, by name Earldred, avenged his father's murder by slaying the killer, Thurbrand. Thurbrand's son Carl in turn avenged his father's murder by killing Earldred. In due course Earldred's grandson Waltheof contrived to avenge that murder by cornering all Carl's sons and grandsons when they were feasting together at a family estate not far from York and killing nearly all of them. This massacre, the last recorded bloodshed in this family feud, occurred probably in the winter of 1073–4.

By introducing a member of the Godwin family to Northumbria, the local balance of power between the northern families would not be disturbed. By assigning an outsider to the post, the eligible youngsters could come to maturity and perhaps re-establish their leadership in Northumbria in due course.

Tostig's years of under-employment might have brought him close to the king, as we have noted. Edward would have had time to appraise the merits of the man who he seems to have recognised as an ally. Tostig certainly escapes all mention in the events leading to the exile of the Godwinsons, possibly because he was already abroad with his new wife. Did King Edward simply see Tostig as a trustworthy pair of hands and an ally in the Godwinson camp?

Relations with his queen, Edith, appear to have improved after her short exile. Edward is reported to have sworn a vow of celibacy following the restoration of the Godwinsons. The royal couple now devoted themselves to creating and maintaining religious foundations. Judith also favoured the Church with endowments, which must have given the royal party plenty to talk about. There are many clues to suggest that Edith favoured Tostig among her many brothers. Tostig was therefore influential in the royal household. With Tostig beholden to the king, Edward might have hoped to enhance his control over Harold.

The continental connection that Tostig had gained through his marriage to Judith might have further endeared him to the king, whose attempts to bring England closer to its continental neighbours had recently failed.

The speed with which the Witan was assembled and the way the case was put against Earl Aelfgar of Mercia to force him into exile suggests some planning and preparation of the events that followed by the southerners.

The chroniclers do not waste any words informing us about the merits of the candidates or indeed who was in consideration to take over the whole territory of Northumbria. We are only told that: 'The king, however, gave the earldom, which Earl Siward formerly had, to Tostig, son of Earl Godwin.'

It is difficult to know what the word 'however' might conceal. The chroniclers use the word 'unintentional' when they describe the outlawing of Earl Aelfgar in the sentence before the king reveals his decision. One chronicler says Aelfgar's confession to the charges made against him was unintentional, and another that the crime itself was unintentional. The circumstance of Tostig's promotion was not an auspicious beginning for a task that was bound to be difficult.

Whether for a single motive, or as an act of politics, King Edward made Tostig the earl of Northumbria, Northamptonshire and Huntingdonshire in 1055. It seems like a reasonable political judgement. The acute shortage of suitable Northumbrian candidates is proved by the choice of another outsider, Morcar of Mercia, when Tostig is ousted a decade later.

The sparse population and the tough living conditions bred an independence that would prove hostile to change when imposed from outside for centuries to come. It was not an area endowed by nature with extensive resources or excellent agriculture apart from the fertile, lime-rich areas of the Wolds between Hull and Scarborough. Where survival is on the margin, there is a reluctance to experiment.

The appointment might have worked well had Tostig been a more adept governor. Northumbria was still not a place where the rules of law accepted down south could be applied. The northerners were no less 'civilised'. The area had traditions that were Norse rather than Saxon. This had been a part of the Danelaw. Jorvik, the capital, was a city where Norse street names had superimposed themselves on the city left by the Romans.

In the Godwin family history, there is a tradition that Tostig was very stern with law-breakers. Earl Tostig attempted to impose order and punished robbers with mutilation or death. While England enjoyed a codified set of laws, a tradition of common law, which respected local conditions, was also developing.

A strict enforcement of Wessex law could lead to conflict with good order. In a part of the world where clans and family 'tribes' were the norm, it was too easy to start an inter-family argument when a punishment was imposed. Tostig slowly lost support among the powerful families because of his style of government.

We are given the name of one *familiaris* of Tostig who was charged with collecting taxes. Tostig's enforcer was a person named as Cospig. The choice of a man of 'inferior status' for this task would be one of the charges brought against Tostig following his overthrow. Employing servants to collect the money evidently gave offence.

We can infer from the objections raised that payments were normally passed from inferior to superior and up the chain until they reached the earl. In traditional societies, each rank takes their cut before passing it on. With the earl collecting taxes directly, the Northumbrian nobility would now have to gather money in their own right. The powerful of Northumbria were evidently not ready for such open government. We might now style the existing Northumbrian system as corrupt, but Tostig's reforms would end in disaster.

SCOTLAND

The continuing saga of relations with Scotland shed some light on Earl Tostig's time in charge of Northumbria. During the time of Earl Siward, King Macbeth appeared content to establish effective control in the area that he could effectively dominate. So Macbeth had moved the Scottish centre of gravity north. This allowed Cumbria, Strathclyde and Upper Bernicia to come under the control of the Northumbrians, and especially the noble house of Bamburgh.

Bernicia was an ancient kingdom which at times stretched from coast to coast and from the Forth down to the Tyne. Earl Siward had been the patriarch of Bernicia. The early history of this area is recorded, as the chronicler Bede wrote his ecclesiastical history in Bernicia. The Viking invasions of the ninth century brought about an uneasy alliance with their southern neighbour, Deira.

Deirian territory ran from the river Tyne down to the Humber. The two 'royal' houses would have to share dominance with the Bernicians, still harking back to the days when they held sway over the fertile lowlands of the border. The rise of a united Scotland had taken these lands and moved the wealth-producing area of the Northumbrian territory to the south and into the land of Deira.

King Macbeth felt able to join with many other continental royals in making the jubilee pilgrimage to Rome in 1050. At the cost of his son's life, Earl Siward defeated Macbeth in 1054 and installed Malcolm as king in Scotland. Macbeth was killed in 1057, and his son Lulach the following year. With his patron dead, King Malcolm was again in a position to look towards securing his southern border.

It might come as a surprise that there should be further hostility, but the event says much about how loyalty was understood. King Malcolm had been nurtured by the Bernicians and owed his crown to the intervention of Earl Siward. But Malcolm owed no loyalty to Tostig or the Godwinsons.

Earl Tostig soon found himself being tested by King Malcolm III. The author of *Vita Edwardii Regis* provides an English perspective on these border raids by the Scots, who. 'since they had not yet tested Tostig and held him more cheaply, harassed him often with raids rather than war'.

The same source describes 'the indecisive and fickle race of men, better in woods than in the open and trusting more to flight than to manly boldness in battle'. Evidently the writer did not approve of guerrilla tactics, although he goes on to praise Tostig for sparing his men 'by cunning schemes'. These must have been diplomatic rather than military. We have no mention of battles or any indication that Tostig himself made any military response.

Malcolm was kin to the leading families of Bernicia, so mobilisation would have divided local loyalties. Northumbria had nurtured Malcolm in exile and assisted him in the overthrow of Macbeth. Did Tostig now threaten to bring an army from Wessex to sort out the Scots and any allies, with the implicit threat that such an invasion would pose to the Northumbrians? Tostig must have fielded some very persuasive arguments against Malcolm, because in 1059 Tostig was able to bring the neighbouring kings together in London.

King Malcolm III journeyed from Scotland to the court of King Edward to conclude agreements of peace which recognised the supremacy of the English king. It is an indication of the manner of Tostig's early government. The apparent success of his diplomatic skill and the border security might have encouraged Tostig to spend more of his time away from his northern base.

PILGRIMAGE TO ROME

In 1061 Tostig felt able to visit Rome with Judith and his younger brother Gyrth, and in the company of Ealdred, the new archbishop of York, plus two other bishops, Giso of Wells and Walter of Hereford, to visit Pope Nicholas II. The primary purpose of the trip was to allow the archbishop to receive their palliums. A pallium was a woollen stole-like vestment worn by the Pope and one was conferred by the Pope on all archbishops.

Initially, Nicholas refused to confer the pallium on Ealdred because he was deemed to have breached canon law when he transferred from another bishopric. The Church of Rome was struggling to assert the rules and authority that it now enjoyed in the Frankish and southern European territories within England. The refusal can be seen as a political expression of the Pope, who wished to have his authority respected in all future appointments.

The papacy was itself recovering its own authority after a decade of military and spiritual turmoil. Stigand was a cleric who rose during the reign of Cnut and managed to amass much wealth. He served six kings and was made archbishop of Canterbury in 1052 when his Norman predecessor, Robert of Jumièges, fled following the Godwinsons' short exile. However, with Norman influence in Rome in its ascendancy, Stigand's credentials were challenged on the grounds that he had wisely held onto his former see of Winchester.

Three years earlier, in 1058, Stigand had been recognised by Pope Benedict X, who was soon deposed and declared the anti-pope the following year. It is relevant to our story that the Normans sided with the party which ousted Pope Benedict. Archbishop Stigand found himself being excommunicated by five more Popes, which is why the archbishop of York is often recorded attending official ceremonies to ensure ecclesiastical legitimacy. Stigand was eventually replaced as archbishop in 1070 by Lanfranc, as the Norman takeover was completed, and he died two years later.

It is easier to describe this sequence of events than to attempt to explain its relevance. This is made doubly difficult when one side exercises secular power and the other is dealing in spiritual power, especially as each of these realms trespasses on the other's territory. The centralised Church based in Rome was becoming an important player in European politics.

On the way home, Tostig's party was attacked by robbers and their possessions taken. The earl and family were held for ransom. Tostig managed to escape and return to Rome. The credit for his escape goes to one of his quick-thinking escorts, Gospatric, who impersonated the earl credibly enough to provide an opportunity for the real Tostig to make a getaway.

Gospatric was a common name but very probably he was a close relative of Earl Uhtred, whose murder at the behest of Cnut had set off a blood feud with the house of Bamburgh. The fact that he was among the group of pilgrims was typical of that age. You kept your friends close but a few key members of any potential rival or enemy family even closer.

Tostig returned to Rome and complained about the lack of order in the surrounding country. The party was compensated for their material losses and the Pope relented. Ealdred was awarded his pallium. To cap it all, Gospatric was also released unharmed, as the robbers respected his bravery. Tostig returned to England in triumph.

However, in his absence, his recently 'sworn brother' Malcolm had not only attacked down as far as Lindisfarne but the gains made over two generations in Cumbria and Strathclyde had been reversed. The Scotland formed by Macbeth had moved south again and re-established itself in the lowlands. The brave Gospatric probably returned at the end of 1061 to discover that his family had been driven from their hard-won land.

This might have been a turning point in Tostig's tenure of Northumbria. He had failed in the key duty of maintaining the borders. Furthermore, the northern half of his territory was closer in kinship and interest to the king of Scotland than to the king of England.

We know that Tostig and Judith were keen to patronise the Church, which would have placed a further tax burden on the people of the north. Church-building by the pious had to be paid for by the poor. Schemes that might have worked in the south where trade and geography yielded better 'rents' were a burden in this more barren territory.

By 1063 unambiguous evidence comes to light of the rift opening between Tostig and those he governed. Two men (we assume they held the rank of thane) by the name of Gamel and Ulf came to see Tostig. The subject of their visit must have been something contentious because it is noted that they had come with the promise of safe-conduct. Safe-conduct operated in a manner similar to that of hostage-taking but on a short-term basis. We know nothing of what transpired before the two visitors were killed in Tostig's hall at York. We do not know if Tostig was present or if he organised the bloody deed. Because there were no repercussions recorded among his staff, we must assume that he had sanctioned these murders. If Richard Fletcher's tentative tracing of the two victims is correct, they were kin to the house of Bamburgh. As such, Tostig had taken sides and joined the lethal blood feud against the descendants of Earl Siward.

These killings look like a 'get-tough' policy. The murder of Gospatric shortly after Christmas, at the start of 1064, must have reinforced the message. This murder took place at King Edward's court and the whisper was that Queen Edith had either connived at or even organised it. Nothing like this seems to have happened since the time of King Ethelred. This was a political assassination. The murder was designed to bolster Tostig by removing a rival and send a message to the northern nobility. It was ominous. This was an arrogant expression of power. It was also out of tune with these more tolerant political times.

This accords well with the assessment of Tostig recorded in *Vita Edwardii* by those who knew the man:

Earl Tostig himself was endowed with very great and prudent restraint although occasionally he was a little over-zealous in attacking evil, with bold and inflexible constancy of mind. He would first ponder much, by himself, the plans in his mind; and when he had ascertained by an appreciation of the matter the final issue, he would set them in order; and these plans he would not readily share with anyone. Also sometimes he was so cautiously active that his action seemed to come before his planning; and this often enough was advantageous to him in the theatre of the world.

The last sentence makes particularly interesting reading for students of spin. What this favourable commentator is saying is that Tostig often rushed in without any planning or consultation and that was al right because he often got away with it. Scholars believe that this work was begun before 1066. However, the writer might have wanted to redraft this passage in the light of future events. One cause of Tostig's problem might have lain in the number of other matters requiring his attention. The last five years of his rule in Northumbria provided numerous distractions. He was involved in campaigns against the Welsh.

Since the incursion that led to the restoration of Earl Aelfgar as earl of East Anglia in 1055, peace seems to have been established along the Welsh border. Aelfgar's restoration was speedily achieved with a fleet, probably through the support of Gruffydd. Once Aelfgar was restored, we learn that the mercenary fleet was still waiting at Chester in November for the pay the earl had promised them.

Aelfgar seems to have arranged the marriage of his daughter to the Welsh leader, Gruffydd ap Llywelyn, when the latter provided him with the necessary support to regain his land and titles in Mercia. The raids, launched from Wales in 1056, had been serious and damaging to Harold's land and prestige. With the Mercian family now allied to the Welsh, there was a real danger of provoking a civil war. On this occasion the circumstances encouraged Harold to favour negotiation.

The short exile of Aelfgar in 1055 had, after all, allowed Tostig to establish himself as the only viable candidate in Northumbria. Gruffydd might have been delivering a message on behalf of his new ally. This was a poke in the eye for the Godwinsons, a house once led by Leofric of Mercia, and Harold accepted it, for the moment.

Wales had been 'unified' by Gruffydd in a pattern that was being matched in many other areas, including Macbeth's, and later Malcolm's, Scotland. From the English point of view this unity had risks as well as benefits. An effective central authority could enforce laws in Wales and prevent raiding. But Wales must have appeared rather like the inaccessible Northumbria to the men of Wessex. Wales was potentially a fourth player in the power politics of England, with Malcolm in Scotland threatening to add a fifth powerful territory.

However, in 1062 we find Earl Harold launching an invasion into Welsh territory. This is so out of character for both the man and the times that it calls for an explanation. The probable answer points to some planning by Harold to secure his and his brother Tostig's position.

Just a year after Aelfgar's return he became the earl of Mercia, upon the death of his father Leofric in the autumn of 1057. The threat posed by the combined power of Mercia and Wales was dealt with by exiling Earl Aelfgar once again in 1058. His speedy return later in the same year, this time supported by the fleet and with Magnus, son of Harald, King of Norway, in attendance, must have caused Harold more anxiety. Harold probably hoped that his brother would be able to deliver the support of the Northumbrians to hold this new alliance in check.

Something must have changed late in 1062. It was shortly after Christmas that Harold, moving from Gloucester, headed for Gruffydd's capital at Rhuddlan. This surprise attack appears to have met with almost complete success, even though travel through the mountains during the winter must have been difficult. One key target appears to have been ships, which were destroyed, presumably to prevent Gruffydd from escaping over the sea to sanctuary in Dublin.

What had provoked this untimely winter attack on a peaceful border? The most likely explanation is the death of Earl Aelfgar. If the earl had been alive, there would have been a Mercian response to the attack on his brother-in-law. The chroniclers have nothing at all to say about the year 1062. The record of the time does not mention the passing of Earl Aelfgar. Nor has any record survived of the king granting Mercia to his young son Edwin.

The destruction of the infrastructure and transport during the first incursion during the winter would have achieved most of the military objectives of Harold. It would not be easy for Gruffydd to launch another raid, so the threat had been removed. The contest was evidently personal, political and urgent, because Harold resolved to launch another attack in the spring of 1063.

There are numerous motives for this second assault. Primarily, it would neutralise a potential ally of Mercia. It would also provide a show of strength aimed at the new young Earl Edwin of Mercia, especially as it would require Tostig to bring his Northumbrian army through their territory.

One cannot underestimate the need for Harold to establish in the eyes of the country, as well as those beyond the borders, as a war leader and not simply a skilled political operator. Earl Harold's military skills had lain mercifully underused for almost a decade. With the king ageing and the succession issue yet to be resolved, there was every chance that a show or perhaps the use of military force would be required to resolve the succession.

So Harold called for Tostig to support him. Tostig's force was mounted, just as Harold's had been on his Christmas raid. Cavalry tactics were again being tried. This time Harold took his army round the coast, presumably hoping to cut off any retreat as the Welsh withdrew before Tostig's force.

> Then in the gang-days went Harold with his ships from Bristol about Wales; where he made a truce with the people, and they gave him hostages. Tostig meanwhile advanced with a land-force against them, and plundered the land.

Once again Gruffydd evaded capture, but his power had been fatally undermined.

> But in the harvest of the same year was King Griffin slain, on the nones of August, by his own men, through the war that he waged with Earl Harold. He was king over all the Welsh nation. And his head was brought to Earl Harold; who sent it to the king, with his ship's head, and the rigging therewith. King Edward committed the land to his two brothers, Blethgent and Rigwatle; who swore oaths, and gave hostages to the king and to the earl, that they would be faithful to him in all things, ready to aid him everywhere by water and land, and would pay him such tribute from the land as was paid long before to other kings.

History has not assessed the damage done to Welsh unity by Harold's destruction of their king in 1063. Wales would struggle to assert itself over the next two centuries, until it was made a principality in 1271 by Edward I and ringed with castles to contain its ambitions.

So by the end of 1063, Wales had submitted not only to King Edward but also to Harold. If Wales was going to become a player in the power politics of England, it would not be on the side of the Mercians. However, early in 1065, the Welsh, despite being sworn allies, attacked a hunting lodge that Harold was constructing to entertain the king, which was within striking distance of the border. Harold was humiliated by this action and the king turned to Tostig to provide him with some hunting that autumn.

In the context of what was about to happen in Northumbria, the hand of the new young earl of Mercia, Edwin, might be detected in the raid on the lodge that Harold was preparing for his king. Some authorities have speculated that Earl Aelfgar was killed during one of the attacks into Wales by the Godwinsons. Aelfgar seems to vanish between mid-1062 and 1065. If his fate was unknown to the Mercians it would explain why Harold and Tostig were able to operate unhindered during their punitive raid of 1063. If 1064 was a year of plotting and preparation, 1065 was the year for action.

In the spring of 1065, the relics of St Oswin were displayed at Durham. He was an early king of Bernicia who had been betrayed and murdered. Richard Fletcher suggests that this was designed as a symbolic way of stirring the people, who would have just received the news of the treacherous slaying of Gospatric. Perhaps Tostig recognised that Gospatric was one of the few members of the northern nobility who could challenge his position as earl. There were still few other eligible candidates.

After a reasonable start, Tostig's rule became increasingly forceful. There can be no doubt that the rebellion when it broke out was planned. The murder of Gospatric would have required a summer of consultation for the families of Northumbria to agree on a suitable candidate to replace him as head of the house. Subsequent events suggest rebellion was also on the agenda.

In 1065, after a decade of rule, Northumbria broke into well-organised revolt. Earl Tostig was away hunting in Wessex. On 3 October 1065, with the harvest gathered in, a force of 200 soldiers led by three senior thanes entered York and occupied the earl's castle. It may be fanciful, but with three leaders the force might have come from each of the 'Thirdings', or Ridings, into which Danelaw had divided the vast extent of modern Yorkshire. Assembling in their separate areas would have helped to hide their forceful purpose and also ensured that all parties in the area were engaged in this rebellious enterprise.

The 'Earlsburgh', or castle, was probably a small fortified enclosure lying a little to the north of the old Roman wall near the minster that Earl Siward had built for St Olaf. There was good access to the river, the city and the old road going north. Earl Siward was buried there: 'He lies at Galmanho, in the minster which himself caused to be built, and consecrated in God's and Olaf's name'. The lane known as Galmanho and St Olaf's church still exist so one can identify the area if not the exact location of these actions. This is roughly in the area where St Mary's Abbey would be founded by William Rufus twenty years later. There was evidently a good supply of weapons and Tostig's treasury secured inside his castle. The first known casualties were two Danish housecarls, Amund and Ravenswart, who were killed.

Pasting the different versions of the chronicles together, a clear timescale of the events emerges:

> Slaying all the men of his clan that they could reach, both Danish and English; and took all [Tostig's] weapons in York, with gold and silver, and all his money that they could anywhere there find.

Another source adds that the rebels slew all of the household servants. There is a strong hint that they went around York to locate all those associated with Tostig's rule. The surprise is that the household does not appear to have been better prepared. It is hard to imagine that Earl Tostig and his agents were not aware of the mounting tension. Yet weapons and treasure had been left with a minimal guard. Only the following day did Tostig's men react. 'Soon after all the thanes in Yorkshire and in Northumberland gathered themselves together at York' is the first mention of the incident in the chronicles of Yorkshire. With these reinforcements, the rebels then moved against the force that Tostig had left. The number of Tostig's force around York is put at 200. They were not able to resist the army of rebels, which we assume had begun to swell, and all Tostig's men were killed.

The rebels then sent for Morcar and chose him as their earl. It is a few days' hard riding over the hills and along the valleys across the Pennines. A journey there and back could have used up a week. So it seems likely that Morcar was briefed and ready to ride in at the head of the army.

We soon hear that Morcar's brother had also mobilised his army and within a week had moved his force south to their rendezvous. This looks like a well-planned coup. Tostig and his men must have been friendless and out of touch not to have spotted the mood or preparations.

Morcar, their earl designate, led the army south to Northampton. This was the territory of Tostig. Earl Edwin was already there 'with his full force'. The chroniclers tell us that they were joined by Welshmen, indicating that Edwin had maintained his close relations with their neighbour.

Earl Harold went to meet the rebels in Northampton. There is no mention of Harold making any special preparation or moving with more than his bodyguard. Harold evidently hoped to defuse the situation and 'would work their reconciliation if he might, but he could not'. The rebels were not willing to negotiate. Instead they were forceful in their demand and 'imposed an errand to King Edward, sending also messengers with him, and requesting that they might have Morcar for their earl'.

Once Harold was on his way,

> the Northern men did much harm about Northampton... either that they slew men, and burned houses and corn; or took all the cattle that they could come at; which amounted to many thousands. Many hundred men also they took, and led northward with them; so that not only that Shire, but others near it were the worse for many winters.

The people of Northamptonshire were paying a heavy price for the unpopularity of their earl.

The news reached Edward where he was hunting at Britford, just east of Salisbury. One chronicle notes that Tostig was with the king when the rebellion broke out. Edward summoned a meeting 'of his nobles'.

The showdown took place at Oxford, which lay conveniently near the boundary of Wessex and Mercian lands. The meeting probably lasted for a few days. The rebels had the opportunity to put their complaint and make their demands.

The first complaints raised against Tostig concerned tax. The available evidence suggests that these were not exceptional, but Tostig had apparently changed the method of collection and might have also been doing some extra fundraising to pay for the church-building and pilgrimage.

The second complaint was also couched in terms that focus on how he discharged his vital role as dispenser of justice. 'He oppressed the nobles with the heavy yoke of his rule because of their misdeeds.' Their complaint was not that they had not done wrong. They owned up to that. Tostig was accused of punishing them 'more from a wish to confiscate their property than for a love of justice'. The rebels asked the king to relieve them of all of these penalties, presumably in the form of an amnesty and restoration of confiscated property.

The rebel's third demand was possibly intended to convey this resentment, because they demanded the renewal of Cnut's law to be the basis for their future government. This had been set down nearly fifty years before. The rebels wanted to return to the certainties and systems operating before Tostig arrived, bringing the ways of a west Saxon among the Northmen.

The other key demand was that Morcar should be made the earl in place of Tostig. They would also have required Tostig to be outlawed, as they could not tolerate the possibility of him raising a force in England to fight his way back. If the king accepted that the charges made against Tostig were valid, there would be no option but to outlaw the perpetrator. The stakes could not have been higher.

At the meeting, some accused Tostig of being responsible for creating the problem, while Tostig accused his own brother, Harold, of backing the rebels. Tostig's evidence was that Harold had ridden out to meet the rebels. Harold was forced to take an oath in order to rebut this charge. The indications are that the king favoured confronting the rebels but practical problems were raised. It was too late in the year. Everybody must have appreciated that the forceful arguments against civil war were even stronger now than they had been in 1052, when Godwin forced his restoration. The king was ailing and there was no obvious heir.

At a meeting at Oxford on 28 October, the king and his council yielded to the rebel's demands. Harold continued the role as go-between that he had adopted from the start of the rebellion. The balance of the available evidence suggests that Harold was acting as an honest broker rather than his brother's ally. Tostig was banished and was abroad within the short time allowed. There was probably little or no opportunity for the brothers to meet and discuss the event. Their next meeting after Oxford might have been on the battlefield at Stamford Bridge.

> Then earl Tostig and his wife, and all they who acted with him, went south over sea with him to earl Baldwin who received them all: and they were there all the winter at St. Omer's.

The power in England was now rebalanced. The brothers Edwin and Morcar, sons of the house of Mercia, now governed the north of the kingdom, with powerful allies in Scotland and Wales, while the Godwins dominated the south. The younger son of the twice-outlawed Earl Aelfgar was now the earl of Northumbria. He would now be responsible for the defence of the northern and north-east coast of England against any invasion.

King Edward would be dead within eight weeks of Tostig's exile. Edward's death might be coincidence, but Tostig was his hunting companion. There were both intelligent men and some commentators have suggested that the impact of Tostig's exile on Edward might have been considerable. One chronicler talks about the king's mind being affected. There have been suggestions, which are supportable by the evidence, that Tostig was well favoured by the king and his queen. The king had, after all, wanted Harold to suppress the rebels to restore Tostig. There can be no doubt that, in this episode, Tostig felt utterly betrayed by his brother.

On 31 December 1065, Edward the Confessor, old and childless, was near death. His council and most powerful subjects were gathered for the consecration of his West Minster. The king was too ill to attend the ceremony and on 5 January 1066 Edward the Confessor died.

Among the last words recorded from King Edward was of a vision of a country being destroyed by an avenging God. There were a number of doom-mongers around at the time. Wulfstan, the bishop in the frontier county of Worcestershire, was delivering exhortations against the habits and fashions that affluence was introducing in England. He railed in particular against long hair, saying that those with long tresses would be weak in the defence of their country.

There must have been years of talk about the royal succession. There was more time to talk as the king lay dying. His burial and the coronation of the new king were speedily accomplished, perhaps because there had been so much time to prepare for these events. Harold was crowned king of England.

King Harold travelled north to York to meet the earls for his marriage to their sister. This is unlikely to have been before the spring, when travel restrictions were eased after the winter. We know that Easter fell on 16 April in 1066 and Harold had returned from York by then. It is significant that the king went north rather than demanding that the bride and her family came south. This was a gesture of respect from Harold to the men of the north.

There must have been much serious talk of the likely threats and how the country would respond. The course of later events demonstrates that King Harold had obtained the complete loyalty of the men of power and their agreement to the plan of defence. The journey to and from York was a useful reconnaissance for Harold, as the events of 1066 would later reveal.

The settlement reached saw Harold marry Ealdgyth. She was the widow of Gruffydd, whose downfall and death Harold had fought for a few years earlier. The Godwinsons were uniting with the house of Leofric. The two other great earls of England became his brothers-in-law. For the young earls of Mercia and Northumbria, this held out the prospect of being uncle to a future king of England. A set of unlikely circumstances had conspired to make this the perfect political match for England.

The views of Harold's lifelong partner and mother to his six surviving children are not recorded. Edith Swanneck, his mistress, seems to have accepted the political marriage. Their love match had lasted through Harold's turbulent career. It was most unusual at the time for a man of power not to be formally allied in marriage. Some have speculated that the Church's strict rules of consanguinity might have prevented a church blessing. Another view is that Harold had been saving himself for a political match; although there seemed to be no bar on nobles setting aside a wife or taking a mistress for the purpose of procuring an heir, the Church would very soon put a stop to this practice.

We hear very little of Harold's new wife, and it is Edith who according to tradition offers to bury the body of the slain Harold after Hastings. If the conjectured time for the wedding is right, and given Harold's absence on campaign through the summer, Ealdgyth would have been noticeably pregnant with Harold's twins at the time of the battles.

It is nowhere stated, but it is probable, that the Mercian brothers made some demands concerning this marriage, as was their right as the family of the bride. One condition would doubtless have been that their children should have a prior claim to the throne over Harold's three existing sons. A second condition might well have been that Tostig should remain outlawed.

Tostig might have felt with some justification that his exile would be short now his brother was the supreme governor in England. News of the trip to York might have kept his hopes alive, believing that the king had gone to arrange his restoration. However, he might have guessed that things were not as they seemed. Kings summon their subjects. It was a supplicant monarch who had gone north to York in 1066.

The return of Tostig would have tested the loyalty of the northern earls who had rebelled in order to expel him from the north. If he was to be allowed back as earl of Wessex, the marriage to Ealdgyth, the loyalty of the earls and the unity of the land would be in jeopardy.

Tostig must have felt thoroughly betrayed a second time when King Harold II, his brother, did not restore him. There would have been no indications or intelligence of invasion at this early stage in the year. Those plots had yet to hatch. So this does not explain why a suitable position was not found for Tostig to keep him on side. Harold had transferred extensive parts of his Wessex holding to his brothers Gyrth and Leofwine, ignoring Tostig. Perhaps the trip to Normandy just over a year before had convinced Harold that a contest was inevitable and he had to be sure that his back was safe. The Mercians and Northumbrians, now united by the grandsons of Leofric, could find many reasons to ally themselves with any enemies of the Godwinsons.

We do not know if Tostig waited to discover how totally he had been excluded. A reconstructed chronology, below, suggests that he was a man in a hurry and did not wait on events in England. His response to all this rejection was decisive. He was the choreographer of the sequence of events in 1066 that would bring to an end the era of Anglo-Saxon England.

PLOTS AND PLANS

The chronicle says that it was Tostig who refused to return – 'Earl Tostig... would not submit to be his own brother's serving man' – but it is not clear if that was before or after he learnt of the marriage.

Because this is a side story for the ever-practical chronicles, we do not have reliable records of Tostig's movements. However, by working backwards from the flow of events in 1066, a confident hypothesis can be constructed of the part played by the embittered Earl Tostig.

His first recourse would have been to turn to his father-in-law, Baldwin V. Flanders was normally a minor player in the events of Europe. But in 1066, Baldwin was regent of France during the minority of Philip I so was, according to feudal law, William's overlord. We know that the French court did not support the proposed Norman invasion and there is evidence of active opposition.

It is probably safe to assume that Baldwin was privy to the decision to oppose William's ambitious proposal and possibly even an architect of the policy. It is likely that Tostig had to content himself with the resources he had been granted when he was exiled. These would provide an entourage and later a raiding fleet.

There are some unreliable sources that report a meeting between Tostig and William, but such a meeting was not vital. Mindful of Harold's visit a few years before, Tostig might have felt that a personal visit was ill-advised. It would be simple to exchange emissaries and there is ample evidence that ambassadors were busy during the early months of 1066.

Instead of making his way west to Normandy, Tostig headed north to Denmark to his cousin King Sweyn. This would have been a difficult voyage to undertake by sea during the winter. As the Godwinson family enjoyed good relationships with the German emperor, Henry, he could have made this trip overland in about a week, given the short hours of daylight.

> The earl now asked King Sweyn for support and help of men; and King Sweyn invited him to stay with him, with the promise that he should get so large an earldom in Denmark that he would be an important chief.

The saga, which can be relied upon to provide much more information about these vital exchanges, suggests that the earl took another tack. Tostig suggested that Sweyn should use his energy and influence to repeat the feats of his illustrious ancestor Cnut. But King Sweyn was not provoked by such flattering comparisons. He was a realist and modestly confessed he had difficulty securing his own domain against the threats:

> So much smaller a man am I than Cnut the Great, that I can with difficulty defend my own Danish dominions against the Northmen. King Cnut, on the other hand, got the Danish kingdom in heritage, took England by slash and blow, and sometimes was near losing his life in the contest; and Norway he took without slash or blow. Now it suits me much better to be guided by my own slender ability than to imitate my relation, King Cnut's, lucky hits.

Tostig was bitterly disappointed and spoke his mind:

> The result of my errand here is less fortunate than I expected of thee who art so gallant a man, seeing that thy relative is in so great need. It may be that I will seek friendly help where it could less be expected; and that I may find a chief who is less afraid, king, than thou art of a great enterprise.

The sagas note that they parted not the best of friends. Undeterred, Tostig headed north to King Harald of Norway, who had moved down to the new harbour he had created near Oslo. If Tostig's party had arrived by horse, King Sweyn would have provided them with the necessary ships and crew to transport them to Norway. Here 'the earl explained his errand to the king. He told him all his proceedings since he left England, and asked his aid to recover his dominions in England'.

The initial response of King Harald was also disappointing, as he replied 'that the Northmen had no great desire for a campaign in England, and to have English chiefs over them there', adding that 'People say that the English are not to be trusted'.

Tostig then reminded Harald of the claim that his predecessor King Magnus had over England and proceeded to deploy similar undiplomatic but provocative arguments to those he had tried unsuccessfully in Denmark.

The king replied:

How came it that he did not get it, if he had a right to it?

Why, [replied the earl], hast thou not Denmark, as King Magnus, thy predecessor, had it?

[The king replies] The Danes have nothing to brag of over us Northmen; for many a place have we laid in ashes to thy relations.

[Then said the earl] If thou wilt not tell me, I will tell thee. Magnus subdued Denmark, because all the chiefs of the country helped him; and thou hast not done it, because all the people of the country were against thee. Therefore, also, King Magnus did not strive for England, because all the nation would have Edward for king. Wilt thou take England now?

Tostig then sets out a plan and promises to bring 'the principal men in England', because they would make him king if he had the backing of King Harald.

King Harald weighed carefully the earl's words, and perceived at once that there was truth in much of what he said; and he himself had also a great desire to acquire dominions.

The debate was a long one and they talked 'long and frequently together'. At last Harold 'took the resolution to proceed in summer to England, and conquer the country'.

We have explored earlier the mixed motives that led King Harald to this decision. It is certain that it was the intervention, argument and perhaps even the provocation and promises given by Tostig that was responsible for the launch of this northern armada.

So King Harald issued the call-up and 'sent a message-token through all Norway and ordered out a levy of one-half of all the men in Norway able to carry arms'. Half the army would be left with his son Magnus, who would be handed the crown before the flotilla sailed.

The saga tells us of the public debate that followed the call to arms:

When this became generally known, there were many guesses about what might be the end of this expedition. Some reckoned up King Harald's great achievements, and thought he was also the man who could accomplish this. Others, again, said that England was difficult to attack; that it was very full of people; and the men-at-arms... were so brave, that one of them was better than two of Harald's best men.

One reputable chronicler, Orderic Vitalis, reports that the Norwegian preparations took six months. To be ready to sail before the winds of winter began to threaten, the summons needed to go out before the end of March. There is no mention of hostages being exchanged, but it would be normal procedure. We have many clues that a long-term friendship developed between Tostig's sons and the younger son of King Harald, Olaf, who all returned to Norway in 1067, and we can speculate that these youngsters spent the summer of 1066 together.

The saga concludes by telling us that Tostig 'sailed in spring west to Flanders, to meet the people who had left England with him, and others besides who had gathered to him both out of England and Flanders'. If Tostig was heading back to Flanders in the spring, he must have set out for Denmark in late February. This should have put him back in Flanders in early April, about the time that Harold was returning from his northern nuptials.

If Tostig did leave on his quest for support as early as February, he might not have been aware of Harold's marriage contract and the alliance with the northern earls. If this is the case, Harold might have been responding to the threat being assembled by his brother rather than provoking it. His Danish family connection would have been quick to inform Harold of Tostig's visit and his next destination.

It should be added that some historians suggest that this trip is a fiction because there is no corroborative source. It would certainly be nice to have another observer, but this is no reason to doubt the record that remains, especially as it is not contradicted by the other sources and does not conflict with any of the known facts. An alternative timing for the visit to Norway is discussed later.

Before the start of May 1066 Tostig landed in the Isle of Wight. The Domesday survey lists the various estates that he held at the south-east corner and eastern shore of the island. His departure in late October had been hasty as well as unplanned. He would still have had some money, supplies, weapons and manpower available to him on the island. Therefore, he would have taken what was his and likely forced other inhabitants to give him money and provisions. We are able to fix the time of Tostig's return to the Isle of Wight, as it was just before the appearance of Halley's comet. On the old calendar the comet appeared for the first time on 24 April. This ominous sign was visible until mid-May.

The attack on the Isle of Wight can be seen in the context of later events as fitting a carefully devised military plan. Given that no such plan is ever supposed to survive first contact with the enemy, one needs to examine the various options that his opening attack offered.

The location was just across the water from the Godwinson family base at Bosham. Perhaps he was able to deploy a spy or emissary to visit his mother, sister or one of his brothers. He would also be able to test the preparations. It is possible that he might even have intended to hold this as a staging post for a Norman invasion. This cannot be easily dismissed, since King Harold would himself occupy the same beaches as he prepared to meet William's invasion from Normandy.

Sources do report that William and Tostig met in 1066. If the conditions were favourable, this was a good opportunity for such a visit. We have to keep an open mind on such a face-to-face meeting. However, in the light of subsequent events, a strong case can, and will, be made that Tostig was encouraging a co-ordinated attack in the north and the south. This joint planning with William (for we do not know that either man employed military staff to act for him) must have taken place at this time.

William's plans were set for an invasion in mid-August. Tostig might have explained that the English army could have dispersed if he postponed, provided he could draw them out with his plan for coastal raiding. He might also have confided the news of the Norwegian plan. Which of these two ambitious and ruthless men would have held England, had matters gone as Tostig had planned, is an intriguing question. The fact that Tostig would not want to address the question while his position was so weak provides the most compelling argument against a personal meeting between these two leaders.

The attack on the Isle of Wight fits in well with the strategy that Tostig would extend through the summer, of stretching the defenders by attacking along the coast. Tostig understood precisely the resources that England could deploy. To improve the chances of success for the invasions, Tostig needed to force some troops to be spread along the coast ready to react to his raids. The demands of coastal defence would limit the size of the main army. Tostig also knew that the period of service was limited to between forty and sixty days. He wanted to force Harold to call out his army as soon as possible, especially if he knew that the attacks would not come until late in the year.

A good commander makes a plan that will succeed even if things do not happen exactly as he wished. The early opening gambit on the Isle of Wight made a great deal of sense. Perhaps the only thing that went wrong was that he found that he was unable to secure it as a base for future operations against England.

After leaving the Isle of Wight he raided along the Sussex and Kent coast, past Dover and into Sandwich Bay. There he met Cospig who was, like Tostig, an outcast. The former had spent the winter in the Orkneys. The sea route back from Norway might well have taken Tostig via Cospig's winter quarters. The fact that they were able to fix a rendezvous is another indication of the plan that Tostig had made for 1066.

The two exiles appear to have spent some time in Sandwich trying to provoke a response from the king. Once news reached them that Harold and his army were on their way, the two retreated and began their raiding up the east coast.

The chronicler also notes that Tostig

> took some of the boatmen with him, willing and unwilling, and went north into the Humber with sixty ships; whence he plundered in Lindsey, and there slew many good men.

Sandwich was the traditional muster place for the English navy. Were the ships taken part of Harold's navy? If so it was another piece of good planning, although the haul of shipping is not that impressive. Depriving Harold of his ships would make pursuit harder and deprive the English of their mobility later in the summer. However, no mention is made of any shipping shortage.

The extra ships stayed with Tostig's flotilla during their brief campaign of raids. The impressed ships and their crew must have added to the menace that was reported as the ships made their way along the coast. Observers would not know how many warriors were on board. Raids are recorded in Norfolk and Lincolnshire. The final raids were along the southern side of the Humber, which would provide useful reconnaissance for King Harald's invasion.

The English version of events talks of the earls Edwin and Morcar driving the raiders back to their boats. From Tostig's point of view, the raiders were achieving their objective of drawing the army to remote parts of the coast. The only drawback seems to be that the raiders did not manage to keep up the attacks for as long as they planned. Tostig and Cospig are reported as being in Scotland for the summer.

The chroniclers also report that the 'boatmen forsook' Tostig. It is possible that some unwilling sailors seized their moment and either sailed away or abandoned their ships. Faced with the power of two substantial armies, his raiding party probably decided to quit with the loot they had gathered. This strongly suggests that the raiders were continental mercenaries rather than house troops.

But it is also possible that Tostig was willing to see them go once the raiding was finished and it was time to head north. However, a mass desertion does look the more likely explanation, effectively bringing the raiding to a premature end.

It was expected that earls who were ejected would return and wreak some vengeful devastation if they could, but Tostig did not raid into Northumbria. One can speculate why he did not attack as he headed north. With so much hostility towards him following the coup just months before, raiding would have encountered ferocious local resistance.

It is also easy to imagine Earl Morcar shadowing Tostig's slow progress north against the tidal drift with his remaining ships. Having been alerted to the danger, the Northumbrians would have been able to destroy Tostig's small force had they attempted to land. The rebel territory would not be spared when Tostig sailed down the coast with King Harald and his Norse army.

The various accounts of what happened next are consistent in suggesting that when Tostig reached Scotland he had perhaps as few as a dozen ships. Some translations suggest that the vessels left to Tostig were not even proper longships but trading vessels. Perhaps those who had fled took with them the best and fastest longships, leaving Tostig with the broad-beamed traders.

Tostig had been on his campaign for about five months by the time he reached Scotland. Fatigue might have been an issue. Tostig must therefore have been grateful that he had parted with King Malcolm on relatively good terms after the royal visit he had organised to the court of King Edward.

Left: 1 King Harold II. This modern statue at the west end of Waltham Abbey represents the association of the Godwinson family with the abbey. It is claimed that a coffin was found with the inscription 'Here lies the unfortunate Harold'. If this is the resting place of Harold's mortal remains then they have been moved three times. However, the church at Bosham also makes a good claim to be the place where Harold was buried after his death at Hastings.

Below left: 2 In Holy Trinity Church at Bosham a large stone coffin was found about a metre from this grave during building work in April 1954. The remains in the grave are missing a leg and the head. As such, the remains are consistent with those of king Harold. The birth and death of this daughter of Cnut are not recorded but she might have been a daughter of Cnut's first love rather than his wife Emma. Local tradition reports that the child died by drowning.

Below: 3 Bosham is an ancient village on the south coast, near Chichester. Before the advent of ships with deep keels, tidal inlets like those surrounding Bosham provided excellent harbours. The spire of Holy Trinity Church can be seen on the horizon. Bosham was the family base of the Godwin family and is where King Cnut, Earl Godwin's patron, is reputed to have demonstrated the limitations of princely power by failing to stop the tide.

Top: 4 The death of King Edward is recorded in the Bayeux Tapestry. It is probable that the tapestry was stitched by the widows of Wessex who had retired to various convents after the defeat of the English army at Hastings. The death of Edward at the start of 1066 started the complex sequence that would lead via the battles at Fulford and Stamford Bridge to William's defeat of an English army near Hastings.

Above: 5 The abbey church of Westminster was built by Edward for the Benedictines. St Peter's became known as the west minster to distinguish it from St Paul's, the east minster. King Edward established his palace near the river Thames on land known as Thorney Island, near the present west door. The church has undergone many additions and the photograph shows the mix of architectural styles. King Edward was too ill to attend the consecration of his abbey on 28 December and died a few days later. Every English monarch since Edward, with the exception of his namesakes Edward V and Edward VIII, who were never crowned, has been crowned in the Abbey, starting with King Harold on 6 January 1066.

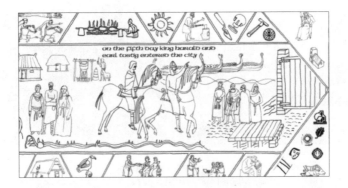

on the fifth day king harald and earl tostig entered the city

Top: 6 This panel from a contemporary tapestry shows King Harald and his ally Earl Tostig accepting the submission of the city of York after their victory at Fulford. The tapestry, designed by the author, shows some events of 1066 missing from the Bayeux Tapestry. It is being embroidered by local volunteers.

Above: 7 This enigmatic scene from the Bayeux Tapestry might have been designed to cast aspersions on one line of English succession from King Cnut. Aelfgyva was the first love of Cnut, although after he became king of all England he took Emma, King Ethelred's widow, as his wife. Aelfgyva's eldest son, Harald Harefoot, was king of England before his untimely death allowed Emma's son Harthacnut to take the throne. The scene implies Aelfgyva had an affair with a cleric, for which there is no evidence. Chronological evidence suggests that the daughter of Cnut buried at Bosham was Aelfgyva's daughter.

Above left: 8 The Isle of Wight played an important strategic role in the events of 1066. Earl Tostig held land at the east end and returned here in 1066 from exile to collect money and possibly recruit men. It is possible that Tostig liaised with Duke William of Normandy while he was here. Much of the coastline is inhospitable to ships, making it an attractive place for raiders who knew the coast and understood the complex tides. The west end of the island is surrounded by cliffs and terminates with the Needles.

Above right: 9 While the west end of the Isle of Wight is marked with cliffs, the east end offers some long sandy bays and some tidal inlets similar to those at Bosham. From Luccombe Cine round past Sandown provides many beaches, harbours and inlets. This is where King Harold brought his army and ships during the summer of 1066 to await the expected invasion from Normandy. The tides and prevailing westerly winds should have carried Harold's army quickly to confront William's troops, perhaps even catching the transports before they beached. William won the waiting game and sailed only after the English army had dispersed, after their rations and tour of duty were exhausted, but he was driven back on the initial attempt to cross.

10 A well-understood system of military obligation had blended the Celtic, Germanic and Viking traditions existing in England. King Alfred had imposed military obligation after the defeat of the Danes. This illustration, which is part of the Yorkshire Preface to the Bayeux Tapestry, shows a messenger bringing the message while a thane musters his men. In practice the army consisted of men experienced in use of arms, although a portion was drawn from the community.

11 The shieldwall would line up many ranks deep. Those with the best armour would be at the front. Behind them would be those with spears who could reach many in the enemy ranks to jab or to hook their shields with the wings on their spears, allowing the front row to slash or stab with their swords.

12 Locking shields would help to resist a charge but restricted the use of swords. It would be the job of those behind, with spear and axe, to blunt a surge. The spearman could handle his spear with one or both hands, depending on the need for the protection of his shield. The work done by re-enactors has allowed much better understanding of how weapons were used collectively and how battles were fought. These photos are of the Wychwood Warriors in Oxford.

13 One tactic employed to break the opposing shieldwall was to form a tight wedge, sometimes called a hog's head, that would force apart the opposing wall. Those following would try to exploit this before the gap was closed.

14 & 15 Scarborough. The modern castle sits on top of the mound that overlooks the north and south sandy bays at Scarborough. This is where King Harald launched his campaign of conquest. The south bay, right, now has the harbour. In medieval times this would have been in the lee of the mound, providing some protection from the icy north wind in winter. The town destroyed by the invaders is believed to lie on this south-facing slope, overlooking the bay. The defenders set fire to the houses by throwing fire down from the mound where a Roman watchtower used to stand.

16 Spurn Head. A remarkable promontory that shields almost half of the 14km-wide mouth of the river Humber, with the North Sea to the right and the estuary to the left. Its existence is precarious. The land is on the move, drifting from East Yorkshire in the north towards Lincolnshire to the south. In 1066 the Norse fleet would have sheltered on the sand bars and islands inside the estuary, while they waited for the troops who had ravaged the coast since their landing at Scarborough. The exceptional tides at the time of the invasion would have allowed the boats to beach close to firm land, making it easy for the soldiers to re-board.

17 At Flaxfleet the rivers Trent and Ouse merge to become the Humber. Because of the immense flow of these tributaries that drain one-fifth of England, there is a perceptible bore at certain tides. On their journey along the Humber and Ouse, the longships could have paused on the foreshore when the tide was ebbing before rejoining the rushing flow that would carry them to Riccall. The extensive mud flats were probably cultivated for flax throughout medieval times.

18 The Norwegian invasion of 1066 coincided with a particularly high tide. The effect was that the tide flowed upstream for about four hours while the ebb lasted over eight hours. However, the speed of the flow was exceptionally fast, allowing the invaders to reach Riccall. The tidal range of the Ouse in mid September is around 5m. The long ebb exposes steep mud banks on the inside bends. The modern flood defence measures are built about 50m away from the natural banks.

North causeway

Modern site of Riccall

Flood embankment

Remains of aggregate extraction

Bank of river Ouse at mid-tide

South causeway

19, 20 & 21 Riccall. This provided a secure base for a fleet of over 300 ships in September 1066. While much work remains to be done, it is probable that this landing was an island connected by two causeways to dry land, making it easy to defend. The fleet would have moored out of the river flow, in the area that is now cultivated. The image at the top is looking north towards York and the bottom image faces south. An embankment now prevents the river flooding the land at high tide. The island itself has been excavated to provide gravel for the flood protection. This base was attacked by the Mercian fleet, which was blocking the river upstream, at the same time as King Harold was surrounding the Norse royal party near Stamford Bridge. The natural banks of the river afford few places where a boat, and certainly not a fleet, could land. The river bank at Riccall (central image) is too steep to allow boats to be 'beached'. The fleet would have to leave the very fast flow of the spring tide, where the hydrology at Riccall had created a 'lay-by' in the form of an oxbow lake, with calm water and gentle slopes. The fleet could be pulled out of the water.

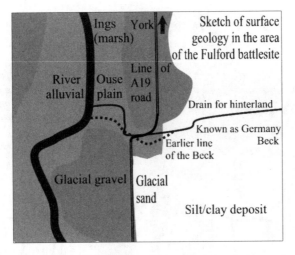

Sketch of surface geology in the area of the Fulford battlesite

Ings (marsh)   York

River alluvial   Ouse plain   Line of A19 road

Drain for hinterland

Known as Germany Beck

Earlier line of the Beck

Glacial gravel   Glacial sand   Silt/clay deposit

22 The battle was fought at this muddy ford because its geology had created an easily defensible position. A glacier retreating about 15,000 years ago left the material into which melt-water carved a deep groove. The sea level was several metres lower then and a deep channel has been cut through this moraine by water entering from the east. Regular flooding has raised the level of the Ings about 2m since the battle. At that time there would have been an broad, fordable area near the site of the modern road bridge.

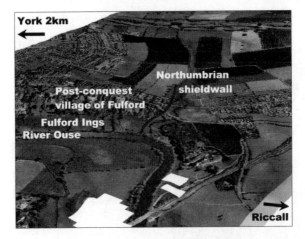

York 2km

Northumbrian shieldwall

Post-conquest village of Fulford

Fulford Ings
River Ouse

Riccall

23 The computer-generated relief map of Fulford shows the breach carved in the moraine around 15,000 years ago with the river Ouse arcing round the hard base material. Germany Beck drained the land at the top of the image which at the time of the battle was wetter than today. The shieldwall ran from this wetland to the river, although there were few defenders positioned across the Ings. Thanks to routine flooding, the site has not been developed.

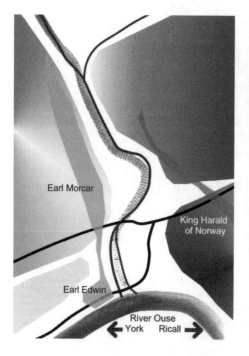

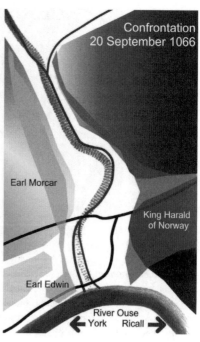

Confrontation
20 September 1066

Earl Morcar

King Harald
of Norway

Earl Edwin

River Ouse
← York   Ricall →

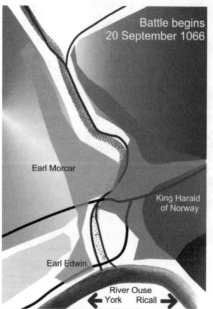

Battle begins
20 September 1066

Earl Morcar

King Harald
of Norway

Earl Edwin

River Ouse
← York   Ricall →

Above left: 24 The sequence attempts to recreate the dynamic of the battle. The first contact was probably near midday and the sides finally separated at dusk. The Northumbrian army arrived early to block the Norse at this 'choke point' at the muddy ford.

Above right: 25 The Norse were based about two hours away so most of the morning would be spent preparing for battle, with the armies separated by the substantial ditch cut by Germany Beck.

Left: 26 The battle opened when the Norse sent a weak force to attack the Northumbrian line, which was driven back.

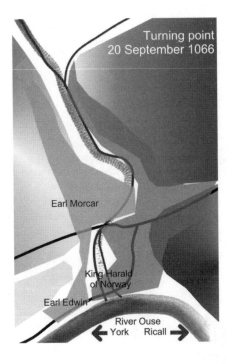

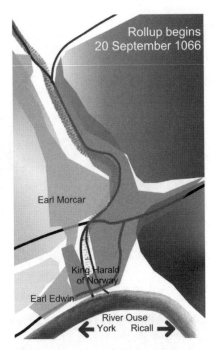

Above left: 27 King Harald ordered an attack along the whole line and then led a charge beside the river and forced Earl Edwin to give ground so that the Norse could cross the Beck.

Above right: 28 Having crossed the Beck, the Norse were able to come behind Earl Morcar's men, who were making good progress at the ford.

Right: 29 There was little opportunity for those at the ford to escape. The rest of the army was forced to retreat across the marshy land led by Earl Morcar while his brother, Earl Edwin, retreated along the river bank back to York.

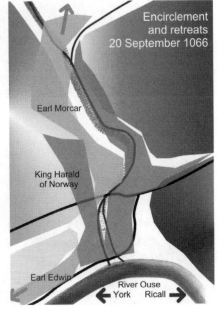

Below and opposite page: Representing a battlefield in a series of images is challenging. However, working with the captions it is hoped to convey an impression of the landscape over which the battle was fought. The sequence is designed to show the English line moving from the right flank beside the river to the left, and the fields across which the survivors retreated.

30 The army's right flank was anchored by the river Ouse. The beck drained into the river here and there might have been a causeway across the sandy delta where the river flowed into the Ouse. Beyond the delta, the banks of the river were steep. As the battle began, one of the highest tides of the year was reaching York.

31 There are now extensive water meadows between the glacial moraine and river bank. This delicate and rare habitat was much wetter in 1066.

32 Looking across the delta, there is an ancient hedge behind which the Norse army could have enjoyed some protection, if it dates back to the battle. The width of the delta would have kept the two sides apart and out of range.

33 This coppiced tree (in France many woodlands are traditionally maintained) would have provided an excellent defensive screen. The remains of coppiced willow trees can be identified along the length of Germany Beck.

34 Looking towards the centre of the battle, the houses along the horizon stand on the elevated moraine. The foreground was about 2m lower in 1066.

35 This featureless landscape has been gradually filled to provide a play area in Fulford, so the rising ground around the edges is now obscured. In 1066 this marked the course of Germany Beck. This was the trap into which Earl Edwin advanced on 20 September 1066.

36 This image looks towards the centre of the battle from the left flank. This is the broad ditch that separated the two sides. It is about 5m deep and 40m wide. The track in the foreground is close to the surface of 1066 and the shape of the ditch is not unlike the way it would have looked at the time.

37 Left Flank. Looking back towards the battle, this image is taken from the marshy land beyond the left flank. The land slopes up on all sides. On the right there is an ancient hedgerow. The English army might have been forced into this marsh to avoid encirclement.

38 This undulating terrain has been levelled for farming. In the bottom of Germany Beck are the remains of a hedge that one source dates at over nine centuries old. Some trees are attempting to re-grow. This would have been the only escape route for the encircled English army.

King Malcolm had connections to all potential combatants and was therefore probably hoping to remain neutral. It made little difference to him who won. So when Tostig came to Scotland the Scots 'entertained him, and aided him with provisions; and he abode there all the summer' at Dunfermline. Malcolm's allies in Bernicia would not have been happy but with an army expected from Norway, the king of Scotland was in a difficult position.

Some have suggested that Tostig took advantage of this lull to make his trip to Norway. However, the timescale is against this. Tostig could not have reached Scotland before the beginning of June and was probably not there until the end of the month. There would not be time, even assuming the earlier date, to sail to Norway and locate King Harald in time for him to mobilise his army and make all the other dispositions of which we are aware, had Tostig not already made the arrangements with the Norwegians.

Tostig's strategy, if that is what it was, had worked well so far. The English armies were at either end of the country, expecting two invasions. There was anxiety in coastal places about more raids and the strain of waiting would be much harder on the defenders than the invaders, who would choose the time of their coming.

The role played by Tostig in the drama of 1066 has been under-estimated. He was the catalyst for the northern invasion and probably devised the only strategy that would enable William to land his invasion force. His intervention with the Norwegians, his coastal raiding and the intelligence he had supplied to William all played a critical part in the defeat of the English. Tostig would have understood how powerful and united the English armed force could be. He would have explained to William that a divided and dispersed army offered the Normans the only possibility of success.

Perhaps only Tostig really understood that it would take the combined might of Norway and Normandy to defeat an England led by King Harold. And for the plan to work, the assaults would have to be co-ordinated; the evidence strongly suggests that Tostig was attempting to choreograph this.

It is unclear what role he saw for himself if both invasions had succeeded. He was probably sharp enough to realise that William's chances of success against an opposed invasion were small, even if his diversions worked as planned, so he would only have to deal with an ageing King Harald of Norway and, of course, his own

brother, Harold Godwinson. The exiled earl might even have pon-
dered the vacuum that would be left if the leading dukes and counts
of Flanders' neighbours were overthrown. His father-in-law, acting
as regent, might even assert some effective central control in France.
Tostig was an inexperienced warrior and would learn too late that
the fortunes of war are a very poor basis upon which to make any
longer-term plans.

In the words of the Godwinson family chronicler:

> Both brothers persevered with what they had begun: but Tostig vigor-
> ously, Harold prudently; the one in action aimed at success, the other
> also at happiness. Both at times so cleverly disguised their intentions
> that one who did not know them was in doubt what to think.

These are perspicacious comments by somebody who knew both
Harold and Tostig. Vigour and ambition had temporarily lost out to
the virtues of prudence and happiness.

5

Preparing for Battle

King Harald of Norway had sent out his war-token, possibly a special war-arrow in the hands of a messenger, around the country in the spring of 1066. Throughout the previous decade they had been used to fighting against the Danes. Now there was a truce or treaty. Harald's Norwegian army had not been summoned during the previous two years.

The 'peace dividend' for the old warrior, Harald, was some domestic unrest which had brought him close to conflict with his son Magnus. The idle warriors were growing refractory. There were, nevertheless, arguments among his veterans about the wisdom of the venture. Half the troops were to stay behind with Magnus. This was normal procedure. They would acknowledge Magnus as king of Norway before Harald's fleet sailed for England.

The local warbands would come together, draw lots and the loser would stay. Why were they prepared to respond to the summons to follow their king overseas?

THE NORWEGIAN ARMY

Owning a weapon was the mark of a freeman in eleventh-century Norway. In the Danelaw, 'wapentakes' were the administrative equivalent of the 'hundreds' created inside Anglo-Saxon-governed

England. Wapentakes were designated meeting places of some spiritual significance, where a vote could be taken by a 'weapon touch'.
Bearing weapons signified rank. The Anglo-Saxon term 'hundred'
itself signified the number of men-at-arms and probably evolved
from the role established for Roman centurions. Administration was
synonymous with military mobilisation.

Carrying a weapon did not mean that everybody was a soldier.
Just as a modern English knight or dame of the realm would not
be expected to take up arms, society at the time of King Harald
of Norway was diverse. Some 'weapon-carriers' specialised in trade,
others in agriculture or administration, while others were full- or
part-time soldiers.

In very rough terms, this might mean that one in twenty were warriors in Norway. Based on a national population in Norway of about
200,000 at the time, these figures suggest an army of 10,000. For
comparison, England's mobilised force of 30,000 was supported by a population estimated at 2.5 million. So there were over seventy-five people
supporting each warrior in Anglo-Saxon England. (The English figures
are based on sampling some Domesday surveys and incorporate many
statistical assumptions.) In addition to the mobilised army there would be
one of equal size that was still dispersed throughout the community. In
England, this levy had been one of Alfred the Great's innovations.

It can be argued that a militaristic tradition had developed among
the Nordic nations and soldiering was just another career option. It
has been suggested that the motive for the Viking expansions of the
ninth and tenth centuries was population growth that exceeded the
domestic resources. Archaeological evidence from Norway certainly
indicates that new farms were cleared in marginal areas at the time of
the Viking raids, so it would appear that the land had more population than it could support.

Norway possessed rich iron ore and abundant timber for the
furnaces, providing an easy source for the materials needed to make
weapons. So a tradition of venturing overseas, equipped to raid,
possibly emerged from the overstretched livestock and arable resources
of the Norse lands. Vikings, and it is too early to give them national
identities, were settlers as well as raiders. The attacks made by Vikings
on religious places have probably been overstated by the scribes of the
time. A monastery might yield one harvest of treasure to trade but fertile land provided a new home. The Vikings established kingdoms in

Dublin and York, and the marks of their Norse origins are evident in Kiev, in the Russian empire, in the Isle of Man and in Normandy.

By the start of the eleventh century, powerful warrior leaders, returning to Norway, were able to dominate the land, and within a few generations a central organisation was emerging. This was not an internal development but one learned by successful raiders as they travelled. Large armies beat smaller ones. The lesson they learned was that the size of the army and the defensibility of the border were what mattered. King Harald doubtless learnt much about organising armies and militias during his decade in Byzantium.

Something of the typicall structure can be seen in the way Harald's predecessor organised his kingdom:

> When the bondes met at the Thing, Magnus was taken to be king over the whole land, as far as his father Olaf had possessed it. Then the king selected a court, and named lendermen, and placed bailiffs and officers in all domains and offices. Immediately after harvest King Magnus ordered a levy through all Throndhjem land, and he collected men readily; and thereafter he proceeded southwards along the coast.

So by 1066 we have an organised Norwegian army with three components. There is the king's household guard at the core, the local appointees with their followers providing the full-time military, and finally the levy.

The system that grew up during Harald's time evidently needed careful man-management, since on several of his campaigns against the Danes we discover Harald releasing some of the 'bonde-troops' while he kept 'his court-men, his lendermen, the best men-at-arms, and all the bonde-troops who lived nearest to the Danish land'. Once they had their spoil, he let some head to their distant homes in the north.

The levy were not farmers who had left their fields. That would be unworkable. Animals and the soil need regular attention. If they were called away from their farms, the nation would go hungry. Soldiering had developed into a career and a good part-time soldier might hope to become a professional. Meanwhile he would help on the farms, depending on how successful the recent campaign had been. Spoil, rather than pay, seems to have been all the reward the levy could expect. What other support they could receive from the community they represented is not known.

It is remarkable that the literature is so uninformative about the numbers involved in Harald's expedition. Ships, and occasionally casualties, are noted but the number left standing after a battle is not listed. We are therefore forced to infer the numbers. This is frustrating as figures, like dates, provide historians with foundations upon which to build their speculations.

This period of relative prosperity and central organisation had seen inflation in the size of fleets deployed by the Norwegians and the Danes in their annual contest. Not for the first time, one side thought it could outbuild its rival and win the final victory. Only when fleets of 150 and 200 are meeting do the sides talk about treaties. With the 'armaments industry' of the time geared up to produce so many ships, the numbers deployed to England are highly credible.

Harald's force at Riccall might have been as large as 12,000 if the final ship-count that reached England is taken as accurate and an average size of longboat is considered. However, a figure of 9,000 is probably more realistic, as not all boats would be filled and there was a good deal of baggage needed for an invading army arriving just before winter. The sagas tell us that 'ships beside provision-ships and small craft' accompanied the fighting vessels.

Not all of those who made the voyage would have been soldiers. There were seamen and perhaps some marines or fighting sailors, referred to as butescarls. There would have been the cooks, foragers and armourers plus the normal complement of sick, lame and lazy. Perhaps a third of the army remained with the fleet at Riccall, a figure that has changed little over the millennium. The fighting strength of Harald's army at Fulford was probably about 6,000.

So to return to the question of why they answered Harald's summons, it was certainly a matter of duty, perhaps even of habit. But it was also 'their job' to be warriors. After a few years of under-employment and a marked decrease in overseas adventures, the prospect of some spoil or the generous Danegeld that Cnut had given to his warriors when they restored him to power was a further incentive. The warriors risked unemployment now there was peace with the Danes.

HARALD ARRIVES

Harald did not depart until late August or early September. It did not really take this much time to gather the force and make all the preparations. The army seems to have been mobilised more quickly on other occasions. In the previous two years, Harald had begun to experience trouble with a few of his bondes who were not paying their taxes on time. If King Harald had to consider the complex agenda of securing the succession of his son, Magnus, he might not have been in a rush to depart. He had a domestic agenda to occupy the summer.

There are other reasons to account for the rather late departure. Arriving late in the campaigning season meant they could over-winter in the north of England and conduct the conquest in two phases. Northumbria was inaccessible once the autumn rains swelled the many rivers. Provided the fleet could guard against the seaborne winter campaign conducted by Cnut, their base was secure.

The mariners might also have advised that the late month often provided a favourable wind, allowing for a quick crossing. However, it is also possible that this was the schedule agreed with Tostig during their lengthy discussions in the spring. It will never be possible to know if this was all part of Tostig's strategic plan, but the case has been argued that simultaneous invasions offered not only the best prospect of a military victory, by splitting the defenders, but also that the winter months could be used to negotiate from a position of strength, whatever happened to the southern invasion.

In 1062 King Harald had ordered a vessel built at Nidaros which would carry about eighty men:

> The ship was built of the same size as the Long Serpent, and every part of her was finished with the greatest care. On the stem was a dragon-head, and on the stern a dragon-tail, and the sides of the bows of the ship were gilt. The vessel was of thirty-five rowers' benches, and was large for that size, and was remarkably handsome; for the king had everything belonging to the ship's equipment of the best, both sails and rigging, anchors and cables.

The invasion would, as far as we know, provide the first outing for this impressive vessel.

We have some dates for the latter part of the journey. Working back, a departure from Solunds in late August is proposed. There are four phases to the journey, culminating in the battle at Fulford: crossing the North Sea, sailing down the Scottish and Northern English coastlines, raiding down the Northumbrian coast and finally the journey inland. Each stage would have called for different seamanship skills.

To cross the North Sea, sail power would have likely sufficed. The swell that often stirs the water surface north of Scotland makes it difficult for any rowers to pull on their oar. The competing high and low atmospheric pressures, arriving from the Arctic and the Atlantic, set these giant ripples in motion across the surface of the sea. The longship would flex to conform to these rolling waves, but it was uncomfortable for the passengers.

These ancient mariners understood their prevailing winds. They knew where each wind would take them. Patience and experience were probably the key navigational aids available at the time, although there is some speculation that they also possessed some simple technology.

If the conditions were unfavourable they would not put out into the ocean. The well-sculptured coasts of northern Europe, with mountain peaks, fjords and headlands, provided excellent landmarks. Without the benefit of a 'crow's nest' for a lookout, the horizon would be scarcely 10km away from the deck of a longship. The Bayeux Tapestry shows a lookout shinning up the mast to look for land. Even a modest elevation can double the distance to the visible horizon at northern latitudes.

The sun is another navigational aid, especially in northern latitudes, as it is never fully lost below the horizon during the travelling months. There are also reports of a calcite mineral called Icelandic spar, which would undergo a subtle colour change when turned towards the sun, even when it was concealed by clouds. They might also have used a magnetic compass, which had already been invented by the Chinese, and which the Vikings might have discovered through their extensive trade links.

Types of floating seaweed, seabirds flying overhead and other sea animals were also indicators used by the seamen. Captive seabirds might be released near land and then followed. A returning seabird might indicate that land was still far off. Speed was relatively easy to assess with experience. Dead reckoning continues to serve seafarers, just as long-haul delivery drivers can predict the precise time they will arrive at the loading ramp, in spite of the variable road conditions they encounter on each trip.

The prevailing wind across the British islands blows from a westerly direction. Under normal conditions, sailing towards England in a longship was impractical. In winter, a north or north-easterly flow of dense cold air can bring bitter weather to the north of England and Scotland. In the winter, when the frozen Arctic wind meets the water-laden westerly air from the Atlantic, heavy snowfall is the result.

However, in the autumn, this same weather pattern can provide some excellent late-harvest weather. The cold dry Arctic air pouring from the cloudless stratosphere creates a high-pressure area that can survive for a week or more.

The pattern starts with a strong blow which pushes all the atmospheric moisture that makes the clouds to the south and leaves a clear blue sky to dominate the weather. The September sun reaches the ground to provide temperatures reminiscent of summer. Like all English weather, it cannot be relied upon, but this 'Indian summer' is a frequent and very welcome part of the patchwork of weather that passes for an English climate.

We have two reasons to suppose that this was the weather pattern in September 1066. The Norse sagas record that when the army rushed from their ships at Riccall to the aid of King Harald at Stamford Bridge, as many died of exhaustion because of the heat as were killed by the English. Running almost a marathon distance, with full armour, in the heat, would certainly have led to dangerous levels of dehydration.

We also know from Norman and English sources that a strong northerly blew William's expedition back onto the French coast and delayed it for sixteen days. At the same time, much of the English fleet sailing back from the Isle of Wight was 'lost', with the lucky ones perhaps ending up on the coast of Flanders, driven there by the northerly wind. Without the intervention of this storm, the simultaneous invasions feared by King Harold, and perhaps scheduled by Tostig, might have materialised.

Support for this weather pattern is also found in Orderic Vitalis:

In the month of August, Harold, king of Norway, and Tostig, with a powerful fleet set sail over the wide sea, and, steering for England

with a favourable aparctic, or north wind, landed in Yorkshire, which
was the first object of their invasion.

A more precise travelogue for the first phase of the journey is
described in the sagas:

> When King Harald was clear for sea, and the wind became favourable,
> he sailed out into the ocean; and he himself landed in Shetland, but
> a part of his fleet in the Orkney Islands. King Harald stopped but a
> short time in Shetland before sailing to Orkney, from whence he took
> with him a great armed force, and the earls Paul and Erlend, the sons
> of Earl Thorfin; but he left behind him here the Queen Ellisif, and
> her daughters Maria and Ingegerd.

Modern replica longships have achieved speeds of 20 knots under
sail, but more realistic experiments have been able to sustain a
quarter of that speed in the open sea. The crossing of 500km of
sea probably took three days if they had a wind blowing from the
north-east.

The second phase of the invasion journey for King Harald and
his new allies also required a favourable wind. It is unlikely that
the experienced seamen would have chosen to go near the rocky
and dangerous northern coast that has wrecked countless ships over
the centuries. Their route would have taken them back out to sea
and well away from the rocks and islands that surround north-east
Scotland.

The slower vessels, such as the traders, would have ignored the
detours and headed direct to southern Scotland. But for the longships, with their warriors available to row the boats onto and off the
sand, an inshore route was practical and the prospect of some time
ashore attractive. The regular beachings kept the warrior-filled boats
together, while the supply vessels sailed on, not as a flotilla, but as
individual ships. Indeed, the northerly wind would have taken the
supply ship straight past the Orkney and Shetland Isles and onto the
benign coast of lowland Scotland.

Longships cannot sail very close to the wind. They sail best when
the wind comes over the stern and fills their square sail. They would
have been happy if the meteorological conditions suggested by the
evidence prevailed during their voyage. These conditions, with the

north wind at their back, would have allowed good progress to be made. The longships could expect to cover 150 to 250km on a day's sailing, the supply vessels half as much. The crossing to a safe harbour in the Firth of Forth probably took about ten days, regardless of the route taken.

Landing in lowland Scotland was possible because long sandy beaches fringe the land that sticks out into the North Sea. The coast near St Andrews would be one possible place to beach. Another would have been on the outer reaches of the river Forth, near Dunbar. King Malcolm kept court nearby so this provided a possible rendezvous with Tostig and his disappointingly small fleet. However, another source suggests that Tostig met King Harald at Tynemouth.

There was time to gather information from Tostig and prepare the plan, while their combined fleet of over 300 ships converged and any stragglers caught up. King Harald was used to moving large flotillas. With perhaps as many as 400 vessels of different designs, it would require a 4km stretch of beach to provide each warband with space for its own camp.

The protocol for landing – who arrived first and who had the best spots – was well established and something about which Harald had been willing to fight his own son, when his royal precedence seemed to be challenged. Harald, as we have noted earlier, doubtless promoted a strong sense of competition among the groups to arrive and camp near their leader and king.

After the Forth, the expedition would once again have moved east, out into the sea and away from another hazardous stretch of the coast. They would be lucky if the wind was much more than a breeze by now. The swell that heralded the arrival of the stable high-pressure weather system would have passed and left the surface of the sea calmer. So the oars might have been called into action during this phase. The men would have been at sea for perhaps a day and a night when they prepared to step ashore in England. The fighting was about to begin.

They arrived in the territory of the English without any mishap:

> Then [Harald] sailed, leaving Scotland and England westward of him, and landed at a place called Klifland. There he went on shore and plundered, and brought the country in subjection to him without opposition.

Anybody who knows the Northumbrian coast will recognise that 'Cliff Land' is an appropriate name for parts of the coast near the mouth of the rivers Tyne or Tees.

THE ENGLISH ARMY

The English army preparing to face this invasion was, like most armies in defence, stretched. Defenders do not know where, or when, the invaders will attack, so they are always at some disadvantage. If they spread themselves along the coast, they could be no more than lookouts. If they stayed in small bands ready to defend their home, they would be swept aside by the attackers. Gathering the whole force together, ready to respond when the invaders revealed themselves, was the only viable option. The job of local defence was undertaken by the half of the warriors that was left behind, but the armour and good weapons would have gone along with those summoned to the main army.

Earl Edwin had brought his force from Mercia. The chronicles inform us that there were some Mercian boats moored in the river near Tadcaster. Their role was to prevent the invaders making their way inland to attack Mercia. With the benefit of history, we know that the invaders launched their attack from Riccall towards the south of York. But the defenders had wisely blocked the river route that would have exposed York to an attack from the west.

It was unusual for earls to muster their army inside the territory of another. They owed loyalty, through their earl, Edwin, to the king, but they had no mandate or obligation to come much further into Northumbrian lands to defend this territory. The task of defending Northumbria fell on its inhabitants. However, the armies of Mercia and Northumbria had marched together in rebellion the previous year and had also answered the summons of King Edward in 1052 in his clash with the men of Wessex. We must also assume that many of the thanes from Mercia knew Earl Morcar, because he was a son of Mercia, and so were willing to come part of the way to support him.

Both Mercian and Northumbrian armies had been called into action earlier in the summer as Tostig raided the coast. It was the Mercians who would have driven off the raids in Lindsey or Lincolnshire, although the *Chronicles* tell us that Earl Morcar was also engaged. The troops used for these actions needed mobility, so it was probably the earls' hearth-troops or housecarls that would have been employed. Perhaps as many as 1,000 mounted warriors from the Mercian and an equal number from the Northumbrian forces had driven off the raids by Tostig in the summer.

These hearth-troops were professional warriors. They ate and lived with their lord. They provided him with protection but were also the means to enforce his will where necessary. The warriors doubtless fulfilled the role of messenger and represented their lord in remoter areas. They sat at the mead-bench along with other honoured guests. There was a practical reason for such proximity. Blood feuds were not unknown in the north.

Warriors could expect to be rewarded with gifts and, in time, grants of land. The rules of land tenure meant most land was granted for the lifetime of the tenant. This gave the king, or earl, regular opportunities to reallocate land and exercise patronage. This land could be used to provide a pension or an estate for loyal members of the household. There seems to have been an understanding that when a trade was reciprocal, it did both parties honour. The hearth-troops maintained by all men of property were honoured and their fate was intimately linked to that of the man they served. These warbands provided the front-line fighters for the earl's army.

Since the loyalty of each warband was to their own leader, it was important that an earl, or indeed the king, maintained the trust of his subordinate leaders. Only by ensuring that they would turn up and fight when called upon could a king field an effective fighting force. At Fulford, in spite of the rivalries between the two great local families, the men of Northumbria were all united against the invaders and bound together by their opposition to the tyrannical Earl Tostig.

The loyalty of these men could therefore be relied on, not so much to defend King Harold or even to save England. In an era of limited education and communications, loyalty was given to the leader that the men knew. Loyalty and motivation among soldiers has been much studied in recent wars. The findings make uncomfortable reading for the generals. Soldiers fight for each other. Starting with the Normans, monarchs would try to persuade their men to fight for an ideal, be it a flag or a person. Ideals all too often provoked crusades and awful civil wars. The rest of the time soldiers continued to fight for their unit, comrades and family. Nothing has really changed in the soldiers' motivation during the intervening millennium.

The bond between fighting men was very close. Indeed, the war-band was expected to avenge the death of their lord even if it cost them their own lives. This was not a casual bargain. The literature cites many examples of the warriors fulfilling their obligation even when they had the opportunity to save themselves.

The size of the permanent force maintained by an earl or a thane has to be guessed at. Earl Tostig had a force of 200 house-troops near York that fought and died for him the day after the coup in October 1065. He doubtless had a small military retinue with him down south, so his full-time force might have numbered 250. The young northern earls might not have built up such a retinue of well-trained warriors at this early stage in their military career. It took time and influence to recruit those who would fight and if necessary die for you. It also required land grants and an income, to recruit men you could trust. Earl Morcar might have had only 100 personal troops plus cousins and others related to the family.

The size of the permanent force controlled by a thane is harder to estimate. The leading families could probably rival the earls with the men-at-arms they employed to administer and enforce order. The hierarchy of thanes has been guessed at through analysis of the Domesday surveys, but any conclusions must be tentative. There might have been over 300 landowners of note in Northumbria. If we allow four armed retainers each, we can add 1,600 full-time warriors to the 100 owned by each of the important landowners as well as the earls. This provides at least 2,000 well-trained and armed soldiers within Northumbria. This would provide the full-time professional core of Morcar's army.

The chronicler of 1066 records that the earls 'gathered from their earldom as great a force as they could get'. In addition to the full-time soldiers, the earls could also summon the fyrd. The organisation of the fyrd, which began as an expeditionary force in Saxon times, had evolved into a sophisticated reserve army by 1066. The term fyrd itself was not fixed, so we find that when this levy was called out in 1006 by King Ethelred, the term meaning 'from the whole of the people'.

The early fyrd had needed reform. The habit of granting permanent tenure to the Church and rewarding an emerging nobility with land in perpetuity had weakened the central control offered by patronage. By the mid-ninth century the ruler had to rely on the three 'common burdens' (namely joining royal expeditions, maintaining bridges and constructing fortifications) that were demanded of all landowners in England. Alfred the Great's difficulties in 878 were due in no small part to his dependence upon these 'common burdens' for the defence of England. Because he did not 'own' the land, and through it the landowners, he could not command a national army.

After his victory at Edington in the spring of 878, Alfred realised he could not rely on the existing obligations to counter the Danes. On the practical front, Alfred built a system of fortified boroughs or *burhs* throughout Wessex. Then he reformed the fyrd, turning it into a standing army. The chronicles tell us:

> The king divided his army into two, so that always half of its men were at home, half on service, apart from the men who guarded the boroughs.

Alfred also designated a mobile and defensive component for the army. There are some clues that two months was the period of service for this levy. A two-month tour of duty would make sense in view of the events of autumn 1066, but it might have been longer. The fleet left Sandwich after mid-June and Harold had to release them early in September, when they had overstayed their obligated service.

The landholders were charged to provide men on the basis of one man from every hide of their land, one hide being a flexible unit of area capable of supporting an extended family. Alfred could muster almost 30,000 to defend the burgh and man the fyrd in 'Greater Wessex'. The days of winning kingdoms with only a few hundred household men were gone.

These reforms did not necessarily extend to the north-east, as this was Danelaw in Alfred's time, where burghs were not established. Frank Barlow has estimated the rentable value of the Wessex holdings, which roughly correspond to £7,000. On this financial basis, Mercia might have had an obligation to provide 10,000 soldiers but Northumbria a mere 2,000. Given the reluctance of the north to pay taxes, the last figure undoubtedly underestimates the size of the army levy the latter could field. The Northumbrian levy is assumed to be much nearer to parity with the other earls. The reasoning for this assumption is that the Northumbrian earl would have been a junior partner in all negotiations if his army was inferior in size, and there is no evidence that this was the case. Given the requirement for some local defence, Morcar might have been able to levy up to 5,000, but it is assumed here that he would have mustered only half this number for Fulford. Earl Morcar probably had 2,000 professional, and about 2,500 soldiers responding to the levy.

Manpower for the fyrd was a scarce resource until the spring planting was done. It was therefore difficult to get your army in the field much before June. A good leader would also try to release his levy army by late August to allow them to make their way home and help gather in the harvest. If he did not respect these timings, he risked desertions the following year. Earl Tostig would have recognised that harvest was a vulnerable time for the organisation of the levy, favouring a late invasion.

It is probable, although we have no confirmation, that those in service would have to be released before their replacements could be summoned. The troops of the fyrd released would return with the weapons and armour and tell their replacements if they were required and where they were to muster. The fact that this changeover was under way in the south might account for the speed with which King Harold was able to respond after Fulford.

Harold had organised his kingdom for this struggle in the short time available during 1066. Coins have survived his brief reign. Perhaps a plentiful supply of coin was prepared to pay for the goods and services the army would require when away from their farms.

By the second half of the tenth century the fyrd was a well-equipped army of infantry. King Ethelred ordered every eight hides to provide a helmet and *byrnie*. The turbulent times of Viking raids therefore brought about the armament of England. The spear and shield remained the basic weapon of the fyrdman, and it was usual for him to have access to a horse, sword, helmet and mailshirt. The death duty set for a thane was two swords and a coat of mail, plus some horses. This was probably less a tax than a way to ensure that weapons were recycled and remained in the hands of the king's fighting men.

Even if the remaining three-quarters of the fyrd mobilised in Northumbria had moved to the coast in small warbands, they could offer only token resistance. Seven thousand men spread along a 200km coastline can do little except provide a flow of information, and they might prevent parties of raiders foraging too far from the main force. These small bands would have to rely on the force of about 5,000 under Earl Morcar to defeat the invaders.

Morcar and his brother Edwin were the sons of Aelfgar and grandsons of the venerable Earl Leofric. Circumstantial evidence leads one to believe that the earls were probably in their late teens as they prepared to face opponents who were twice their age. The earls' grandmother was the redoubtable Lady Godiva. She is best remembered for the story of a naked bareback ride on a horse in Coventry. It is impossible to settle the accuracy of this event, however. Naked can be interpreted as without finery and ornaments, rather than literally nude. Lady Godiva also had substantial landholdings in her own right around Coventry so there was no need to make a bargain with her husband. However, this was a time of high national tax in order to pay the Danegeld. Lady Godiva also joined the monastic building spree of that time and founded Stow Priory near Lincoln, for which she would have needed to do some fundraising. Perhaps her ride was a bet or bargain made with Leofric. But there is no tradition of the lords of this period exposing their wives to ridicule, so it might have served the Normans to spin such a story when her two grandsons were later rebels against William.

Ultimately, it would be unwise to dismiss this tradition, which seems to contain some grains of truth. Godiva came from a tradition of powerful matriarchs and knew that an oath was binding on the giver so, whatever the reason for the bet and the precise definition of nakedness, this lady might well have challenged convention in some remarkable way. She would live to see the downfall of Anglo-Saxon England.

LANDFALL IN ENGLAND

The sagas suggest, but do not exactly tell us, that Harald's first Northumbria landfall was in the mouth of the river Tyne, where the remains of the monasteries at Tynemouth and Jarrow would have been a visible reminder of Viking raids two centuries before. The army did not pause long on the beaches of Tynemouth or Cullercoats but moved on down the coast. This landing has been dated to 8 September. One source also suggests that this was where Earl Tostig had arranged to submit to King Harald. Perhaps this was some ceremonial submission by the earl now that he was back in territory he claimed was his own.

The third phase of Harald's journey began moving after this first landfall in England. Assuming the weather pattern persisted, it would have allowed the seamen to advise that it was safe for the boats to proceed down the coast without the need for all the oars to be manned. By moving with the flow of the tide, the sea would add an extra knot to the progress provided by the wind in their sail. Progress south would be good, provided they went with the tidal flow. With the tide near its autumn peak, there would be a flow down the Yorkshire coast of almost a knot.

However, they would want to beach their boats. Moving past the coast at perhaps 3–5 knots, each six-hour tidal flow would move them roughly 30km down the coast. This would have necessitated returning to land, although moving away from land and into deeper water would take them out of the coastal drift-current. The tidal flow down the coast is reversed twice each day, so they would lose most of the gain if they stayed at sea. Landing would also give them time to rest and time to feed. The coast down which they were passing has some of the longest sandy beaches in the country. For boats of shallow draught, most of this coastline was remarkably benign.

Although the longest day was nearly three months past, the northern latitude still provided sixteen hours of enough light to steer by. The supply ships would have adopted a different strategy. Without the oars, they would have relied on the light winds and perhaps sailing close to the cost to catch the tidal drift south, before going further offshore when tidal conditions were against them. The effect of this coastal tidal flow is minimal 15km offshore. So the traders might not have stayed with the warriors.

Some sagas report a landing in the river Tees. This would be another convenient spot to pause. Each of the landings would provide an opportunity to gather information and allow the warriors a little time for plunder. When the fleet reached Scarborough they paused in their progress, perhaps because of the wind. The Orkney Saga tells us that 'the weather fell calm and they lay there the night over'. This certainly fits the pattern of the autumnal high-pressure system.

The warriors came ashore in force the next day at Scarborough. The raiders could have landed in the north or south bays, either side of the castle mound where Scarborough had been built on the slopes. An Icelandic saga says two brothers called Kormak and Thorgils were the first men to 'establish the fort called Skardaborg', exactly 100 years before. Thorgil's nickname was *Skardi*, meaning hare-lipped. Scarborough is 'the fort belonging to Skardi'.

The chroniclers record that the town resisted strongly from inside their fortification. There is some evidence that this was a modest burgh with a fortified ditch. Because of the view and micro-climate on the steep slope, Scarborough made Scarborough a popular convalescent spot centuries later. However, these attributes were not enough to save all those who sought shelter under the castle. The weather-beaten church that served the old town of Scarborough contains the grave of Anne Brontë, who died there while convalescing with her sister Charlotte in 1849.

A small force had been left to guard this fishing town of perhaps fifty family homesteads. The town refused to submit, which appears foolhardy, but perhaps they were confident behind their defences. While some Norsemen attacked the town's defences, others apparently climbed the hill that dominates the town. The Romans had chosen this prominence as a location for a signal tower. From this high point they threw fire onto the thatched roofs of the houses and farmsteads below. It is hard to imagine that the resistance lasted long, but they held out long enough to necessitate the barrage of fire. It appears that an example was made of those who resisted, as a warning to others:

> Then he [King Harald] brought up at Skardaburg, and fought with the people of the place. He went up a hill which is there, and made a great pile upon it, which he set on fire; and when the pile was in clear flame, his men took large forks and pitched the burning wood down into the town, so that one house caught fire after the other, and the town surrendered. The Northmen killed many people there and took all the booty they could lay hold of. There was nothing left for the Englishmen now, if they would preserve their lives, but to submit to King Harald; and thus he subdued the country wherever he came...

The warriors, who had been travelling for about fourteen days, would have been eager for the opportunity to find fresh food. The month was September. The harvest from land and sea was being gathered in so there were good pickings for the early arrivals. Ravaging the countryside was commonplace, and it is well illustrated in the Bayeux Tapestry, which recounts the events after the Norman landing a few weeks later.

The army continued overland in their accustomed fashion as raiders. Their next target was Holderness. Today we recognise Holderness as an administrative district. Maps of the eighteenth century show the wapentakes of Holderness, and it is still a parliamentary constituency, although if a place with that name ever existed it has vanished. But in 1066 it was the power base of one of the noble families of Northumbria, so Tostig would not have spared the property of those who had rebelled against him. The chance to seize or destroy their wealth was too tempting to resist.

The raiding served another purpose beyond that of revenge or re-supply. The destruction of the territory would oblige the young Earl Morcar to come out from York to meet them in battle. This was a clever tactic. Some have suggested that William employed exactly this tactic to entice King Harold to battle near Hastings before his force was ready. The earl from Mercia would quickly lose support if people saw their undefended homes being destroyed by the enemy. The local thanes would expect an effective and immediate response.

Scarborough provides the only valley-route towards York. The temptation to set out to meet the invaders must have been strong. Did Tostig already know just how swiftly the army could be moved by water along the rivers to threaten the regional capital at York? He had lived there and the traders or seamen who steered Harald's ship would have known it was possible to take the fleet right into the capital city of Northumbria. If the invaders could draw Morcar's army out in an attempt to prevent the raiding, the Norsemen could perhaps slip into York while it was unprotected by its army.

We can only speculate upon the strategy of the opposing generals. However, there is no evidence that Earl Morcar ever planned to leave York to intercept the attackers, in spite of the provocation offered. Both sides evidently had cunning commanders and probably enjoyed a good flow of intelligence.

The reluctance of Morcar to come out to chase the invaders was wise. The Norse army was soon heading for a rendezvous with the boats that had sailed on after setting the soldiers down on the long, sandy bays either side of Scarborough's mound. While the longships made their way in stages along the coast, the warriors rampaged their way south rather than west.

Two days' sailing would have brought the fleet to Spurn Head. On the seaward side of the point, the longships would be exposed to the waves that pound the shore and currently consume nearly 3m of the shoreline annually. Although the weather was probably benign, experienced seamen would have appreciated the sanctuary offered by the promontory of Spurn Head once they rounded Spurn Point.

The great river Humber receives the waters from the Ouse and Trent basins. It drains one-fifth of England, from Birmingham in the south to Swaledale in the north. On an average day, 13 million cubic metres of water will flow out into the North Sea, but over fifteen times that amount (160CuM) flows in and out of the mouth as the tide turns, twice each day. The salty seawater is able to reach 45km upriver when the tide is flowing, bringing it to the site of the modern Humber bridge.

At its mouth the Humber estuary is 14km wide, with the remarkable Spurn Head jutting 5½km out from the northern Yorkshire bank, constricting the mouth of the river. We do not know the precise shape of the coast and this promontory in 1066. This spit of land is built of boulder clay, much of it washed down there from the Holderness coast, which is eroding at a rate that varies from less than a metre near Bridlington up to 2.8m each year near Kilnsea. The coast of the East Riding down which the invaders of 1066 passed was about 2km further out to sea.

HARBOUR IN THE HUMBER

The nearest sanctuary for the sailors in their longships was just inside the mouth of the river Humber. Once round Spurn Point, the seamen and their ships would have still been subject to the tides but the waves of the North Sea would no longer reach them. For a seaman accustomed to the perils of the wind and the sea, the estuary was a sanctuary.

By rounding Spurn Point, the boats could also cut at least 15km off the march for the warriors coming to meet them. The area of Sunk Island would have been an ideal rendezvous. The links to the land were limited to a number of causeways. This made it easier for the seamen to defend the fleet that had brought the invaders from Norway and the Orkneys.

Behind Spurn Head they would have still had to contend with the tide that rose and fell twice a day. But around the island, they were in slack water. The 'island', with its modern sea defences now in place, is part of the mainland and is excellent agricultural land. Following the natural route through the Yorkshire Wolds, the Norse army would have rendezvoused with their ships after perhaps two or three days of destructive progress down the coast.

Sadly we have no record of where the warriors re-boarded the boats. Safely moored on Sunk Island, the longships could have easily embarked the warriors. However, to beach all the longships at a place where the army could easily re-board limits the locations. There are suitable havens along the Yorkshire coast, but they were all subject to the tides that would expose a kilometre of sand at low tide, leaving the longships high and dry. To be stranded on the shore for up to six hours was far from ideal, especially when the main body of troops were ashore.

The slope of the sandbars behind Spurn Head provided a better option. The approaching 'spring' tides meant that this was the time of some of the highest tides of the year. This allowed the longships to get close to firm land so the army could embark easily, with the added bonus that the next, even higher, tide would lift the loaded ships off the mud to resume their journey inland. They were now ready for the final stage of their ambitious voyage.

With the warriors safely aboard, it was time for the judgement and skill of the seamen to be tested. They had two challenges. The first was to get down the river to a safe place where they could rest while the tide ebbed. The second was to ensure that they did not collide with another longship in the narrow channel.

RECONNAISSANCE

There is a military maxim which states that time spent in reconnaissance is never wasted. It is unlikely that this wisdom was denied to the ancients. Battle sites were often the careful choice of one of the combatants, who hoped that 'home advantage' would improve the chances of victory. Evidence for active reconnaissance is sadly lacking, but it is inconceivable that a commander, let alone one with the experience of King Harald, would have launched his boats along the Humber or Ouse without having checked that the route was not only safe but secure against ambush.

The first part of the reconnaissance would confirm that the army could safely reach Riccall on the turbulent tides. The next part of the mission would be to secure the route. A simple ambush party on the banks of the river could have caused havoc to a flotilla as the boats sped along on the tidal flow up the Ouse. Moving at 3-6 knots, in a channel that allows no room for manoeuvre, landing or passing gives enormous advantage to any ambush party.

To prevent this, the Norsemen would need to be in control of both banks. It must remain a matter of speculation, but the Norse commander may have sent an advance party to secure the landing area and the banks. This force could also have identified the presence of Earl Edwin's fleet that was blocking the river Wharfe near Tadcaster.

The reconnaissance force might have numbered ten or more boats. These chosen troops might have numbered at least 300. This force would have been sufficient to block the causeways at the planned landing stage at Riccall and send parties out into the countryside to secure supplies or give warning of any approaching raiders. Such a reconnaissance in force would also have 'warned' the English commanders that the Norsemen were coming. This would certainly help to explain why Earl Morcar did not leave York to stop the invaders raiding after their landfall at Scarborough. If they knew that the invaders planned to make their way inland they could spend their time preparing to meet the Norsemen.

While Harald's men made their violent way down the east coast, there would be just enough time for a small group to report back on the possibility of riding the tide to the gates of York. It was a remarkable plan. Only a full appreciation of the tidal flows in September 1066 made it possible.

THE HUMBER BORE

The river Humber is oriented from west to east. Twice a day, the gravity of the sun and the moon compete, causing the direction of flow to flip in a dramatic but predictable way. The funnel shape of the Humber estuary produces an interesting effect.

A bore is produced when the tidal flow entering the river is opposed by the water flowing down the river from its catchment towards the sea. The result is a rise in the level as water is fed from both ends. At some point, the might of the sea overwhelms the force of the river and the flow is suddenly and dramatically reversed.

The shape of a river can amplify the magnitude of the ripples that result from the resolution of the opposing flows. Sometimes, the results can be spectacular. The bore on the river Severn provides a continuously breaking wave many metres high, where surfers compete for the longest surf ride in the world. From the 1970s until recently, the river Severn in Gloucestershire provided the record ride. The current bore surfing record is 10.1km on a tributary of the Amazon.

The river Humber is not well known for the bore that each day marks the turning of the tide. This is not easily seen in a river as wide as the Humber. But the effect on mariners, ancient as well as modern, is considerable because of the way the tides behave in a river which has a bore. First, the change in the tidal flow is sudden. There is no lengthy time of slack water during which ships can manoeuvre into or out of the stream, waiting for the tide to turn. Second, the tide would normally flow upstream for six hours and then ebb for six and repeat this cycle with two tides each day. Instead, in the Ouse/Humber system, the water flows upstream for just over four hours with an ebb lasting eight. What the flow upstream lacks in duration it makes up for in speed. The volume of water that ebbs in eight hours has to flow upstream in half the time. As a result, the speed of the flow is alarming.

To negotiate the Humber takes skill and courage. To provide the ships with manoeuvrability, some extra stability and a bit of extra speed, the sea master would have ordered the benches to be manned and the oars to be deployed. As the tide began to rise, some of the ships floated off the sandbar near Sunk Island, ready to move out into the flow at exactly the right moment.

To prepare for their journey, the longships would have to be loaded before the tide peaked. This would lift the laden ships off the mud. However, now was not the time to get into the stream. For the eight hours of the ebb tide, the ships would make their way cautiously off the sand bar. If they moved too far, they would be caught in the ebb. If they moved too slowly, the keel would ground and they would soon be stuck fast in the mud until the next tide.

By positioning themselves close to the channels where the river narrowed at Hull, the loaded boats could have made steady progress towards the stream. When the moment was right they could join the flow and soon they would be moving along at what must have been a thrilling speed when the tide turned. Those who misjudged the move would be pushed back towards the Point. Even rowing hard they would make little progress against a 4-knot ebb tide. Once inside the fast-flowing channel they would have been able to add another few knots to their speed by bending on their oars. From the bank they would appear to be moving at 10 knots.

With so many laden ships about, any collision would have been catastrophic. The water of the Humber is notorious for the amount of mud it moves. Anybody tipped into the water risked being dragged down as the folds of their clothing filled with silt. The oars allowed the ships to manoeuvre and be kept apart as well as to drive the longships into the fastest part of the channel. The man on the steer-board would not want his longship cast onto one of the sandbanks that still menace sailors in the Humber estuary, where the force of water could flip it over.

Rowing was important because the steer-board at the rear of the longship was useless in still water. If they did not row, the ship would simply be drifting in the current. With the oars, the longship would have been moving through the water instead of just floating along like a log.

The tidal flow in the Humber estuary is impressive. This great body of water would have been moving at between 3 and 5 knots in the channels. The seamen had to watch for a short while to let the turbulent bore go past. Once they started rowing they risked overtaking this tidal front, so they had to hang back a little, using up some of the limited time that the river would be flowing. It would take each longship around five hours to cover the forty sea miles to the sandbars at Trent Falls.

There were some fine judgements to be made by the military leaders and the mariners. A commander wants to keep his army together. But if the ships are not given some space the risk of collision increases. The mariners would also have told him that if the ships joined the flow at the rate of one each minute, the whole fleet could not be underway before the tide turned. It would take at least two tides to move the fleet forward and the timing of the tides allowed only one journey in daylight.

At Broomfleet, the rivers Trent and Ouse meet to make the Humber. There is an extensive sand flat known as Whitton Sands, where some longships could have sheltered. It is impossible to know the hydrology of 1066, but the Sands appear like an island with a small tributary of the river flowing round to the north, mirroring in many respects the landing places at Riccall and Sunk Island.

The longships could have kept pace with the tide, and a few at the head of the flotilla might have ridden the fast-flowing tide straight into the Ouse but, after five hours of rowing, most crews would have needed a rest. There was no point in those further back in this procession going on if the tide risked overtaking them. If they did not use the high water to make it to the bank, they would be carried backwards by the ebbing tide. Here they could have waited as the waters flowed towards the sea.

Again they would need to move carefully off the sand as the tide fell to avoid being left stranded. During the afternoon, the fleet would have been left beached, resting and perhaps eating before the procession up the Ouse began when the tide returned in the late afternoon.

There would have been some anxious moments as the level rose and they could propel themselves into the river Ouse. Discipline would have been essential for, once the force of the tidal bore hit them, they would have to go with the flow. This time there would be even less room for error. The Ouse was too narrow to allow longships to travel, or pass, abreast. One collision in the narrow river would have been catastrophic for the fleet. Following ships would have no way to avoid any vessel that foundered or rammed its prow into the bank and was turned across the flow.

Of one thing the invaders could be confident. There would be no traffic in the opposite direction. The tide in the river ensured that.

The sagas make little mention of the seamanship required to sail up the Humber and into the river Ouse. This is all the kings' saga has to say on the subject: 'Thereafter the king sailed to the Humber, and up along the river, and then he landed.'

As the width of the river is restricted, the water reaches it peak speed. Beyond Goole and heading towards York, the speed in the Ouse in September is typically 6-7 knots, not simply in the centre of the river but from bank to bank. With a little help from the oars they would be passing the nearby banks at speeds approaching 10 knots. It would take them three hours to reach Riccall, 45km away.

The small ripple that marks the turning of the tide takes three hours to reach Riccall. Once again, the longships had about three hours to join the flow. If the mariners kept the one-minute spacing, then half the fleet could make the final stage of the journey on this second surge of the tide. Their journey would take them past some low-lying land at first and then onto some faster sections, where the river had cut through the ancient clay. The last hour would be past steep banks of mud that offered no place to stop, until they reached the final strait that would take them to their landing at Riccall.

RICCALL

The lower Ouse is a meandering river. However, around Riccall there is a straight stretch of nearly 3km where the 300 longships could safely land the army. Mooring the ships along the steep banks would be impossible. There were two problems. Carried along by the tide, the ships would be moving much too fast to stop. There is no way to ease a ship gently into the bank as the fast tide rips past the face of the mud, sculpting these forbidding banks. The second obstacle is the bank itself. Depending on the height of the tide, boats would be travelling with a steep wall of mud on either side. Even if the boats could be brought to the bank, it would be impossible for the crew to haul the boat up the bank and out of the river's flow.

However, the layout at Riccall offers a safe way to leave the fast-flowing tide. At Riccall the river Ouse takes a sharp turn to the south after passing the end of the Escrick moraine. This had created a swampy hinterland something like an oxbow lake. This remarkable piece of hydrology had created a lay-by out of the main flow of the river.

Boats would be able to leave the river through what was effectively a breach in the bank. Because this was a period of high spring tides, the boatmen would then able to row their longships in the slack water until they came to the site where their warband could beach its boats and set up camp. This is where the discipline of the mariners would again be so important.

The manoeuvre to leave the fast-flowing stream needed to be well judged. If they got it wrong and turned the ship across the river, the racing water could soon swamp the boat. If the prow dug into the steep bank instead of entering the quiet channel, the ship would be quickly pushed round by the force of the water. With help from the bank, they might have been able to drag the ship into the other entrance to the slack water.

The worst fate would be to miss the turning altogether, as the Mercian marines were only a short distance further along the river and a longship would be powerless to prevent itself being swept towards their enemy. But we have no reports of any ships overshooting.

If these assessments are correct, the main Norse army arrived spread over at least two tides, and probably four. They secured their boats during 18 and 19 September. There are two tides each day and, if the timing was perfect, they could hope to travel upstream for up to four hours on each tide. The one-minute spacing would be just enough time to make sure that one boat had been moved out of the channel and onto the bank at Riccall before the next arrived. The slower trading vessels would have followed along over successive days.

Viewed with the eye of a landscape archaeologist, the riverside landing at modern-day Ricall appears to have been an island about 3km long and up to 300m wide. There is no sign of the oxbow lake now, but two causeways leading to the higher land where the modern village is sited are evident. Safe behind the river defences, the land has been cultivated for many decades. The 'island' itself has been exploited for its gravel, leaving the surface with many water-filled holes, and there is evidence of several jetties, presumably used by those extracting the aggregate.

Riccall was not simply a good mooring for the invading army. It must have appeared almost perfect. It was not too far from the road to York. There were two good routes along high ground leading towards the city. If they had travelled further towards York along the Ouse, the path of the river would have actually taken them away from their destination for another half hour on the fast-flowing tide. It would take a full hour to reach suitable flat ground where they might land their boats, and that landing would be almost at Fulford. So if the invaders went any further upriver than Riccall they would certainly have been attacked as they landed, by the troops from York and the Mercians who had effectively closed the Wharfe to them.

The natural defences at Riccall were also perfectly arranged for the benefit of the invaders. To the east, the oxbow lake provided a moat. To judge by the length of the causeways, this marshy hinterland might have been over a kilometre wide. To the west they were protected, first by the river and, beyond that, on the inside of the acute bend, there was more low-lying marshland over which the river doubtless spilled at times of exceptional tide. There was no land over which any force could approach to attack them and the river guaranteed that an assault from that direction could be ruled out. Earl Morcar's scouts might have witnessed the build-up of Norsemen but they would have had to report back that the position at Riccall looked unassailable with such a force to protect it.

The location selected at Riccall was not unlike that chosen by Norse invaders when the brave Brithnoth confronted the Vikings at the battle of Maldon in 990. On that occasion, the chivalrous lord allowed the Viking party to cross the causeway and come to dry land before battle was commenced. Virtue was not rewarded and he was slain. As Earl Brithnoth doubtless appreciated, the invaders had to be confronted in battle in order to destroy them. Earl Morcar was about to face the same necessity.

At Fulford there is no evidence of any parlay. No embassies were exchanged. King Harald did not send to demand submission and ask for hostages. In all the other disagreements on English soil in recent decades, a confrontation had not ended with a battle but with negotiation. Something was different about the coming clash, as we have no hints that any contact was made between the armies. In a pattern that would be repeated at Hastings, there was no attempt to see if there was any scope for negotiation.

One is forced to conclude that all the parties must have recognised that a battle was the only way to resolve the two issues in dispute. King Harald was out to conquer England and Earl Tostig was planning to destroy those who had evicted him ten months before.

News of the burning of Scarborough would have reached York by this time. Earl Morcar of Northumbria and his brother, Edwin, the earl from neighbouring Mercia, were both in York with their housecarls. There had been enough time to ensure that Earl Morcar had his full army assembled. Earl Edwin was with his brother now that the location of the invaders was clear. His ships were moored at Ulleskelf, a short distance up the river Wharfe, a tributary of the Ouse. These armies were less than a quarter of an hour's journey by boat from each other.

Speed was a weapon used by all good commanders. King Harald had seized the initiative and he was not about to relinquish it. Entrusting his expedition to the immense and uncontrollable power of the tide was a gamble but one that was typical of his style of leadership. And as a very good general, he undertook the risk only once the route had been proved and secured.

Harald's army did not rest at Riccall on that Tuesday night of September 1066. His forces prepared for battle. In the morning, his army was moving across the causeways and on to York, where he hoped to make his winter base, preparatory to a campaign for England the following year. Wednesday would bring him a hard-fought victory as his army forced its way towards York at Fulford. But before a week had elapsed this great warrior would have the six feet of English earth promised to him by King Harold of England when they met near Stamford Bridge.

6

The Battle at the Ford

There is a ford half an hour's walk south of York, which was to provide the setting for the last great battle between two shieldwalls on English soil. Halfway to the ford was the collection of farmsteads named as Sutton (South Farm) and later Gate Fulford when mapmakers first set down the location. In 1066, the area around the ford was duck-hunting and grazing land.

Three kilometres north of the ford were the city walls of York that had stood since Roman times, although the city had expanded beyond these bounds. A defensible boundary could have been prepared to withstand a siege, had that been the plan. There had been some time to prepare. With King Harold preoccupied defending the south coast, such a defensive strategy might have appealed. However, there is no evidence that this was even considered as an option.

It would have been intolerable to remain behind the fortification while the enemy was free to ravage the country. The young Earl Morcar seems to have had no doubts that a confrontation was the only way to settle the conflict. Ironically, it was precisely a strategy of constructing and defending strong points that would soon allow the Norman conquerors to dominate England.

Battle was not the only option available in this period. A force that was clearly inferior might well accept terms and submit. The honourable exchange of hostages from the family of the weaker party was normal. Bede records another approach that avoided the need for battle. King Oswin of Deira simply sent his army back to their homes when he realised the overwhelming force that King Oswy from the neighbouring Bernicia had assembled against him. Battle was a choice. So Earl Morcar was both willing and felt able to give battle.

Earl Morcar enjoyed the support of the leading families in Northumbria. He was not from one of their factions. He had been elected or selected by the lords of Deira and Bernicia when they rebelled against Earl Tostig the previous autumn. With the regal succession following weeks after the overthrow of Tostig, the warriors would have remained alert. Trouble often followed the succession of a new king. Tostig had been 'sworn brother' to King Malcolm on their northern border, so trouble might even come from that direction. They were well prepared.

In fact, it was the summer raids by Tostig that had kept the army active, although he had not attacked his old earldom. Perhaps he wanted to send the message that he would not attack what was right-fully his own. The raids on the Norfolk and Lincolnshire coasts by Tostig also had the effect of drawing Earl Edwin to the east coast in order to defend Mercian territory.

Earl Edwin would probably have brought his army over to help his brother even without Tostig's raids. York had been the centre of national life earlier in the year when King Harold had married the sister of the brother earls. Edwin was now doubly bound to fight any invaders. There was also a very personal component for Edwin and Morcar in the fight with the ousted Tostig, who had led a cavalry army through Mercia three years before to destroy Gruffydd, the ally of their father in Wales. The circumstances surrounding the death of Edwin's own father, Earl Aelfgar, left room for some suspicion to attach itself to Tostig.

Earl Edwin positioned his main force ready to meet the invaders if they chose to head west and into Mercia. From their location, it would take a day to march and join Morcar's army once the intentions of the invaders were known. Did King Harald intend to launch an attack to the west from his base at Riccall? Only those Mercians who had horses would be available to move quickly enough to join the army at Fulford once the intentions of King Harald were clear. Most of the Mercian foot soldiers would probably have missed the battle.

However, the support of his brother and a contingent of the Mercian force was part of the plan to defend the ford. The lie of the land on the battlefield that Morcar had chosen gave Earl Edwin and his best men a crucial role. Ultimately, it would be their failure to hold this ground that would play a critical part in the defeat of the defenders at Fulford.

Much of what follows will remain forever a matter of speculation. The description of the battle is based on the Norse literature and five years of physical investigation. There are grounds for considerable confidence in this interpretation, not least because the physical evidence has illuminated some of the remarks contained in the only commentary of the battle, the *Heimskringla* or *The Chronicle of the Kings of Norway*. Sadly, the most verbose English chronicler describes the course of the battle in just seventeen words, which is only slightly more than they take to provide the date for the battle. 'And this fight was on the eve of St Matthew the apostle, which was Wednesday.'

Forewarned of the landings at Riccall, the earls and their experienced military commanders had doubtless spent some time selecting ground that would favour them in the battle to come. They did not march to Riccall, where the invaders occupied a position from which it would be hard to dislodge them.

Instead they waited south of York, having chosen a spot that was excellent from a defender's point of view. The ford crossed a stream or beck that ran all year. In the summer it was a few metres wide and in the winter months it could flood the land around. At the ford the ground was marshy. On the defenders' side, the land was firm. There was some good ground on the opposite side but, at the ford, the defenders overlooked anybody who wanted to attack them.

The beck had carved its way into the landscape. Any attackers would have to cross a deep ditch which was wider than the distance a man could throw a spear, and then fight up the slope, which was about 4m above the ford itself. This natural moat formed the front of the defenders' position.

At the ford, the earl's flanks were both secure. Flanks are a preoccupation of every commander. They are always extremely important because the English did not want the Vikings to get round the end of their line and attack them from behind. The weapons, arms, leadership and training were all designed to fight a battle along the shieldwall. If the enemy could get round the line they could cut the warriors down from behind. Secure flanks remained important until manoeuvrable forces such as cavalry became available. Only mobile troops could be moved to oppose any attack that threatened to go behind their main line.

Morcar's right flank was protected by the river Ouse, and beside the river was an extensive marsh, known as the Ings. The left flank on the attackers' side was swampy. It could be crossed with some care, but this was not a place where troops would choose to mount an attack. The course of many streams that have been buried by modern agriculture can still be picked out in this area using special photography.

To the left was wetland, to the right was the river, and to the front there was a wide, peat-filled ditch. The invaders would have to cross this ford to reach York. This was a good choke point where Morcar could effectively block King Harald and bring him to battle on terms that seemed to favour the defender.

It is doubtful that King Harald would have wanted to bypass the defenders, but even had he wanted to do so, his options were limited. A long, looping march to the east would bring them to the city, but there they would have to cross another extensive marsh with few causeways. In fact, the city was surrounded by low wet land apart from the two moraines deposited where the retreating ice paused about 15,000 years ago.

Nature had indeed constructed a good defensive position for the English. Trapped between two separate but related moraines, a lake had been created. The only drain where this wetland pierced the moraine was at the ford. This was where the water from the extensive catchment could reach the river Ouse. The meltwater of the retreating ice had cut a deep groove through the hard moraine material which, over the succeeding millennia, has been filled first with boulder clay and then with peat.

Around the time that the Romans left Britain, alluvial sands and mud from the Ouse found their way along the beck, as the regular flooding of the river raised the river banks and the level of the Ings. Since 1066, the land beside the river has risen about 2m. In another few thousand years it will backfill the beck. But at present, the land where Earl Morcar formed his shieldwall is virtually the modern surface.

This glacial drain is known as Germany Beck. It will play a central part in the day's drama. A possible source of the name 'Germany' has been suggested as the Celtic word *Germani*, which means 'shouters'. Tacitus, writing in the first century, say that the same word was 'self-invented' by the Celtic tribes who occupied the Rhine basin, who began to call themselves Germani. There would seem to be some significance to the word that is not yet understood. This beck might well have provided a clear boundary between two tribes, as it was destined to do again, leading to the adoption of this ancient name.

In the Domesday survey of 1086, holdings are noted in 'Foleford' and 'Fuletrop'. Early maps call the area nearer the city Foule Sutton. Water Fulford and Gate Fulford are both names that have been applied to this area, and the separate villages can be identified. In 1828 the two villages were called Fulford Ambo (i.e. Both Fulfords). According to Joan Pikering in her *History of Fulford*, the place was also called Fulleford, Foulforth, Fowforth, Magna Foulford, Fuleford Parva and Overfolforth in various documents. The present village of Fulford is a post-Conquest settlement located to take advantage of the gradual modification of the area of the ford by the flooding referred to earlier.

'Gate' has also been prefixed to two village-names, Gate Fulford, and Gate Helmsley, in each case from their situations on a Roman road', according to Kenneth Cameron writing in *English Place Names*. However, the identity of the Roman road is suspected but has yet to be confirmed. Evidence is mounting that Gate Fulford was about 1km north of the ford and the site of the battle.

> Ford, is one of the commonest topographical place-name elements, as indeed we might expect, in view of its importance to the new settlers in any area. It is also well-represented in English documents recorded before 731 and it is likely to have been used to form place-names from an early stage in the Anglo-Saxon settlement of Britain.

Cameron continues: 'Further, most names [ending] in -ford must have had a local significance and it has been pertinently said they can only reflect routes by which villagers communicated with their neighbours'. He goes on to postulate that -ford was so common that it came to be understood as 'a settlement'. The name was not often compounded with the river it crossed, but more often with the type of road crossing there. The type of tree or the main crop or animal using the ford provided the likes of Ashford, Oxford and Gosford. However, it 'has been shown that the commonest word compounded with ford are descriptive of the ford itself'. So long, broad, stony, shallow and deep are all common. 'The water was "clear" at Sherford, "slaggy" (muddy) at Slaggyford and "foul" at Fulford, a name found in at least six counties.'

A ford seems to have been a popular place for a battle, to judge from the entries in the *Anglo-Saxon Chronicles*. Fulford joins Cracganford (458), Cerdiceford (519), Biedcanford (571) and Beoford (752) as battle sites. A ford was suited to the weapons and tactics of the time.

The gap between the river and the marsh at this point was just 400m wide. With about 2,000 fully trained and equipped troops, a powerful shieldwall could be prepared that could be three or four ranks deep. Behind this strong wall of warriors and their shields would be the 3,000 fyrdmen, less well armed and armoured but ready to lend their lives to hold the line and kill any who tried to break it.

The scene was set for the first of the three battles that would decide the fate of King Harold Godwinson, England and the Anglo-Saxon nation.

The sun rose shortly before six o'clock on 20 September. In September, daylight comes quickly in Yorkshire. The halo of light that hovers near the horizon during the summer nights was gone. At Riccall the camp would be stirring while it was dark. It was not only the prospect of a battle that might have roused the warriors that morning, but the penetrating damp-cold along the river bank that prevented a good night's rest. Perhaps an hour after first light, Harald's scouts and patrols would have begun to report back what they had seen by the first light of that dawn.

From early times, war leaders have deployed scouts ahead of their main force. The Grand Old Duke of York is immortalised in a mocking rhyme for marching his 10,000-strong army up the hill and down again. There is no better way to forfeit the trust of your followers than to get lost or lead them into a dead end. One would expect any competent commander to deploy parties of trusted troops, probably on horseback, ahead of the main body to watch for the enemy.

Once the sun was up, the evidence that the earl was making his stand at the ford would have been clear. Even in the dark, the fires of those who arrived early at the ford would have told the scouts that an army was assembling. Earl Morcar would not have wanted thousands of strangers staying in his main city. The warriors would have been welcomed and moved on to the ford with some provisions for the morning.

The warriors would have been living near enough to the city to be summoned when they were needed. The network of kinship and remembrance of favours owed ensured that everybody had a place

to stay. They could be summoned and assembled as soon as the route
of the invaders was known. Only those from north of the river Tyne
would have sought out some kin in the south with whom they could
wait. Everybody else could assemble within a day or two. It was now
at least five days since the attack on Scarborough announced the
arrival of the invaders.

We hear that King Magnus, Harald's brother, 'ordered the whole
army to be gathered by the war trumpets into battle array, and ordered
all the men to arm, and to lie down for the night under their shields;
for he was told the enemy's army had come to the neighbourhood'.
So it was evidently good practice to be in position early. Perhaps many
of Morcar's men slept with shield and cloak as their shelter the night
before the battle at the ford.

King Harald would quickly have had his first men on the way. The
causeways would slow their departure and it would take several hours
for his full force to reach dry land. Now that it was clear that the
English had taken a defensive position, he did not need to form up
the troops before they approached the site. It was clear that the English
plan was not to launch an attack on them. Harald might well have
told Tostig to lead the way, as this was familiar territory to him.

King Harald had three armies under his control. The smallest
belonged to Tostig and his ally Cospig, reinforced by a small contingent from Scotland. They could probably only count on a few
hundred good warriors. Then there were the troops from Orkney and
Shetland with their earls. There is no account of the size of this force
but they might have added 1,000 fighters to Harald's army. Harald
would trust these troops less than those he knew and would expect
them to prove themselves.

Finally, Harald had his Norwegians, perhaps 6,000-strong. Many of
these would be his veterans from the Danish wars. It is probable that
he would have held these as his reserve. The tactic he had developed
fighting for the Byzantine Empire was to allow the mêlée to develop
and then strike with his most potent force. He knew the quality of
his Norwegians and that he could rely on them. It was Earl Tostig
and the earls of the outer islands whom he would expect to lead
the attack.

We know a great deal about the military sophistication of Harald.
As the army walked towards Fulford, a distance of about 16km, his
trusted lieutenants would be providing him with more information

about the ford and the master tactician would be working out his plan.

When the first Norse reached the ford they would see a line of shields. The English might be sitting or squatting but their shields would be facing the assembling enemy. The edges of their shields would be set to overlap, to make sure that the gaps for missiles to enter were as small as possible.

A shield was the warrior's friend. Before the battle it acted as a mask behind which the warrior felt concealed. In the heat of battle, the shield provided some sense of invulnerability. It was a weapon but it might also save their life. Shield design was a compromise between weight and protection. Depending on the type of wood employed, the shield would be about 6mm thick. Experiments have shown that this is too thin to stop the thrust of a spear and a few sword swipes would soon hack a shield to bits. There are no records of reserve shields being held ready to replace those damaged. The protection provided was therefore somewhat illusory. King Harald fought without one, boasting in one of his poems that his swinging axe was his shield.

The use of the shield had a fundamental effect on tactics. The shield is not only for personal defence but provided collective protection for those around. The duke of Cumberland trained his troops to work as a team and use their bayonets to stab the man to their right once they closed up to the Scottish army at Culloden in 1746. When the sword was raised to strike, the left side of the attacker's body would be exposed. This same advice must have been drilled into every army since man made an art of warfare.

However, the loss of one's shield would require a very quick rethink if one was to survive. Stripped of its limited protection, attack was probably the only form of defence. A glorious and defiant burst of aggressive energy might just create a gap into which your comrades could pour and behind which you could retreat, perhaps to see if you could recover a usable shield from the wounded. The constant cry within the ranks must have been to reform a solid wall of shields.

Evidence suggests that the kite-shaped shield associated with the Normans was familiar among the English and Vikings of the eleventh century. The advantage of the kite shape was the protection it afforded to those on horseback, as well as the vulnerable lower limbs. There is always an element of fashion in arms and armaments and it is possible that the kite shield was more popular in the south. The housecarls were better travelled and able to invest more in new weapons, so they might well have had a kite shield among their collection.

There is an assumption that shields were made with flat boards, even though most illustrations portray them as domed. Curved shaped shields would have advantages. If a blow was not perpendicular, it might be deflected.

As the deposed English Earl Tostig and his troops reached the ford, a cry would have rippled along the line of shields when he was identified. That would have put an end to any casual behaviour. Instead of relaxing, the defenders would have quickly formed their line, with shields overlapping, the boss of one shield touching the edge of the one beside. Each warrior in the front rank would have to stand with his shoulder towards the emerging enemy. Perhaps a front rank of a thousand iron-clad eyes stared across the beck at the man they had come to fight. Behind stood more English warriors, now arrayed about five ranks deep.

The vital role of morale and psychology among an army cannot be overstated. We have no record of any speeches delivered but the leaders would have made sure that their troops understood what was at stake. The serious talking would have been done in the weeks before the battle. Communication during the battle was limited to a few calls sounded on a horn and banners to mark the position of the leader. We only hear of the horn being used to sound a charge, but other sound signals might have been employed.

On the other side of the beck, Tostig and his men would appear level with the defenders as they reached the top of the opposite shoulder of moraine. Only the valley, cut by the water of the retreating glacier, separated the armies now. One hundred metres divided the sides as they came into view. Both sides would study the other, as more warriors crested the ridge to see the awesome sight of the English shieldwall arrayed for battle. Soon the walls would be shouting their war cries. No man is so fearless as to be unimpressed by such a formidable sight.

The Norse army would do little more than spread along the ridge until their leaders took them to their positions. It was probably a little after nine o'clock when the first of the invading army arrived on the battlefield. It was a three-hour march from Riccall and the priority was to have a drink. The battle itself would be thirsty work so it was important to go into battle well prepared. The river was nearby. It was safe to go and fill their water skins ready for the task ahead.

It would also be another three hours before the full force of the Norwegians arrived. Earl Tostig was noted as an intelligent and scheming man. He would have recognised that he did not want to provoke an attack before the full force was ready. He would display the same caution five days later at Stamford Bridge. He would stay out of range. Only the taunts of the Northumbrians would have reached him. Leaving his men positioned along the ridge, Tostig could have moved to the end of the ridge and had good time to walk round the southern side of the battlefield.

From the shoulder of the moraine cut by Germany Beck, he could see in front of him an amphitheatre of mud through which the water of the beck had chosen its meandering path. The English also enjoyed a grandstand view of this arena from their shoulder of the moraine. This was the place where people and animals forded the river. If there had been a causeway, the defenders had probably removed it.

Beyond this loop, carved out by the water of the beck, the land rose again, but not to the height at which Tostig was standing on the moraine-top. He could see that the English shieldwall extended beyond the point where the land on his side fell away again into marshy land. Along the side of the beck occupied by the English he could see that the willows had been coppiced. But on his side the birch, willow and alder trees told him that this was a good area to hunt waterfowl but not a place to deploy his troops.

The English line looked solid all along the high ground back from the ditch. However, for some 70m at the right flank of the English there was scarcely what he would call a shieldwall at all. Once the beck burst through the moraine it spread out in a wide delta and made its way to the river in many small streams. The delta quickly widened, so that solid ground on which soldiers could stand and fight was 50m or even 100m wide. This was an impossible place to attack as the mud would grip a warrior's legs even up to his knees, making him an easy target for the archers. The English shieldwall effectively ended where the firm ground of the moraine met the damp land. There was only a thin wall along the delta.

Behind this thin line lay the Ings. This provided good hunting for ducks and in a dry summer, excellent hay could be taken off and then sheep and lambs put on to graze before the winter. It looked so tempting. A man could wade through the Ings slowly, but it was no place for soldiers to fight. Beyond the Ings it was possible to see smoke curling up from fires that were burning in York, perhaps baking the bread that someone would certainly need before the day was over.

As Tostig completed his survey he would notice that along the bank of the river there was a sizeable force to guard the levee which ran along the riverbank. This raised walkway was made by the action of the river itself each time it flooded. The heavy material, such as stone and sand, would fall out of suspension. Later, the feet of people and animals would consolidate this riverbank, which then acted as a dam to trap the fine material and form the Ings. This walkway was narrow enough for a small band of determined warriors to hold, provided they kept the shieldwall intact. Tostig would not have been able to see who had been entrusted with holding this isolated flank but might have guessed that it was Morcar's brother, Edwin, plus his best Mercian housecarls.

By the time Tostig had completed his reconnaissance, the army had swelled to several thousand. Now they could begin to deploy against the English. The troops began to move along the ditch that separated the armies. Now they would come within range. Their shields would help to provide protection from arrows and slingshots.

Bows were a common weapon, whose everyday use was for hunting. However, they could be employed in battle like a sniper weapon or to harass an assembled force by firing over the shieldwall. A good bowman could loose ten aimed arrows in a minute. The epic poem *Beowulf* mentions 'the iron-tipped arrow shower'.

Little is known about how these 'long range' weapons were employed, as they were used by the rear ranks who were likely to be farmers and craftsmen, not trained in the arts of war and so not figuring in the epic poems or sagas. However, King Harald of Norway would be killed by an arrow in his throat when he left the protection of the shieldwall at Stamford Bridge.

With the opposing armies now forming up only 30m apart along most of the shield wall, an iron-tipped arrow would have the power to penetrate a shield. However, the energy would be taken out of the arrow, making it an inconvenience rather than a danger. The Bayeux Tapestry shows the shields of those in action with arrow shafts embedded in them. At this stage the warrior might snap the head off, to avoid injury if the shield walls met for some pushing and shoving.

However, some arrows would have hit legs and shoulders unprotected behind a shield. The casualties would have eased their way to the back of the line for whatever remedial treatment was available.

This dangerous game might have lasted for over an hour at Fulford. There was no incentive for the English to make a move. The invaders would have to make the costly move into the ditch where they would become the targets for javelins and spears.

Two concerns might have troubled the young earl, Morcar, as the hours rolled round towards midday. The first was the continuing stream of warriors arriving from Riccall. The second was the impatience of his men. After an hour of arrows, the archers would probably have exhausted their supply. It is hard to keep an army standing about.

King Harald could have moved most of his troops to Fulford before midday. He too would have had a good look at the location. At Stamford Bridge the two leaders conferred about the battle and they took time to make their plan. However, the cunning plan that would be followed at Fulford bears all the marks of Harald's planning. Like Tostig, he was someone who kept his own counsel. In all probability, Tostig knew nothing of Harald's plan to cross the ford.

As it approached the middle of the day, Harald sent his least experienced troops into the attack. The place chosen was the ford. This was offset to the right, perhaps 50m away from the centre in the English line along the beck. The troops chosen to lead the attack for King Harald would probably have been the islanders he had brought with him, led by their earls and with Earl Tostig's men at the front. Harald expected little of these troops as they advanced into the muddy amphitheatre around the ford. Indeed, the ground was so boggy that it was difficult for them to move. But once they had waded into position they would certainly not be able to run away.

King Harald kept his good troops near the riverbank where the land was much firmer. The shape of the moraine meant that he could keep his army, and his presence, concealed in dead ground. Here the Norwegians were out of sight and out of harm's way. If the cunning King Harald did keep his best troops off the battlefield, it would have helped to make the English more confident, which is what he required for his plan to work.

The time for shouting and psychological warfare from both sides was over. Now the battle had begun. The next weapon to be employed was the javelin. These were light throwing spears similar to the Roman *pilum*, to judge from those found buried in graves of the tenth and eleventh centuries. The tactic for their use was tried and tested.

A shower of javelins was unleashed when the enemy was perhaps ten seconds away from contact. This would bring down some men, pierce the shields of others and render them useless, so opening up the charging enemy to a counter-attack. This appears to be what the English did. The English shieldwall easily pushed the fractured shieldwall that had advanced against them back down the slope. At this point they should have stopped.

However, the saga tells us that:

> When the earls [Morcar] advanced downwards into the fen, the arm
> of the Northmen's line which was at the ditch gave way; and the
> Englishmen followed, thinking the Northmen would fly. The banner
> of Earl Morcar advanced then bravely.

The English evidently succeeded in repulsing the opposing shieldwall. This incident was not quite at the 'arm' or flank of the invaders but close to their right flank. This was likely to be achieved in the normal push and hack of close-quarter fighting. Only much later in a battle, when tiredness and lack of replacements became a factor, could the shieldwall be penetrated. At this stage of the battle, every gap in the shieldwall was quickly repaired.

To break the wall the English would have launched a series of small charges. One shield formation recognised in the literature is a wedge shape often called the pig's or boar's head. The wild boar, a close relative of the domesticated pig, was well know for breaking cover and charging those threatening it. The momentum of the charge would knock the spear-carrier back even as the beast impaled itself on the hunter's spear. This formation relied on momentum to burst through the shieldwall.

Experimentation by re-enactors has demonstrated how effective this formation could be. The warriors at the point of the wedge would lean back into the rest of the wedge to make sure it was a compact formation. This wedge would give the attackers a numeric superiority at the point of impact. If the wedge succeeded in breaking the opponents' shieldwall, they could attack the wall from its unprotected sides and rear until the protective line reformed. These exhausting and lethal mêlées would last a few minutes, each one denting the defenders and pushing the line back. This was like the attrition of trench warfare, with thin shields providing the only protection.

In spite of the mud at the ford, the English steadily pushed the invaders back. Each time the English broke the line of the opposing shieldwall, it would have to withdraw and reform. The way to defeat this stratagem was to form an arc, or counter-wedge, that would envelop the attackers. The English had been drawn into the amphitheatre where the Norsemen now lined the slopes. The arc carved by Germany Beck had also stretched the English line. To keep the shieldwall intact, men had been drawn into this hollow at the crossing from other parts of the line. The numbers were still sufficient to allow this but the English line was getting thinner.

Fighting is an exhausting business. Those at the front of the shieldwall could be expected to maintain contact for no more than five or ten minutes before pausing for breath. So after a rush, those at the front would attempt to change places with those behind. If their shield had been hacked by sword or axe it would be imperative to move behind those who could afford some protection.

However, there was plenty of killing work for those just behind the front shields. They could stab in many directions with a battle spear and this required both hands. The axe was another two-handed weapon for those deprived of their shield.

An army equips its men with a mixture of weapons to meet the different conditions that develop during the fight. The heavy axe might have had a shaft measuring over 1.5m. Used from behind, and with the protection of a shieldwall, an opportunist axeman could split skulls and shatter shields. However, any two-handed weapon user would be vulnerable to a counter-jab from an opposing spearman. Fighting was team work.

A heavy axe is not easy to steer so would have been employed in diagonal or horizontal strokes. If the axe embedded itself in a shield or entangled in the armour of its victim it might have to be abandoned. However, the axeman was ideal for plugging any breach in the shieldwall. The lethal axe could provide vital moments for those around to close the gap.

Axes might have had a peaceful as well as a martial role. However, the carpentry tools that have survived we know as adzes. The majority have the blade set perpendicular to the shaft or parallel, allowing them to be employed rather like a wood-plane. War was a serious business and those who practised it were properly armed with war axes, not the tools of a woodworker's trade. The 'bearded axe', so called because the base of the blade seems to protrude rather like a beard, is not the natural shape for chopping wood, when a flatter blade would be more suitable. The angle would make it well suited for slicing whatever came in its path.

During a battle, danger came from many directions. Those wielding their swords at the front had their focus on the man opposite them. However, behind the front man might be a warrior armed with a spear whose long shaft of ash would allow him to jab any one of half a dozen warriors fighting in the first few lines of the opposition. They could attack not only those to their front but those on either side.

Many of the battle spears found have wings. These could be used to hook behind a shield and expose the carrier to a sword thrust. Both shieldwalls would be engaged in this lethal search for some exposed body part that they could attack.

For protection warriors wore an iron helmet and armour. Any blow to a head encased in iron would have been traumatic. The effects could have been reduced by some wool padding to act as shock-absorbing material. Thick hardened leather helmets would have been more comfortable and also effective. The few helmets that have survived have protective metal flaps over the ears and holes around their base, which it is conjectured were used to suspend pieces of chain mail to protect the neck.

Professional warriors would all expect to own what the Vikings called a 'byrnes'. This suit, made from rings of wrought iron, would mitigate the effect of a slashing blow. However, it was the padded jack below the armour that would absorb and spread the energy and reduce the damage to flesh and bone. Experiments have shown that chain mail would not be effective at stopping a spear but might limit the penetration. Even members of the levy who stood well behind the shieldwall would expect to wear a padded jack to reduce the effect of blows.

This iron armour would be excellent at limiting injury during close-quarter battle. If the opponent could not swing his axe, make an effective stroke with his sword or was limited to prodding and poking with his spear, the riveted links could prevent serious injury. Lethal as the fighting looked, the chances of survival were good so long as the shieldwall and the cohesion of the formation remained.

After an hour of progress, the leading English fighters would have been exhausted and the Norse formation was still holding. The stretched line of the English had spent this hour driving into the

Norsemen's line, fighting in the mud at the ford. While they were accomplishing this, King Harald was preparing his attack, when he 'saw his men retreating along the ditch'.

The situation might have looked good for the English. However, King Harald had managed to get Morcar to leave his strong position and cross the ditch. Morcar had also been forced to thin his line, to cover the extension as his line stretched around the amphitheatre at the ford. This salient had meant the English shieldwall was now about 600m long, half as long again as the original formation. Earl Morcar was also on the lower ground. He would not be in such a good position to observe what was going on.

King Harald would have compounded his advantage if he had kept his best troops largely out of sight. We do not know much about the vegetation at the time but the shape of the land would make it impossible for Morcar to observe any troops forming up near the river.

This is what Harald was doing:

> [Harald] had the standard 'Landwaster' carried forward and made so hard an attack that all were driven back. Morcar's brother had had his standard brought along the river, downwards against the army of Harald, but when the King hardened his attack, the Jarl and his men fled along the river.

King Harald had spotted the weak point in the English defence. If he could force his way across the beck beside the river, he would be in a position to surround the English. The sagas make it clear that this attack was led by King Harald himself. He composed a poem about the way he could break through a line. He abandoned his shield and took his two-handed axe that could split skulls, even those encased in iron.

As a prelude to this attack Harald 'ordered a war-blast to be blown and urged them on'. Up to this point in the battle, three-quarters of the warriors had been spectators. Apart from the exchange of arrows and insults, the only action had been at the ford. Now all along the line the Norsemen jumped into the ditch and began to wade towards the English shieldwall on the other side. In some places the separation was only 30m, but in most places the lines along the banks of Germany Beck were 50m apart.

The effect of this attack along the whole line would be to cause great confusion. Under cover of the noise and the intense focus that

English warriors would now need to ensure their personal survival, the cunning King Harald could launch his attack. The full-frontal attack would also prevent any warbands going to aid parts of the line that were yielding under the pressure. There would be no fresh reinforcements fed into the overstretched line at the ford from now on.

This sequence of events was not haphazard or exploiting a sudden opportunity. Harald had offered an attractive sacrifice to Earl Morcar, knowing that he was bound not only to accept it but then to continue the advance because it must have felt to the English as if they were winning. Now was the moment to strike and cross the beck.

The saga tells us that the banner of Harald went with the king. He had identified this as his most precious possession. He called it the 'Landwaster'. We are not told when or where he acquired it but it was with him during his service with the Varangian Guard. Most illustrations and commentators note that the Vikings had the raven for their symbol. The *Anglo-Saxon Chronicle* of 878 notes 'there also was taken the war-flag, which they called Raven'. The Norse term for these banners was *gunfani*, from which the Norman and later French word *gonfalon* derives. The raven was a symbol of Odin, a fickle Norse god whom it was unwise to trust. Odin watched over his followers, making them invincible until granting them a heroic death and a place in Valhalla.

The reputation of these banners evidently impressed the author of *Encomium Emma*, who records that:

> ...the Danes had a banner possessed of a wonderful property, which although I believe it will seem incredible to the reader, nevertheless, because it is true, I will insert it for him for the sake of truth. For although it was woven of a very plain bright silk and had no figure embroidered on it yet always in time of war a raven seemed as it were to appear on it, in victory opening its beak and beating its wings, restless in its feet, but very quiet and drooping in its whole body in defeat.

The track beside the river must have seemed an easy place to defend. There was no wide ditch cut through the moraine where the beck crossed the Ings to reach the river. Here the flow broke up into smaller streams, before tumbling into the river. Along the bank of the river Ouse there would be many small streams, rather than one ditch to cross. The saga implies that this was undefended and Earl Edwin responded rather slowly to the threat posed.

This might best be interpreted as telling us that the earl did not recognise the danger that the loss of this location would have on his position. When King Harold led his charge along the riverbank, it might have taken less than half a minute from the time the charge began until the full weight of King Harald's 'best men' hit Edwin and the Mercian guards. They would inevitably have given ground. The key was how quickly they could recover the situation.

Faced with such an attack, all the Mercians could do was reform their shieldwall. The loss of the riverbank might not have appeared too serious at first. This was a rather isolated outpost of the battle. The main action was off to their left. They had seen the line advancing, but from their position very little of the battle was now visible on the moraine, which was 6m higher then their position at the riverbank. With the invaders pressing along the whole line, everybody would be very focused on their survival.

King Harald soon had his best troops on the firm ground that formed a causeway on the defenders' side of the beck. This was also the place where the defenders were thinnest on the ground. The delta had not seemed like a place that needed much defending. The sources tell us that the earls were slow to respond to this threat. Given the circumstances, it was understandable.

From his position near the ford, the events next to the river would not even be seen by Earl Morcar. Once he was made aware of the threat, his options were limited. The fact that he survived is a credit to his leadership and the quality of his fighting men. The time was probably a little after one o'clock and a slightly higher tide than had brought the fleet up to Riccall on the previous days was just peaking at York.

The thin shieldwall along the delta was being driven back along the ditch and up towards the track, where Morcar's men were still getting the better of the Norsemen. All that was saving these men from annihilation was the Mercians and their leader, Earl Edwin, who were fighting alongside the river.

But once enough of King Harald's men had crossed the beck's delta, Edwin had to fall back. The Mercians were secure from attack on their right as that flank still lay alongside the river, now swelled with fast-flowing water. They could only make their left flank safe by retreating to where the Ings were too soft for the Norwegians to come round and attack them from behind. If they did not make their open flank secure, their fate would be to be driven into the river. This was not a viable option for a warrior clothed in heavy iron armour.

Once Edwin and the Mercians retreated to secure their own position, the right flank of Morcar's army was exposed. Earl Edwin might have spotted this but it was impossible to send for reinforcements, as the only way to reach them was along the river bank, and that would now mean rushing several kilometres to bypass the Ings.

Earl Edwin's battle along the levee lasted through the rest of the day. As long as they held the shieldwall, the Mercians would be impossible to defeat. The Ings extend halfway back towards York. The Norwegians would have to charge their line repeatedly to force it back. The Mercians could yield a kilometre or more before there was any risk to their flanks. That would take hours.

They were probably helped because King Harald was now set on the destruction of Morcar's much bigger army. The 'Landwaster' moved away, and with it the pressure on the riverbank. Even if Earl Edwin could fight his way back towards the beck, the Norwegians were already across in strength and preparing to surround the unsuspecting English.

Edwin's Mercians were now a sideshow for the battle at the ford, and at dusk they would be able to slip back to York, after perhaps five hours of fighting.

It might have taken the Norwegians half an hour to cross in sufficient numbers to force the Mercians back and then to fight their way to the ford. While this was going on, the rest of the Norsemen were suffering appalling casualties as they attempted to cross the wide, boggy ditch to the English bank. This was the battle that Morcar had wanted to fight. For his men, overlooking the ditch and dealing out death to any of the attackers who reached their bank, eventual victory must have seemed within sight.

SURROUNDING THE MEN IN THE FORD

The first many of the English warriors would have known of the trap that was about to enclose them might have been when those behind them were felled by Norwegian warriors. Having pushed Edwin's Mercians back along the bank, fresh legs would have raced the 80m along the English side of the beck and up the incline, to appear at the backs of the English. The drama beside the river had been concealed from them by the fold in the land.

As the minutes passed, dozens more Norwegians arrived to attack the defenceless backs of the English. The confusion would not have lasted long. Even amid the noise of battle, the English would have heard, or been alerted to, the disaster looming.

Retreat was a particularly dangerous phase in any battle. Controlled and conducted carefully, it is possible to extract troops with few casualties. Retreat is not the same as running away. Turning your back to your enemy presented the attacker with almost every advantage. Instead of a shield to parry the blows, the enemy had an open target to hurl any available missiles at. The fugitive is largely ignorant of any dangers as they cannot see behind except by turning round. If they turned, momentum would also be with the pursuer. At the battle of Brunanburh, it is recorded in the chronicle that 'the west Saxons hewed the fugitive from behind terribly with their sharpened blades'.

The real danger comes if a retreat becomes disordered and turns into a rout. This is a situation that can turn defeat into a slaughter. So long as the army maintained its cohesion, it could avoid the slaughter that would result if it ran away. One soldier surrounded by three enemies is bound to die as he cannot face them all. Two soldiers have a chance as they can protect each other's back. This crude military logic can be extended to show that it makes sense to stick together.

The situation for the Anglo-Saxons was now becoming perilous, although it would still have been hard for many of them to perceive the danger which was approaching from behind and beyond a small hill. There might have been a short respite for the defenders as the first of Harald's troops arrived rather out of breath, having fought their way up this small hill. Perhaps Earl Morcar was able to stem the flow, but soon the weight of Norwegian numbers would have ensured their success. Within the space of another hour, the defenders had been dislodged from their position along the beck.

Perhaps two hours after the battle had begun, the men who had pressed forward earlier at the ford were being surrounded. They could not break contact and run because they would have been felled by spears from their opponents. The ground on which they were standing did not allow any rapid movement and, if they had a chance to look round, they would see that the Norsemen now occupied the ridge that they had held that morning. Within a short while, the men at the ford were isolated from the rest of the army.

The English were now under attack on three fronts. The battle along the river, as we have seen, was of no further significance to the battle at the ford. The English, who had stood their ground all day and dealt out destruction to any who made it across the ditch, were still an effective force with Earl Morcar as their leader.

The final front was in the amphitheatre at the ford. Here the fate of the Northumbrians was being sealed. Those who were not cut down were crushed. Tales that the beck ran red with Saxon blood are credible. With the hard clay lying only a short distance below the mud around the ford, when the saga tells us that one could walk 'dry-foot' across the bodies, it might also have been an accurate account. There was no escape route for these men. They had been fighting longer than any others and death was inevitable.

For Earl Morcar, now reduced to half an army, the situation was perilous. Florence of Worcester, using a source that is lost to us, provides this commentary: the English 'fought so bravely at the onset that many of the enemy were overthrown; but after a long contest the English were unable to withstand the attacks of the Norwegians and fled with great loss'. He adds, 'More were drowned in the river than slain on the field.' A very similar comment about drowning appears in the Nordic saga report of another battle, at Stamford Bridge. It would be difficult to drown in the Germany Beck of 1066. However, the coincidence of a very high tide might have brought half a dozen surges of muddy water up to the ford over the next few days, possibly providing a macabre spectacle of bodies pressed into the mud at the ford and along the delta, appearing to have drowned.

The comment that the English 'fled' might also be accurate. One of the chronicles agrees that the English 'fought that host and made great slaughter of them; but a great number of the English were either slain or drowned or driven in flight, and the Norwegians had possession of the place of slaughter'.

The saga and several Nordic poems about the battle agree that, after a long fight, the English fled, 'and they soon broke into flight, some running up the river, some down, and the most leaping into the ditch'. However, although the sources agree about the English fleeing along the ditch, this could just as easily describe their escape route as their running away. There are many ways of translating the words used, as well as interpreting what they mean when they describe how the battle ended. The words can be placed in the context of the real landscape where these events took place, to explore what is being described. Earl Edwin's Mercians could be portrayed as fleeing up the river, but it was probably a tactical retreat or a stand-off.

It is possible that, after the outflanking move by King Harald, Earl Morcar and the rest of the army simply took to their heels but this seems unlikely, not least because of the fatal consequences of a rout outlined earlier. The battle may have gone into a final phase.

Earl Morcar, with a force of perhaps 3,500, could have turned to meet the Norwegians who were outflanking them. These troops had relatively fresh legs. This shieldwall would have been in danger of being outflanked.

Their only option was to fall back. This action would make sense of the landscape as well as the literature. The best route open for Morcar was to retreat along the line of the beck. Remember that the English left flank was secured at the start of the battle by the marshy land. In this area, there are a number of streams and what might well have been numerous areas of higher ground that were relatively dry. Moving back across this landscape, serious fighting would have been difficult but a relatively safe retreat from the battle should have been possible for the English.

This battle could have gone on into the mid-afternoon, but this was no longer a battle of shieldwalls. The English were in retreat through the fenland. It would make no sense to delay their departure once they realised that there was no way to fight back. Had Earl Tostig known that Earl Morcar had survived, he might have organised a more effective follow-up. However, the saga reports that Earl Morcar was killed at the ford. Perhaps his banner had fallen among the dead at the ford. This was certainly the story that was carried back to Norway by the survivors.

The direction of Morcar's retreat would lead him towards the village of Heslington. From there the survivors could make their way out into Holderness or find a route back to York. The retreat was, however, drawing the invaders away from the direct road to York.

Whatever the course of this final phase, the victory at the ford went to King Harald. All of the key players had survived this long and hard battle. The records all agree that the casualties on both sides were high. Given the reckless charge undertaken by the Norsemen across the exposed deep ditch of Germany Beck, high casualties were to be expected. The English would have lost about a third of their number in the battle at the crossing once they were surrounded, as this represented 200m of the 600m of stretched shieldwall.

The battle was over and the way to York was open to the invaders even though Earl Edwin and his contingent had made their way back into the city. But it was probably not any fear of this small party of exhausted defenders that prevented the city from being stormed and sacked. Everybody was tired and the victors were pursuing Earl Morcar's force as they retreated some 4km from the walls of York.

Instead of heading into York, the Norwegian army returned to Riccall. There was much repair work and healing to be done. King Harald's brother had evidently set up a military medical service:

> After the battle the king [Magnus] ordered the wounds of his men to be bound; but there were not so many doctors in the army as were necessary, so the king himself went round, and felt the hands of those he thought best suited for the business; and when he had thus stroked their palms, he named twelve men, who, he thought, had the softest hands, and told them to bind the wounds of the people; and although none of them had ever tried it before, they all became afterwards the best of doctors. There were two Iceland men among them; the one was Thorkil, a son of Geire, from Lyngar; the other was Atle, father of Bard Svarte of Selardal, from whom many good doctors are descended.

Those wounded earlier in the battle would be able to withdraw in the lulls that followed each assault. They could pass back through the line to receive attention. A small collection of skeletons excavated near York can be dated close to the time of this battle. Some show multiple wounds, including a high proportion delivered while the victim was prone, and probably already dead. It is conjecture, but these might have been a few who had left the battle as walking wounded but who had been overtaken and killed later in the battle.

The issue of these few mortal remains is mentioned because the fate of the estimated 3,000 other casualties is not known. This represents

27 per cent of participants as fatalities, which is acknowledged by many sources as an exceptional casualty rate.

The value of the salvage of arms and armour ensured that the bodies would be collected. The victors, especially their comrades and kin, would want to honour the dead, but nothing is known about the ritual. The moraine over which the battle was fought would resist any attempts at proper burial. Two extensive zones of charcoal staining in the soil at a level consistent with the period of the battle have been identified near the ford. Perhaps cremation was employed. We do not know much about the fate of the fallen.

The city quickly came to terms. Earl Edwin was in the city but Earl Morcar was, wisely, elsewhere. King Harald and Earl Tostig went into York themselves to arrange for hostages, provisions and support before returning to the ships. The inhabitants recognised Harald as their king and agreed to assist him against Harold Godwinson. Harald agreed that 150 hostages would be exchanged between the victor and the vanquished. They had the customary few days to deliver the hostages. Monday was the day agreed. King Harald and Earl Tostig left, content 'that all would go southward with them, and gain this land' the following year.

The battle at the muddy ford appeared to have settled the issue of England's government. However, two more extraordinary battles over the next few weeks would bring about different resolutions. Instead of becoming one of the iconic battles of the English story, Fulford, like its victims, would soon be lost.

7

Postscript

The northern invasion had made landfall in Northumbria on 14 September. Trotting along the rough roads and covering about 10km each hour, messengers would have been in York the following evening. Further messengers would have been dispatched at daybreak to carry the news into the kingdom on 16 September. The breeding of horses had reached Europe, along with much science and technology, after the Arab invasions of Iberia. The Normans had established themselves as breeders and suppliers of horses for Europe, adapting the Arab stock. Special breeds were developed for all the different types of fighting, but as yet there was no horse capable of cantering the length of England to bring the news to London or on to King Harold.

An exhausted housecarl from among Earl Morcar's men might have reached Harold's home at Bosham, near Chichester, late on 18 September if the messenger had travelled via Oxford. The dating evidence suggests that Harold had already left the coast, heading for Westminster, which, with its proximity to real money in the kingdom, was becoming the new administrative base of the king.

Another messenger, dispatched direct to London, might have announced the first instalment of bad news about the Vikings landing sometime during 18 September, a Monday. But there was some good news. Word would have just reached Harold that William's fleet appeared to have been hit by his own fleet, as well as by the storm of 12 September, and scattered. Harold had a decision to make.

King Harold might have assumed that William's fleet had suffered badly, and the storm would have made accurate reporting difficult. It was probably safe for Harold to assume that William's invasion was on hold for the year. However, he might also have been alarmed that William's attempted invasion had been so well synchronised with the dismissal of the levy from the Isle of Wight after a frustrating summer of inaction, and with the Norse invasion.

Denis Butler, among others, suggests that the English fleet encountered the Norman invasion force on their final sweep of home waters after a summer patrolling the Channel. There is good evidence for a sea-battle, as both English and Norman sources record casualties following this encounter. However, it was probably the northerly storm, as much as the English fleet, that defeated the Normans' attempt to cross.

This encounter, to which Norman sources make no direct reference, would account for what must otherwise be interpreted as a serious misjudgement about the weather by the Norman sailors. The original decision to sail from the river Dives makes a lot more sense if this naval encounter did take place, forcing the heavily laden invasion force to take evasive action.

We can give a name to the thane from Norfolk who in September 1066 emulated the deeds of Francis Drake and defeated an armada. He was called Eadric and had commanded the fleet through much of King Edward's reign, but sensibly took himself into exile in Denmark when England submitted to William later in the year.

The news from the north was unwelcome but not unexpected. The northern threat was the reason that Harold had not been able to gather the mighty army of England together to confront William.

With one threat seemingly defeated, Harold could have felt confident that it was safe to leave the south unguarded. During the next two days the preparations would have been made for his army to be gathered, if indeed it had not already been summoned.

Listening to the reports from the seamen, King Harold could feel optimistic that William's force was spent, at least for this year. It was another gamble, but the quickest way to gather an army was to assemble the fresh troops now positioned to defend the coast. The vulnerable landing places were mostly only one long day's ride away, so he could have his army very quickly.

The messengers would have returned north to tell the earls that support was on its way. Even if the exhausted messenger had set out at dawn on 19 September, he could not have reached York in time to advise Morcar to play for time. The news probably reached the Mercian force near Tadcaster the day after the battle.

Exactly who received the news and how the anonymous messenger decided to handle it is critical for what happened next. On 21 September, the Mercians were probably uncertain about their status. Their earl, Edwin, had been on the losing side at Fulford. Edwin would have returned to show himself to his army and try to reassure them. Did he speak to the messenger? Even if Edwin had remained in York, the messenger would have sought him out in order to discover the whereabouts of his brother. Assuming that it was one of Earl Morcar's Northumbrians who had been dispatched to London, he would have wanted to deliver his message to his own earl.

Edwin would almost certainly have been briefed on the king's intentions. As a trusted member of staff, the messenger was probably able to tell Edwin how those in the south had responded and what they planned to do. If he was carrying a sealed letter from the king, its contents would have remained unread by Edwin. But is it possible that these two men realised not only the dangers but also the possibilities the situation presented to catch the invaders off guard? So the saddle-sore emissary was probably heading south again on the Friday, 22 September, with the latest news and possibly the suggestion of a plan from Harold's brother-in-law, Edwin.

Earl Edwin realised that he had to stay in York. If he did not agree to submit, the Mercians would be the next target for the invaders and York would pay a high price. To do anything other than to encourage the populace to agree to the lenient terms being offered by Harald and Tostig would alert the Norsemen. It was agreed that 150 'sons of the leading men' of Northumbria would be given as hostages, while the same number would be given by the Norwegians in exchange.

This was a substantial number and would have represented members of all the important families of Northumbria. Earl Tostig was gathering the effective reins of government into his hands. No family would be able to risk revolt and the young men given in exchange would be privy to any disquiet in Northumbria. Tostig was not going to risk a second coup. If we assume that the two days after the battle were spent by the victors in recovering their dead and making arrangements for their weapons and armour to be repaired, suggestions of a feast at Riccall are credible, and Sunday would seem to be the earliest that this could have taken place.

Embassies from the town would have been hearing the terms set by the victors on the Thursday and Friday. It was probably unwise for the locals to go to the battlefield until the Norsemen had completed their recovery work there. The high tides would allow the Norsemen to bring some longships to the battle site to carry away any spoils or the fallen warriors and return them to Riccall. The sad business of recovering those who had been dead for three days could have taken place on the Saturday, while the victors were preparing to celebrate their hard-won victory.

With the victors due to parade to the city the next day, the citizens would have especially wanted to clear those slaughtered at the ford. King Harald's whole army would be passing the ford on the Sunday.

We do not know how or where King Harald received the news of the defeat at Fulford on his way north. It was probably when he was about two days' ride south of York. Harold understood one of the foremost principles of war: the need to maintain momentum. If he allowed Harald to gather his strength in the north over winter, he would be difficult to dislodge when the campaigning season began in the spring.

It is often said that it would not be easy to muster a force to march north. The warriors had only two days to gather in London. The levy had been dismissed almost a fortnight earlier. If the system set by King Alfred was still functioning effectively, the new army of fresh men would already be assembling before news of the Norse invasion reached the south. The evidence of this and many other episodes of this time suggest that there was indeed an effective system for summoning an army. The autumn of 1066 was testing the system to its limits but it was evidently working well.

The army would have to be on its way north no later than Thursday 21 September. With each man carrying his equipment on one horse and mounted on another, they might have covered 80km each day. It was an impressive act of logistics to marshal and feed the troops and horses on their journey north at such short notice. Somewhere along the route, the much-travelled messenger returned with the news of the defeat at Fulford and the plans for the submission on the Sunday. Meanwhile, the English army was about a day's march from York, assuming that they were able to cover ground at about two-thirds of the speed of the unencumbered messengers.

On Sunday morning the saga tells us of Harald's arrangements at Riccall:

> So that on Sunday the king proceeded with the whole army to the castle, and appointed a Thing of the people without the castle, at which the people of the castle were to be present. At this Thing all the people accepted the condition of submitting to Harald, and gave him, as hostages, the children of the most considerable persons; for Earl Toste was well acquainted with all the people of that town.

This was King Harald's victory parade and, more pertinently, his show of strength. Another meeting was apparently arranged 'within the castle early on Monday morning, and then King Harald was to name officers to rule over the town, to give out laws, and bestow fiefs'. However, the same source later shows that Harald had other plans for Monday. This illustrates the problem that can occur with interpreting the information that has been left for us. Nevertheless, the sequence of events after the battle reported by the sagas, and in several chronicles, brings the events in the north to a dramatic climax. There is some conflict about the details but they all agree about the important timings.

Late on Sunday 24 September, only four days after leaving London, Harold's army rode into Tadcaster, where he could cross the river Wharfe. Harold himself moved on to York.

> The same evening, after sunset, King Harold Godwinson came from the south to the castle with a numerous army, and rode into the city with the good-will and consent of the people of the castle [York]. All the gates and walls were beset so that the Northmen could receive no intelligence, and the army remained all night in the town.

Concealing an army of perhaps 5,000 inside medieval York was not feasible. This was probably no more than a breakfast pause for the troops heading west.

Earl Edwin's ships were, as far as we know, still moored at Ulleskelf. The sailors might have been able to tell Harold that the Vikings would soon be split between Riccall and Stamford Bridge. This was good news.

According to one version of the *Anglo-Saxon Chronicle*, Harold's army left Tadcaster early on Monday morning, 25 September, and rode via York to Stamford Bridge. The Norwegian scribe Snorri records that King Harold of England spent the night before in York. He then goes on to describe the events of Monday morning:

> On Monday, when King Harald Sigurdson had taken breakfast, he ordered the trumpets to sound for going on shore. The army accordingly got ready, and he divided the men into the parties who should go, and who should stay behind. In every division he allowed two men to land, and one to remain behind. Earl Toste and his retinue prepared to land with King Harald; and, for watching the ships, remained behind the king's son Olaf; the earls of Orkney, Paul and Erlend; and also Eystein Orre, a son of Thorberg Arnason, who was the most able and best beloved by the king of all the lendermen, and to whom the king had promised his daughter Maria. The weather was uncommonly fine, and it was hot sunshine. The men therefore laid aside their armour, and went on the land only with their shields, helmets and spears, and girt with swords; and many had also arrows and bows, and all were very merry.

If we accept these figures and the casualty rates discussed earlier, King Harald set out with something short of 3,000 lightly armoured men, some carrying wounds from Wednesday's battle and all suffering from the feast the night before. There is a good route to take them to Stamford Bridge along the line of the Escrick moraine. This would keep them well clear of York. This was a substantial march with over 28km to cover. If they set off soon after first light, they would expect to reach Stamford Bridge in the early afternoon.

Quite why King Harald marched his army to Stamford Bridge is a mystery. It was not an especially good communications centre. York or Tadcaster were much better placed. Perhaps Stamford Bridge was not the destination. There was a significant junction of roads some miles north of Stamford Bridge itself. This might have been the location nominated to complete the formalities of submission and the exchange of hostages.

The invaders evidently had no plan for a fight. The chroniclers agree that it was a warm September. Because the days were hot, and combat was not expected, the men left most armour and weapons behind at Riccall. Doubtless some equipment needed repair after the first battle, but with Earl Morcar and a significant contingent of his army at large, considerable caution was important for the invaders. The fact that they went unprepared was surprising.

They appear to have left a significant force to guard each crossing point, as you would expect from professional soldiers. There were no easy fords and two other bridges, at Kexby and Elvington. What better ploy than to cut the army in half by capturing one of the bridges between Stamford Bridge and Riccall?

It is hard to credit that Harald knew nothing of Harold's progress northwards, but the evidence is compelling. The actions of the invaders only make sense if they are completely ignorant that a swelling English army is stalking them. Maybe Earl Edwin was a convincing performer. The river would have directed all foraging activity towards the east and it is to the east that any scouts would have deployed, looking for fugitives from the battle.

Perhaps Harald relied too much on the council of Earl Tostig. Possibly the earl did not yet have the confidence to try and re-establish his contacts, so his security advice was over-confident. Maybe the truth is that he had no allies in the north. His was going to be an army of occupation.

While the invaders were making their way north-east, the English army was in fact heading due east on a collision course. Their route from Tadcaster was about the same distance. Those who spent the night in York had only half the distance to cover. The legacy of the last ice age provided the armies with separate routes to Stamford Bridge. There might have been nothing alarming about the sight of many men on horseback on the adjacent ridge heading in roughly their direction. They had, after all, been summoned to submit to King Harald and their restored earl.

This is not the place to discourse on the numerous issues raised by the events later in the day. In outline, the vanguard of the English captured the crossing at Stamford Bridge after a hard fight. Negotiations followed, with both sides playing for time. It would take several hours for the English to get across the river Derwent and even longer for reinforcements to arrive from Riccall. The negotiations show that there was still some love between the brothers Harold and Tostig but the latter was not persuaded to betray the Norwegians.

The reinforcements from Riccall would make slow progress on their 28km dash from Riccall in full armour and on a hot day. This was precisely two-thirds of the modern marathon distance. The train for Harold's army must have stretched back to York if half of the warriors were mounted. With the one bridge to cross, it would still take about three hours to assemble the army, even if the horses could ford the river.

It was afternoon when the battle began. The English mounted soldiers charged at the Norsemen, who were clearly outnumbered and, unable to secure their flank, had formed a circle or wedge. The attacking horsemen rode round in a circle, not pressing home their attack, simply skirmishing. The Norwegians responded with arrows. It is reported in the sagas that 'their horses were clothed in armour'.

Later, the Wessex cavalry adopted a different tactic and charged the line before falling back. This was an advanced tactic that had arrived with the horsemen from central Europe. Harold and his military commanders had evidently been modernising the English army to incorporate the horse. Eventually the Norse shieldwall broke open, possibly in order to attack the retreating cavalry. This was what King Harold wanted. He ordered his army forward to keep the breach open as the horsemen rode back.

The battle reached its first climax. King Harald rushed to restore the situation and led a charge into the thickest of the fighting. He 'fell into such a fury of battle' that he rushed forward ahead of his troops, 'hewing with both hands neither helmets nor coats of mail could withstand him, and everyone in his path gave way before him'. At this point, King Harald was struck in the throat by an arrow. This was his death-wound. Those around him were cut down as they tried to protect their dying leader, but Tostig made it back inside the formation, clutching the 'Landwaster' banner. Only those close to Harald's standard made it back to the protection of the shield circle that was now restored. Both armies had fought themselves to an exhausted standstill. The sides drew back to reform and catch their breath.

The style and tactics of this battle are remarkably prescient of the battle to come with the Normans, although the position of the English would be reversed. King Harold's cavalry did not appear at Hastings so it was perhaps still recovering after this battle in the north.

During the lull in the fighting Harold again offered quarter to his brother Tostig and the survivors. Tostig again refused, saying they would 'rather fall, one across the other, than accept quarter from the Englishmen'. The Vikings responded with their war cry. Harold renewed his attack and the invaders were steadily ground down. Harold gave permission for the survivors to recover their dead but this time there were not enough to attend to the fallen invaders and the bleached bones on the battlefield are reported by later visitors.

The reinforcements fared no better. They fell easy victims to Harold's mounted soldiers. The reinforcements were not able to form the tight groups where each could support his neighbour with his assorted weapons. The sources suggest that perhaps 90 per cent of the invaders were killed. The high casualty rate perhaps demonstrates the effectiveness of the armour that the Norsemen were not wearing, and the advantages of fighting on horseback.

There is an ambiguous passage in several sources that might indicate that, while the battle was raging at Stamford Bridge, the seamen of the Mercian fleet sallied in among the ships at Riccall, destroying the base there. There is mention of many dying by burning. Perhaps the women and the wounded took refuge among the ships where, by accident or design, fire spread among the tightly packed vessels.

The ships required to take the survivors home do not appear to have come from Riccall. 'Olaf, the son of King Harald Sigurdson, sailed with his fleet from England from Hrafnseyr, and came in autumn to the Orkney Isles...', according to the Orkney Saga. This might suggest the future site of the city of Hull as the point of departure for the survivors, because the name Hrafnseyr can be interpreted as 'the port on the Seyr'. Sayer's Creek is one of the founding rivers of Kingston-upon-Hull.

Back in the Orkney Isles this sad sequel is related in the sagas: 'Maria, a daughter of Harald Sigurdson, died a sudden death the very day and hour her father, King Harald, fell.' The writer could also have noted that her husband-to-be, who was lauded by Harald as the fairest and cleverest in Norway, also perished as the leader of 'Ore's

Storm' to try and save King Harald. Olaf, Harald's son, returned to Norway the following spring and was made co-king with his brother Magnus, reigning until 1093. There were further Danish, rather than Norwegian, attempts to support English uprisings in 1070, 1075 and 1085, but these were short-lived and defeated with Danegeld rather than in battle.

King Harold's victory in the north was complete. The English king had shown himself to be a formidable and decisive commander.

WILLIAM OF NORMANDY ARRIVES

On 27 September, the wind apparently turned, if one accepts the Norman version of events. William's fleet, re-assembled in the estuary of the Somme, crossed the 100km stretch to England at night, reaching Pevensey the following morning. A night crossing might have been the only way to persuade the nervous fleet to sail, after their mauling a few weeks earlier. Duke William's ship had a lantern on the mast to help the fleet stay together, but it was not altogether successful as some ships landed too close to English defenders along the coast and were 'slaughtered'.

They would have heard this news in London that same night, but it would be Monday 2 October before Harold learned of the landings while he was still in York. However, Harold was back in London, organising another campaign, by Friday. England had used up three armies and much of the equipment was still in the north. The effects of the northern invasion would be felt when Harald confronted William.

On 6 October, Harold Godwinson sent out a call to raise more troops. In spite of the other campaigns, the best estimate of Harold's army that lined up on Senlac ridge is 2,000 housecarls plus 5,000 summoned as part of the levy. The limited clues about the casualties in the subsequent battle suggest that East Anglia and the south-east provided this last contingent. It was another sizable force but it could have been half as large again without his northern campaign and at least twice as big if Edwin and Morcar had been able to provide their full force. The two battles had taken a heavy toll among the professional warriors. Harold's army assembling at Senlac was short of the experienced soldiers who could make the levy an effective army.

For six days Harold sent forth the summons to call the people to arms
from all quarters, and, having assembled vast numbers of the English
he led them by forced marches against the enemy. It was his design
to take them unawares, and crush them at once by a night attack, or,
at least, by a sudden onset, and, that they might not escape by sea, he
caused a fleet of seventy ships, full of soldiers, to guard the coast.

On 11 October, Harold left London. According to Orderic Vitalis, he
had a clear plan. It was a repeat of his strategy at Stamford Bridge to
take the enemy unprepared. The position at Senlac finds a geographical parallel at Fulford. It was another blocking position through
which William, safe on the peninsula at Hastings, would have to
pass to invade England.

The same source says Harold's mother and at least one brother
wanted him to rest. Earl Gyrth, his younger brother, offered to lead
the army. Gyrth was cursed for his suggestion:

But do you, my brother, rest awhile in peace, and wait the issue of
the contest, that so the liberty which is the glory of England, may
not be ruined...

Harold even ended up kicking his mother when she clung onto her
son in order to prevent his departure. Sadly, the family were right,
and on 14 October the English army was badly defeated and King
Harold killed along with all of the Godwinson earls.

After his victory, William waited at Hastings, perhaps expecting
the English to surrender, but instead a resistance party began to form
around Edgar Aetheling, the grandson of Edmund Ironside, whom
the dowager queen Edith had nurtured at court. The cities of Wessex
did not hold out long with their earls all dead. William employed
some 'exemplary violence' against Romney to send a message to
others. The chronicle notes William's army 'inflicted such punishment as he thought fit for the slaughter of his men who had landed
there by mistake'.

William's progress towards London was blocked and, when an
advanced party of 200 knights reached London Bridge, his knights
were driven off but Southwark was left in flames. Troops, possibly
those summoned to Hastings but who had failed to arrive in time,
were in London. Edgar Aetheling was also reported to be in London

and might have led the force to oppose the approaching Normans. At this stage the battle for England still appeared to be on.

William changed tack and stopped terrorising the neighbourhood in the hope of forcing submission. Instead, he now behaved as the consummate politician that he was. He took 'great pains to appease everyone' as he visited the towns that had submitted to him, leaving a small garrison behind to ensure their good behaviour.

The Witan that had so recently appointed Harold to be their king now supported the claim of Edgar, giving the lie to the durable Norman propaganda that Harold had somehow seized the throne of England. The teenager Edgar's claim had been set aside earlier in the year rather than dismissed by the Witan. Nevertheless, this fiction of 'Harold the Usurper and Oath-breaker' would be used to define all those who had fought at Hastings as rebels whose property, titles and lives were forfeit to William. William kept most of the Godwinsons' lands.

The English resistance was not all armed defiance. The monks at Peterborough elected one of their own to replace their recently deceased abbot and sought the consent of Edgar Aetheling, whom they declared was the true king. William was not amused and sent armed men to communicate his wrath. Fortunately, William was gold-hungry and allowed himself to be bought off with a hefty fine.

Winchester, the site of the royal treasury and home to the late King Edward's widow, Harold's sister Edith, promised submission. This act is not easy to understand. Edith was the first significant noble to submit. One might have expected her to move the treasury to a place where it might have helped her surviving nephews in their quest for the throne. It would be left to her mother to lead the Godwinson rebellion.

The submission of Winchester started the surrender of southern townships to William. As his grip tightened round London, the peace party in the city of London won. William accepted their plea for a pardon and was conciliatory in his reply. Pragmatically, William now made use of those who had held office under King Edward to run a rather complex economy. He needed their administrative and financial support to pay his army. Those who had received their appointments during the short tenure of Harold did not keep their jobs.

In a move that was out of character, William offered major con-cessions. The London merchants, the clergy, and southern English nobility submitted in the accustomed fashion and on terms that they felt they understood. So, almost three months after his landing, William was recognised as king at a ceremony in Westminster Abbey church.

The Norman Conquest was not over. The process of conquest would take the rest of William's life. He set his builders to work on the tower in the trading heart of London. The rulers would henceforth live behind thick walls. Until this bastion had been constructed against the 'inconstancy of the numerous and hostile inhabitants' William preferred to stay at Barking, outside the city. It was to Barking in January 1067 that the earls Edwin and Morcar came to surrender.

A modern survey shows that about forty stone structures were completed during the first decade after 1066. There were also untold numbers of wooden towers, built on top of a hill or motte. Although these structures were little more than watchtowers, such stockades provided a refuge for the outnumbered occupiers where they might hold out and hope for relief.

There is little surviving evidence, but these fortified barracks might have had a considerable psychological effect. Previously, a local ruler could be overthrown by ambushing the guard that protected him and enforced his authority. Now the enforcers were able to scurry to their fort and pull up their ladders behind them. These invaders could not so easily be removed, so their authority remained. Removing an unpopular local governor had suddenly become more difficult. Acquiescence or grudging consent of the populace was no longer required. This was developing into an army of occupation that, quite literally, watched over the people.

In March 1067, William returned to Normandy and took with him all of the English leaders, claiming that they were needed to bear witness to his lawful election as king of England by the Witan. During the visit Earl Edwin was also promised one of William's daughters as his bride, according to some sources.

By 1068 it was already evident to Edwin, still the earl of Mercia, that this political marriage would not happen. When the leading English earls did homage to William, the latter understood that in submitting to him they became his vassals. Therefore their property, honours and titles belonged to William, and he naturally expected them to re-purchase these from him if it was his wish that they should be restored. Their failure to share this feudal outlook spelt disaster for the English earls.

The English custom of submission was superficially similar to the Norman one. A man would bow his head and on bended knee promise to his overlord to 'shun all that he shuns and love all that he loves...'. But there was a condition. If a person was unable to maintain themselves due to mismanagement or misfortune, they could submit to their lord, who in return would maintain the person who had given themselves into his custody. Just as a peasant could place themselves at the disposal of their lord, so others in the social hierarchy could submit to their superior in a ceremony known as 'commendation'.

The key difference was that to the Normans the oath meant subjugation. For the English it had only meant that they were placing themselves under his protection.

Both customs made one subordinate to the superior. There was, however, in England no expectation that the supplicant would abandon all that he had to his superior, or that the latter would actually exercise any rights to take land or titles except in accordance with the laws. There was a serious clash of cultures. The brutal rule of feudal supremacy would displace the accustomed system of heritance that had evolved over centuries to meet the needs of good governance.

As far as William was concerned, Edwin and Morcar, plus their titles, were now his to dispose of. As such, any dissent was tantamount to rebellion. A short stay in Normandy showed the earls the true nature of the Norman occupation, and they joined those already in open rebellion after their return.

Edgar Aetheling took refuge in Scotland. King Malcolm III married Margaret, one of Edgar's sisters. This successful union, to a descendant of King Alfred, founded the dynasty of the House of Canmore, which lasted 200 years until displaced by the House of Stewart. Margaret introduced English customs and language into the Scottish court and Church procedures. Malcolm made two more raids into England in 1079 and 1091 in support of Edgar but was eventually forced to submit to the English ruler. But King Malcolm did not give up and in 1093 was killed in another invasion.

Separate rebellions broke out led by the Godwinson matriarch, Gytha, in Exeter. During the summer of 1068 Godwin, Magnus and Edmund, Harold's sons, launched raids, but they did not meet with the support they needed to sustain them. Had this attack been synchronised with the rising of the cities of the south-west, the outcome might have been different. However, the merchants were increasingly supportive of the new order.

In 1068, King William appointed Robert de Comines, Earl of Northumberland, instead of Morcar. Soon after, the men of Northumberland voted with their swords and massacred Robert and 900 of his men whilst they were staying in the city of Durham. Edgar Aetheling came from Scotland and was received by the men of Northumberland at York. William moved up quickly from dealing with a revolt in the Fens led by a local landholder, Hereward the Wake, and surprised the Northumbrians. Hundreds were slain and the city of York torched.

1069 marks the end of William's plan to govern with consent. His strategy had bought him time and enabled him to take over the administration of England. Rebellion was, however, endemic. There are numerous reports of Norman soldiers being slain as they moved through the woods and lanes of England. To stop this trend, the 'murdrum fine' was introduced. The concept lives on in the language and law of England. Murder is seen as premeditated, unlike manslaughter. A fine of '65 marks' was to be levied on the hundred where the dead Norman was found if the community failed to find, and hand over, the culprit.

This is the era when the stories of 'Robin Hood' begin. Many interpret these stories of greenmen as a generic tale of resistance. These folk heroes lived in the wood where they harassed the occupiers and exploiters of the poor. The occupiers preferred the term 'outlaw' for those who left their community and the intrusive enforcement system. Orderic notes that the English 'groaned aloud for their lost liberty' and plotted to get rid of 'the yoke that was so intolerable and unaccustomed'.

In 1069 rebellion is everywhere. Harold's sons were back, raiding the West Country. The Welsh had taken Shrewsbury and then Chester. Resistance in the Fens was strong and now Morcar and Edwin rebelled, with the support of the Danish king, Sweyn, who was now staking the claim to the English throne that Tostig had reminded him of three years before. The Northumbrian earls Waltheof and Gospatrick, together with Edgar Aetheling, slaughtered the Normans in York. Earl Waltheof's exploit of slaying a hundred Frenchmen with his long-axe as they fled a fire was immortalised in verse. William moved north again, laying the land waste as he went. This was the start of the harrying of the north.

The revolt in the Fens, led by Hereward, had been strengthened by refugees from the harrying of Northumberland, including Earl Morcar. Although Ely fell in 1071, Hereward escaped and, with a band of followers, remained an irritant for King William for many years.

By 1073, William felt that at last he had conquered England. Just as well, as his subjects in Maine were revolting. The army that William took with him to bring his French subjects to heel was largely composed of English soldiers. The next storm broke in 1075 with the 'Revolt of the Earls'.

In view of the strength and longevity of the English resistance to the Conquest, it is surprising that it failed. William's immense energy, his use of patronage, his deployment of force and fear, his willingness to play politics in the short term and ability to extract money through feudal patronage all contributed to his survival. By contrast, the failure of English resistance can be attributed to a lack of leadership. The battles of 1066 had eliminated a generation of national and regional leaders. Somehow the northern earls, who were still young men, could not command the necessary national support. The loss at Fulford might have damaged their reputation badly.

After the surrender of London late in 1066, the northern earls took their sister, the widowed queen, to the Mercian capital at Chester, where she gave birth. One source suggests there were twins, but there was certainly one son who was named Harold. The young family moved to Ireland and is then lost to us. Earl Edwin was to die in an ambush, probably on his way to join the rebellion in the Fens but possibly going to the rescue of his brother, who had been captured.

The rest of our cast faded from history. Tostig's two sons appear to have taken refuge in Norway, and his widow Judith remarried Welf, Duke of Bavaria. Queen Edith retired to the convent of which she was a patron at Wilton, which is one of the likely locations where work on the Bayeux Tapestry was undertaken. Edith died in 1094 and was buried with Edward in Westminster Abbey.

The rest of the Godwinson women moved to Flanders after their involvement in rebellion. The youngest son of Earl Godwin remained a captive. Wulfnoth, and we suspect Morcar, benefited from the deathbed releases of all those held in custody by King William.

His son, William Rufus, set off immediately to secure the precarious throne of England and took the important hostages with him, although the term 'prisoner' is also applied by some scribes. Wulfnoth died still in captivity, respected by the few who record his life. Morcar also died in captivity.

The historian Orderic Vitalis composed the following confession for the dying William. There is no evidence that he expressed these sentiments at this time but they perhaps capture the consensus of those writing with the benefit of hindsight.

> I treated the native inhabitants with unreasonable severity, cruelly oppressed high and low, unjustly disinherited many, and caused the death of thousands by starvation and war, especially in Yorkshire.

Four years after these events a tariff of papal penances was issued for those who had taken part in the Norman invasion. The best interpretation of this is that Cardinal Hildebrand, later Pope Gregory VII, who had advocated the justice of William's cause in Rome, realised that he had been tricked or misled. The papal blessing given to William's mission had been to impose his rule over England but not to engage in a bloody conquest. The suggestion is that William misrepresented the invasion as a crusade to gain papal support. Participation in a crusade gave automatic absolution of sins committed to all those who took part.

The Norman dynasty in England lasted from late 1066 until 1154, when King Stephen died. Their impact on Britain was significant. They introduced a new architectural style, empowered the ecclesiastical system, altered the system of land tenure and left a legacy within the language and legal system which have outlasted the turbulent family that introduced them. However, it is harder to distinguish the changes wrought by the Normans on Anglo-Saxon institutions. Much that was essential England survived.

Another regal line from continental Europe arrived with Henry II, the first of the Plantagenets. The echoes of the Norman invasion would continue until King John lost the duchy in Normandy to the French king, Philip Augustus, in 1204. The language at court was Norman for the next three centuries. Henry IV, who came to the throne in 1367, was the first king of England whose mother tongue was English.

Conclusion

Having followed such a complex plot, it would be unfair not to reveal who, in my opinion, 'dunnit'. My view is that neither King Harald of Norway nor Duke William of Normandy set out with a master plan. I strongly suspect that it was Tostig who choreographed the events of 1066, thinking he could outwit these experienced tyrants.

Sadly, Tostig abandoned the consensual government that was developing in England and soon discovered, to his cost, that battle is a very uncertain way to resolve important affairs. Quite how Tostig expected to turn the situation to his advantage if more than one king was left standing after the three battles we will never know.

The heroes of this story are Harold Godwinson and the English people. I cannot detect any selfish ambition in Harold's actions. He was a good servant of England and his death at Hastings was a blow to the country. The willingness of the English to produce four armies to defend their country suggests that they felt they had something worth fighting for.

1066 was a setback, but one from which the people of England quickly began to recover. Achievements such as the Magna Carta and the creation of a representative forum were only postponed, rather than prevented, by the killing of the legitimate king of England, Harold Godwinson.

The omission from the national narrative of the battle at Fulford is one that historians need to answer. We hear it is the victors who write history. If so, it is time to rebel and insist that a correct record of events is made.

Glossary

Aetheling   The *æðeling* was originally the member of the royal line who could
               command the largest warband and so was chosen for the office of
               king – a recipe for war in early Anglo-Saxon kingdoms.

Anointing   With the coming of Christianity there is evidence that the act of
               anointing a king or queen was seen as conferring special, almost
               mystical, status.

Byrnie   The mailshirt worn by warriors.

Ceorls   Pronounced 'churls'. In spite of the connotation of 'churlish', ceorls
               were freeborn men. These distinctions of rank were not rigid. A ceorl
               who accumulated five hides of land became entitled to the rights of
               a thane, and this rank became hereditary after three generations, in
               theory. (From Danish word *carl* or the Saxon *ceorl*, a free man).

Gang-days   Icelandic origin, used to describe a warband. According to Webster's
               Dictionary, 1913 edition, 'gang-days' means 'A number going in
               company... for a particular purpose'.

Hide   The amount of land needed to sustain one family. Varies according
               to the land and agricultural practice in the area.

Housecarls   The Saxon or Scandinavian chief's immediate band and bodyguard
               were the house- or hearth-troops who lived at his hall and were
               bound by personal and traditional bonds of loyalty.

Knights   Knights rarely feature in the narrative but the word derives from
               the Old English word *cnicht*, meaning household retainer or even
               servant, so similar to housecarl. However, the term knight developed
               as Christianity and feudalism affected the post-Conquest social
               order.

Nithing   Outlaw.

Thegns   'Thanes' is preferred to 'thegns'. These men provided the warrior class

	in Anglo-Saxon England. They held land from their lord (who might also be their king) and their title was hereditary.
Fyrd	The Old English word *fyrd* meant 'a journey or expedition'. The meaning of the word evolved as the central organisation improved, and by 1066 is probably used to describe the military levy.
King	The word *cyning* literally means 'of the kin' and denoted a member of the royal line. The office was expressed by titles such as loaf-giver, landlord and warlord.
Riding	Derived from the 'thriding' or 'third part'.
Skald	A poet associated with the Scandinavian courts.
Thing	The governing assembly of the free men in Germanic societies, presided over by lawspeakers. In many Scandinavian countries legislative bodies are still known as 'things' or 'tings'.
Udal	A system of freehold tenure found in Scandinavia and subject to the payment of tax but no service. Ownership is established by unbroken possession for thirty years or by three generations.
Wapentake	A sub-division of a 'riding', equivalent to the southern counties' 'hundred'. Became obsolete around 1900. The word was probably derived from an assembly or meeting place, usually at a crossroads or near a river, where a vote was taken by a 'weapon touch'.
Witenagemot (or Witan)	Derives from the Old English for 'meeting of wise men' (*witan*, wise man; *gemot*, assembly). It was a convocation of the land's most powerful and important people, including senior clergy, ealds and leading thanes. A political institution in Anglo-Saxon England which operated between approximately the seventh century and eleventh century. As a token of resistance, or perhaps a recognition that Witan was the correct term, the chroniclers continued to use the word for a century after it had officially been abolished and replaced by the 'king's counsel'.

Naming and Date Conventions

NAMES

Anglo-Saxon names had two parts. The first part of the name was descriptive, such as Ead or Ed, meaning 'blessed', while Ethel or Elf meant 'noble'. The second part is less well understood. Suffixes such as '-gyth', '-red', '-stan' or '-flaed' were added, and these might have been part of a local or family tradition. Some, such as 'gifu', are understood as meaning 'gift of'. The terminal letter 'a' was often added for a female, a habit possibly acquired from the Romans.

Adult males often used their patronymic as a second name or surname, such as Haroldson or Godwinson.

SPELLING

Language and writing have moved on, so the forms of name adopted in this book have been guided entirely by modern usage. There is no agreed authority on how these names should now be spelt. The English alphabet does not include some of the letters and possibly the sounds used to represent the names. The names used here have been adopted simply as an aid to reading and comprehension. There is neither logic nor consistency in these choices. The choice is pragmatic.

To avoid confusion, Harold Godwinson, King of England, is called Harold with an 'o', while Harald, King of Norway is referred to as Harald with an 'a'.

There are two Olafs in this story. They were both Viking raiders. The first is Tryggvasson, who took Christianity to Norway and united the north. The second, Olaf Haraldsson, was Harald's half-brother, and later became known as Saint Olaf.

USE OF NICKNAMES

These have generally been used. When they came into use cannot always be determined. The motive for adopting nicknames is to make it easier to identify the key players.

Some, such as Ethelred 'Unraed', which translates as 'no counsel', were probably near-contemporary. But there are no contemporary references to King Harald of Norway being called 'Hardrada' or 'hard ruler', perhaps because none exist. This does not mean that the nickname was not in use when its owner was alive. We see William of Normandy being called William the Bastard by a Norman monk soon after his death and it is hard to believe the tag was intended as a compliment to his memory.

The term 'aetheling' is reserved for its original sense, which equates to a modern title such as 'heir apparent' or perhaps 'crown prince' to indicate an official designation. If the course of history ran straight and true, these aethelings would have become kings or queens, but many never converted their title.

DATES

The dates used are those the participants might have recognised had they possessed a calendar. I am reliant on the unnamed scholars who have, over the centuries, converted the date references in the texts that have survived for us to study. These dates were specified in terms of the ecclesiastical calendar which, thanks to the excellent record-keeping by clerks in holy orders, allow us to provide some key dates.

The reforms to the date system, caused by a miscalculation in the need for leap years, were many centuries away in 1066. Because the seasons did not respect the calendar devised by man, it might be convenient to add six days to the dates used in the book to appreciate the seasonal-equivalent date. This has been done when carrying out the tidal calculation referred to in the text. You might find the dates quoted in some sources prior to 1753 differ by up to eleven days.

On Thursday 4 October 1582 Pope Gregory XIII decreed that the following day would be Friday 15 October. Most Catholic countries obeyed but it was ignored by the Eastern Orthodox church and most Protestant countries. Between 1700 and 1753, northern Europe switched to the Gregorian calendar, with Great Britain and its colonies, including America, being the last of this batch to switch. This date-jump accounts for many of the date discrepancies.

At the same time, it was agreed that the year began on 1 January, as determined by the Roman calendar. The legal year used to begin on 25 March. To avoid landowners losing any rent, the legal year was moved to take account of the lost eleven days, giving us 5 April as the start of the tax year. Because the Orthodox Church in Russia used the Julian calendar, their October revolution of 1917 took place in November.

I have checked most of the dates where original sources can be found. I am disappointed to report that I frequently computed a date or days of the week that disagreed with other published sources. It was also possible to find several dates reported in these secondary sources. I have not been consistent and have sometimes deferred to the majority view.

The timeline provides the dates used in compiling this book. I recognise that some of the dates will be wrong but would argue that in many cases precision is not vital. It probably does not matter if somebody was appointed to a role but did not actually arrive until the following spring. However, it is vital to know not only the day but the time when Harold, King of England and Harald, King of Norway set out for Stamford Bridge.

QUOTATIONS

Full quotations have been set apart, but where they are a part of the sentence they are included within the flow of text. Any words inserted into the quotations for the purpose of clarity are enclosed in square brackets. On a few occasions, the convention of multiple full stops [...] is included where a piece of text is omitted from a quotation.

Dateline

Timetable Autumn, 1066		*=conjectured or uncertain Julian date + 6 = Gregorian date
28 December 1065		Abbey Minster of St Peter consecrated, with Queen Edith and Earl Harold 'dux et subregulus' present
January		
3		Edward slips into coma
5	Thurs	The dying king has a fit but wakes and makes final dispositions and relates his prophecy of doom
6	Epiphany	Funeral and coronation have to rushed to be completed before the end of the Christmas festival
20*		William's ambassador tells King Harold that his 'usurpation' will be challenged
30*		Harold rejects William's demands, effectively accepting that they are going to fight

February		
5★		Gilbert sent as legate to ask for papal blessing on an enterprise to punish King Harold
15★		The leading lords of Normandy agree support but ask William to call a counsel of all knights to get their assent for an overseas attack
20★		Second Norman ambassador demands Harold marry William's daughter as agreed
★		Tostig heads to visit his cousin, King Sweyn of Denmark, seeking support
25★		Harold and Bishop Wulfstan head to York
March		
Early★		Tostig moves on to persuade King Harald of Norway to invade England
1★		Northumbrian Witan is swayed by Wulfstan to support Harold and England
Mid-★		Tostig with King Harald in Norway
Mid-★		Wedding ceremony and festivities in York for Harold's marriage
		Harold tours Northumbria to cement loyalty
Late★		War token sent to summon Norwegian levy
April		
Spring		Tostig sails back to Flanders from Norway
16		King Harold back at Westminster
20★		Tostig attacks Isle of Wight
24		The 'hairy star' appears
May		
Mid-★		Tostig attacks and holds Sandwich after raiding south coast
Late★		Tostig leaves Sandwich when Harold mobilises and starts raiding
Late★		Progressive mobilisation of fyrd begins

June		
Mid-★		Tostig's raids defeated by response of Mercian and Northumbrian armies
Late★		Tostig reaches Scotland
July		
Mid-★		King Harold's army installed on Isle of Wight
August		
12		William's fleet is completed and gathers in the estuary of the river Dives
30★		King Harald's fleet sets sail from the Solunds, Norway, with 200 warships and many supply vessels
September		Harvest time starts
8		King Harold releases his army after the summer and autumn waiting on the Isle of Wight
12		Harold's fleet leaves the Isle of Wight
12		William's fleet attempts to cross the Channel but is driven into St Valery-sur-Somme
11/12		King Harald of Norway visits Orkney and Shetland Isles. His fleet swells to 300 longships
14★	Thurs	The Norse fleet makes landfall, probably somewhere near Tynemouth
17★	Sun	Scarborough is attacked and burnt
18★	Mon	Holderness, the base of one of the northern earls, is destroyed; Riccall occupied
19	Tues	King Harald re-boards the ships and rides the tides to Riccall on the river Ouse
19★	Tues	News of the northern invasion reaches Harold
20	Wed	King Harald of Norway defeats the combined army of the northern earls at Fulford
21★	Thurs	Southern army sets out. 10 hours x 8kph = 80km x 4 days = 320 km
22	Fri	King Harold gets news of defeat at Fulford

23	Sat	Feast at Riccall for victors
24	Sun	King Harald parades army and accepts the submission of York
24	Sun	King Harold II arrives in York in the evening and takes steps to ensure that the presence of his army, resting at Tadcaster, is kept quiet
25	Mon	King Harold defeats and kills Harald and Tostig at Stamford Bridge
26	Tues	
27	Wed	William's fleet sails from the Somme at dusk
28	Thurs	William lands near Pevensey after a night crossing of the Channel
29	Fri	William moves along the coast to Hastings
30	Sat	
October		
2★	Mon	News of William's landing reaches Harold
3	Tues	
4	Wed	
5	Thurs	
6	Fri	Harold reaches London
7	Sat	
8	Sun	
9	Mon	
10	Tues	
11	Wed	Harold leaves London
12	Thurs	
13	Fri	The English muster on the valley road some 10km from William's camp
14	Sat	Battle with Norman invaders results in the death of Harold II and much of the south Saxon nobility

Timeline

	English kings	Godwinsons	Other	Norse
911			Normandy granted to Rollo	
947			William finally establishes control of Val-ès-Dunes near Caen	
950			William marries and is placed under an interdict by Pope Leo IX	
968	Ethelred born?		Leofric, future earl of Mercia, born	
975	King Edgar dies on 8 July			
978	King Edward the Martyr is killed; the boy Ethelred becomes king on 18 March			
982	Ethelred marries Aelfgyva			

	English kings	Godwinsons	Other	Norse
985			Ethelred's mother, Aelfthryth, sent away	
986			Sweyn becomes king of Denmark (and Norway) after death of his father, Harold Bluetooth	
987			Louis V, last Carolingian king, dies; Hugh Capet becomes king of France, 3 July	
988			Sweyn Forkbeard overthrows his father, King Harold Bluetooth Gormsson, King of Denmark	
991			Viking raids in Kent; battle of Maldon	
993		Godwin born?		
994		Cnut born?	Viking raids on London repulsed; south-east raided; Olaf Trygvasson converts to Christianity, sponsored by King Ethelred	Olaf Trygvasson and Sweyn of Denmark raid London, September 8
995			Olaf Trygvasson proclaimed king of Norway in the autumn; Olaf Haraldsson born	
996			Richard I of Normandy dies	

	English kings	Godwinsons	Other	Norse
998			Viking raids	
1000				Olaf Trygvasson drowns rather than risk capture
1002	Aelfgyva, Ethelred's first wife, dies; Ethelred marries Emma, daughter of Richard, Count of Normandy		13 November: St Bryce's Day massacre; 17 November: Elfrida, mother of Ethelred, dies at Wherwell	
1005	Edward born to Ethelred and Emma(?)	Palace revolution?	Macbeth born	
1006			Aelfgyva's father, Aelthelm, murdered by Eadric. Her brothers were later blinded	
1007			£36,000 Danegeld paid	
1008			Fleet of 300 ordered with Eadric the Acquisitor	
1009			Thorkell the Tall invades	
1011		Wulfnoth rebels?	Vikings capture Canterbury and in a drunken rage murder the Archbishop, Aelfheah, who had earlier baptised Olaf Trygvasson	

	English kings	Godwinsons	Other	Norse
1012			£48,000 Danegeld paid: Thorkell the Tall and 45 ships hired to defend east coast, perhaps in response to Aelfheah's murder	Olaf Haraldsson receives confirmation from St Alphege, Bishop of Winchester
1013	Sweyn subdues England	Ethelred into exile	Sweyn lands in August and western thanes submit at Bath	
1014	Sweyn's sudden death on 3 February; Ethelred returns	Godwin has lands restored	Olaf Haraldsson hired to defend east coast; hostages mutilated by Cnut, who returns to Denmark (April); 25 June: Aetheling Athelstan makes will and dies soon after	
1015	August: Cnut returns with fleet	Harold Harefoot born?	Harald of Norway born	
1016	Ethelred dies in April; Edmund Ironside dies in November; Cnut takes over after battle of Assandun	Cnut arranges the murder of Earl Uthred at Wiheal	Spring: Edmund's resistance	
1017	2 July: Emma returns to marry Cnut		Four English earldoms created	

	English kings	Godwinsons	Other	Norse
1018	£82,500 Danegeld paid to King Cnut who feels secure enough to send the invasion fleet back to Denmark with a payment of £72,000	Harthacnut born	Climate improves; Harold II of Denmark (*c.*994-1018) dies	The English preoccupied, allowing Malcolm III of Scotland to avenge defeat at Durham by winning the battle of Carham
1019	Cnut in Denmark to secure throne	Godwin helps Cnut suppress Danish rebellion following the death of his brother Harald. Cnut becomes king of Denmark		Cnut on Danish throne
1020		Godwin's daughter Edith born		
1021	Cnut returns and outlaws his regent, Thorkell			
1022			Cnut's daughter buried at Bosham, after dying in an accident aged eight	
1023	Cnut takes his son Harthacnut to be king in Denmark			Thorkell made regent for the three-year-old Harthacnut
1024				Magnus, son of Olaf, born
1025	Cnut in Denmark			Cnut's brother-in-law, Ulf, takes over as regent; Cnut 'driven off' at Holy River battle by Norway and Sweden

	English kings	Godwinsons	Other	Norse
1026			Richard II of Normandy dies (Emma's brother), succeeded by Richard III	Ulf murdered for conspiracy with Swedes and Norwegians
1027		Harold born?	William the Conqueror born in Normandy in September; Richard III of Normandy dies, succeeded by Robert	Cnut's pilgrimage to Rome directly from Denmark, perhaps as a penance; he attends the coronation of Emperor Conrad II
1028		Cnut conquers Norway with a fleet of fifty ships from England and a deal of bribery, and becomes king of Norway	Henry, son of Conrad, Holy Roman Emperor, betrothed to Cnut's daughter Gunhild; Richard III murdered(?); Robert I becomes duke of Normandy	
1029		Tostig born	Hakon, regent of Norway, drowned; Aelfgyva appointed regent for her son, Sweyn	
1030	Cnut defeats Olaf at battle of Stiklestad: Harald exiled			Death of King Olaf of Norway on 29 July
1031	Cnut's second trip to Rome; expedition to Scotland			

	English kings	Godwinsons	Other	Norse
1034				Fresh revolt in Norway forces Aelfgyva to flee: Harald reaches Constantinople
1035	Cnut dies on 12 November at Shaftesbury		July: Robert of Normandy dies at Nicaea, returning from pilgrimage to the Holy Land	Magnus becomes king of Norway
1036	Harold Harefoot takes full control after death of brother Sweyn	Edward and Alfred attack their half-brother Harold Harefoot	Gunhild, Cnut and Emma's daughter, marries future Emperor Henry III; Sweyn, Cnut's son by Aelfgyva, dies	
1037	Harold accepted as king		Alfred, Emma's son, is captured by Godwin and dies	
1039			Harthacnut makes a deal with Magnus of Norway and sails to Bruges	
1040	Harold Harefoot dies; Harthacnut becomes king			
1041	Edward returns from exile and is 'sworn as king'			
1042	Harthacnut dies at Lambeth; Edward's reign begins on 8 June			Magnus assumes kingdom of Denmark after Harthacnut's death
1043	April 3: Edward's coronation at Winchester		Emma deprived of her treasury	

	English kings	Godwinsons	Other	Norse
1044			Fleet at Sandwich after invasion alert from Magnus of Norway	
1045	Edward marries Edith Godwinson on 23 January	Harold marries Edith Swanneck	Magnus of Norway fights battle at Helganes. Winter: Harald marries Elizabeth, the Ruse princess	
1046			Harald's breach with Sweyn of Sweden	King Magnus of Norway offers Harald joint kingship
1047			Sweyn, nephew of Earl Godwin, is named as king of Denmark in Magnus' will: William and the king of France win the battle of Val-ès-Dunes, securing Normandy; Eustace II, Count of Boulogne, takes over after death of father	Magnus of Norway dies on 25 October; Harald becomes sole king
1048				Harald takes Thora, daughter of Thorberg Arnason
1049			Papal council at Rheims; Edward's sister, Godgifu, married to Eustace II, dies	

	English kings	Godwinsons	Other	Norse
1050		Macbeth in Rome for papal jubilee		
1051	Cinque Ports established	Tostig marries Judith in Flanders	Godwinsons exiled after 21 September	
1052		Return of Godwin family from exile on 14 September; Sweyn, the eldest son, dies returning from pilgrimage on 29 September	Edgar Aetheling born (son of Edward the Exile); Stigand made Archbishop of Canterbury when his Norman predecessor, Robert of Jumièges, flees	
1053		Easter: Earl Godwin dies	William of Normandy and Matilda married	
1054			Siward tries to oust Macbeth. His son Osbeorn and nephew are killed	
1055		Aelfgar, Earl of East Anglia, exiled on 19 March; Tostig given Northumbrian earldom; Aelfgar and Gruffydd raid Hereford but a peaceful settlement leads to Aelfgar's restoration	Siward of Northumbria dies on 26 March	

	English kings	Godwinsons	Other	Norse
1057		Earl Leofric of Mercia dies on 31 August	Edward the Exile dies on 19 April just after returning to England; Macbeth killed at battle of Lumphanan Malcolm III crowned at Scone on 25 April	
1058		New earl of Mercia, Aelfgar, outlawed again but is restored with help of Norsemen, under command of young Magnus	Stigand excommunicated when Benedict X declared anti-pope	
1059		Malcolm III of Scotalnd visits King Edward	Pope Nicholas II makes the de Hauteville family dukes of Apulia; Benedict X driven out with Norman help; William and Matilda make peace with Pope	
1060		Abbey at Waltham consecrated on 3 May		
1061		Tostig and Judith go with delegation to Rome. Back in the autumn?	Conquests by Roger I to capture Sicily from the Arabs begin	
1062			King Harald has a great ship built	

	English kings	Godwinsons	Other	Norse
1063		5 August: Gruffydd killed	Harald wins Danish/Norwegian sea-battle of river Nissa; William conquers Maine	
1064		Harold's trip to Normandy; Gamel and Ulf complain to Tostig about taxes and are killed	Walter III, Count of Mantes, last surviving nephew of King Edward, dies a captive of William	Thorfinn, Earl of Orkney, dies, and territory in Scotland reverts to chieftains; Gospatric murdered on 28 December
1065	28 December: Westminster Abbey dedicated	Harold invades south Wales in late summer after Gruffydd raids Chepstow; Tostig invites Edward to hunt on his land; northern insurrection starts on 3 October; Tostig exiled	Over 200 senior thanes meet in York on 3 October and rebellion begins; confrontation in Oxford on 28 October	Harold concedes; Harald and Sweyn reach peace deal
1066	Edward dies on 5 January; coronation of Harold on 6 January	Harold marries Gruffydd's widow Edith	*Vita Edwardii* probably written	
1067			*Carmen de Hastingae* probably written	
1069			Edgar Aetheling in revolt against king, along with Sweyn, Morcar and Earls Waltheof and Gospatrick; Harrying of the North	

	English kings	Godwinsons	Other	Norse
1070		Papal agent issues penitential terms for William's soldiers	Harrying of the North continues	
1075		Queen Edith dies on 18 December	'Revolt of the Earls'; Waltheof beheaded after a revolt	
1082			Eustace II dies	
1083			Queen Matilda dies	
1086			Edgar Aetheling is again in revolt	
1087	William dies in Rouen on 9 September			
1093			King Maclolm and his son die in battle with William Rufus; Queen Margaret dies	
1094		Wulfnoth, the last of Godwin's children, dies a captive		
1097			Bishop Odo dies	
1125	Edgar Aetheling dies in exile			

Maps and Genealogical Tables

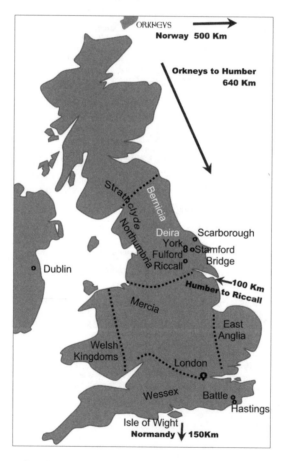

1 Outline of England in 1066. The boundaries between the main earldoms were not fixed.

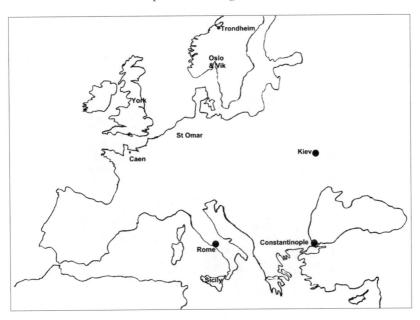

2 The Mediterranean and north Europe at the time of Harald Sigurdson.

3 The rulers of England's neighbours in 1066.

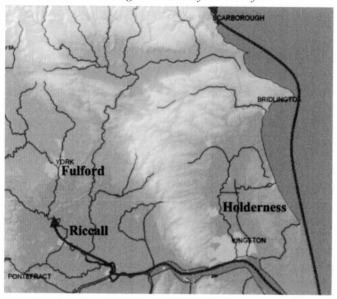

4 The Yorkshire rivers and high ground provided one obvious route to York from the coast. However, the invaders after landing at Scarborough did not move inland but raided down to Holderness before re-boarding their longships to ride the spring tidal flows to Riccall, within easy striking distance from York.

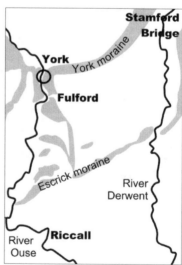

5 The glacial heritage that formed the ford, cut by Germany Beck, is apparent from the surface evidence left by the retreating ice. At Fulford, the water trapped by the hard moraine material escapes to the river Ouse. The moraines also illustrate the parallel routes leading to Stamford Bridge.

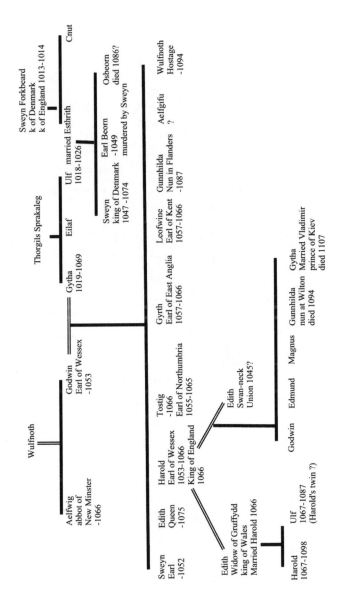

6 The Godwin family

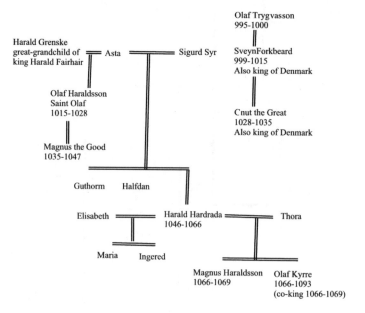

7 Kings of Norway

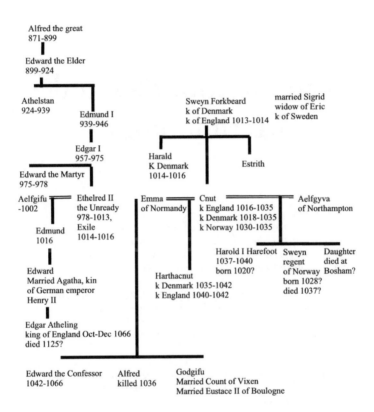

Alfred the great
871-899

Edward the Elder
899-924

Athelstan
924-939

Edmund I
939-946

Edgar I
957-975

Edward the Martyr
975-978

Sweyn Forkbeard
k of Denmark
k of England 1013-1014

married Sigrid
widow of Eric
k of Sweden

Harald
K Denmark
1014-1016

Estrith

Aelfgifu
-1002

Ethelred II
the Unready
978-1013,
Exile
1014-1016

Edmund
1016

Emma
of Normandy

Cnut
k England 1016-1035
k Denmark 1018-1035
k Norway 1030-1035

Aelfgyva
of Northampton

Harold I Harefoot
1037-1040
born 1020?

Sweyn
regent
of Norway
born 1028?
died 1037?

Daughter
died at
Bosham?

Edward
Married Agatha, kin
of German emperor
Henry II

Harthacnut
k Denmark 1035-1042
k England 1040-1042

Edgar Atheling
king of England Oct-Dec 1066
died 1125?

Edward the Confessor
1042-1066

Alfred
killed 1036

Godgifu
Married Count of Vixen
Married Eustace II of Boulogne

8 Lineage of Alfred

Literary Sources and Methodology

I learnt a lot about historical sources when I transcribed my grandfather's trench diary. He kept a record while digging his way towards the coast of Flanders in early 1915 and somehow survived in what became the Ypres salient. I had an opportunity to compare his journal with the contemporary war record held in the Regimental Museum in Aberdeen.

As a novice, I was surprised that many dates did not tally. Key events were often recorded for different days, but there was a pattern. For example, the death of a member of my grandfather's platoon might not be recorded at HQ until the following day.

My grandfather, a cabinetmaker by trade, sharpened his pencil before making each entry, so I could see where each entry began and if it covered a few days because the soft pencil quickly lost its sharp point. He had clearly taken out his penknife to make his point and record the spectacular sight of a Zeppelin being shot down in front of his trench. The regimental war diary had it recorded on a different day. When I checked the German records I was provided with a third date for this unique event.

Professional historians attempt to apply tests to documents to assess their accuracy. The first rule is that the record should be made as soon after the event as possible, so any direct observations contained in letters or reports are deemed highly credible. I quickly learned that it was necessary to form a judgment on a balance of all the available evidence, but accept that an element of uncertainty will often remain.

I was also struck by the use of the word 'authorities' in earlier works of history. In this context, the word 'authority' has implications with which I am not happy. The modern term is 'sources', with a distinction being drawn between primary and derivative writings. However, my grandfather showed me that those observing events can see and record different things. There were, sadly, no equivalents to my grandfather at the battle of Fulford.

What this taught me was to take on board as much data as possible and accept that it was my responsibility to extract a coherent story. What I have tried to do below is list the sources used and how they were assessed.

ANCIENT SOURCE MATERIAL

The Nordic Sagas

All the Nordic sagas have been used, especially *Heimskringla* or 'The Chronicle of the Kings of Norway', as recorded by Snorri Sturluson. Snorri was a lawyer by training and rose to be the lawspeaker in Iceland around 1200. He was well travelled, meeting other Scandinavian lawyers of his time. He was the author of many works and an early social theorist.

Several versions and translations of the sagas were used and some sections were re-translated when it became important to understand whether the writer was referring to a ditch, dyke or marsh. The Online Medieval and Classical Library (http://sunsite.berkeley.edu/OMACL/Heimskringla) was especially useful.

Interpretation is important when examining the sagas, as the excerpt below illustrates. The first part is accurate, possibly because the subjects were of Nordic stock. However, the listing of the children of Earl Godwin is inaccurate, but nevertheless interesting because of some of the details it suggests.

> Edward, Ethelred's son, was king of England after his brother Hardacanute. He was called Edward the Good; and so he was. King Edward's mother was Queen Emma, daughter of Richard, earl of Rouen. Her brother was Earl Robert, whose son was William the Bastard, who at that time was earl at Rouen in Normandy. King Edward's queen was Gyda, a daughter of Earl Godwin, the son of Ulfnad. Gyda's brothers were, Earl Toste, the eldest; Earl Morukare the next; Earl Walter the third; Earl Svein the fourth; and the fifth was Harald, who was the youngest, and he was brought up at King Edward's court, and was his foster-son. The king loved him very much, and kept him as his own son; for he had no children.

I agree with Kelly DeVries' favourable assessment of the Nordic tradition and its value as a historic source. He quotes the compiler of the *Heimskringla*, Snorri, who opens his chronicle with the following observation on his own methodology: 'In this book I let be written old narratives about rulers… which I have heard from well-informed men, also certain histories of previous generations as they were taught to me.' Snorri also encapsulates the dilemma of every historian when he recognises the need to exercise his judgment: 'And although we do not know the truth of these, we know that old, learned men judged such to be true.'

But, referring to the many tales surrounding King Harald of Norway, Snorri notes 'these came not as history and these were not included, because we will not put unsubstantiated stories into this book'. Other recorders of the sagas took a different approach: 'Although we have heard, many things talked about, and even circumstantially related, yet we think it better that something may be added to, than that it should be necessary to take something away from our narrative.' The point is that these writers are open about the approach they are adopting. This allows the reader to assess the credibility.

It is perhaps a shame that the term 'saga' has attached it to the recording of a rich oral tradition. There is certainly nothing pejorative in the word 'saga'. The OED suggest that a saga is just a 'long, involved story'. It is unfortunate that many scholars have seen the oral poetic format as less reliable than western forms, even though inserting verse into the narratives was common during the transition from oral to written records.

The Anglo-Saxon Chronicles

In the popular mind, the *Anglo-Saxon Chronicles* are a single, homogenous document. They actually consist of six major manuscripts and two fragments. Versions D and E are classified as northern in origin in contrast to A, which is believed to have been written at Winchester.

Version E has been traced as the source for many of the derivative works. Henry of Huntingdon, John of Worcester and William of Malmesbury probably used it as a key source for their histories. This version was also copied from an original document that has been lost. Because they have been rewritten, we cannot exclude the possibility that they have been censored. There are several additions of local events, and it was updated until 1154. Written in Peterborough, it is now located at the Bodleian Library, Oxford.

The chronicles have a very limited focus. They were written by clerks in holy orders who brought their bias to the perceived significance of events. There is much more about bishops than about kings in these chronicles. Success or failure is often expressed in terms of the effect an event had on the Church. So the views expressed by these chroniclers cannot be taken as definitive. However, the chronicles provide a wonderful skeleton for our story and scholars have been able to provide dates for many of the events by interpreting the ecclesiastic calendar. The matter of dating is discussed later.

The version of the chronicle is only mentioned when it is relevant, and the term 'chronicler' implies that the source is the *Anglo-Saxon Chronicles*.

Vitae Edwardii Regis

This work was commissioned by the dowager queen, Edith. The writer would have had access to Edith's views, and after 1068 also those of her mother Gytha and possibly other women, following their exile to St Omer in Flanders where this work was written. Edith commissioned the book in order to put across the Godwinson family view, just as her predecessor, Queen Emma, had commissioned her *Encomium* to justify her actions. Both must therefore be read as pre-digested history.

Historia Ecclesiae Dunelinensis

Composed by Symeon of Durham, this history provides a readable commentary of many of the events around 1066 but neglects Fulford completely. This is sad, as Symeon is otherwise a good commentator on northern affairs. Henry of Huntingdon, writing perhaps ninety years after the battle, says that the battle site is still visible, although his limited text is taken from version E of the *Anglo-Saxon Chronicle*. However, this monk might have had cause to travel from his base in Lincoln to York and the best route would take him through Fulford. So the additional comments he makes are valuable.

Ecclesiastical Historii

Orderic Vitalis was the son of an English mother and a priest from Orléans. When he was sent to Normandy to train for monastic life at the age of ten, he records that he felt like an exile as he spoke no Norman. 'And so, a boy of ten, I crossed the English Channel and came into Normandy as an exile, unknown to all and knowing no-one. Like Joseph in Egypt, I heard a language which I did not understand... In place of my English name, which sounded harsh to the Normans, the name of Vitalis was given to me.' What his history illustrates is just how 'English' the conquerors had already become. Orderic Vitalis tries hard to be objective, analytical and informative but was reliant on Norman sources covering the events of 1066.

The Carmen de Hastingae Proelio (Song of the Battle of Hastings)

This is a poem of which approximately 800 lines survive. It is attributed to Guy, Bishop of Amiens, who was an intimate of William's court, and it was completed in time for Matilda's coronation in May 1068 but could have been composed a year earlier. Sadly, the manuscript of the *Carmen* was lost early in the twelfth century and not rediscovered until 1826.

Orderic Vitalis speaks of the bishop as composing a poem 'abusing and condemning Harold but praising and exalting William', which I take as his commentary on the bias in the *Carmen*. However, it does provide a Norman perspective. Subsequent Norman writers such as William of Poitiers put flattery and storytelling above any need for historical accuracy and these writers are regarded as unreliable.

In the generations after the Norman Conquest a strong interest in history emerged in England. The early historians are able to contribute much to our understanding of the later Norman period but rely on the *Anglo-Saxon Chronicles* for much of their information before that time. The twelfth century was a good time for chroniclers. William of Malmesbury produced *Gesta Regum Anglorum* in 1125. Henry of Huntington completed his *Historia Anglorii* about 1139.

However, these ambitious projects had to please their patrons. They also introduced legends, anecdotes and amusing stories to leaven the accurate but stodgy style of Bede in his *Historia Ecclesiastica Gentis Anglorum* or the scribes of the various *Anglo-Saxon Chronicles*. Henry, for example, tells the tale about Cnut commanding the tide not to rise to illustrate the king's awareness that his power was limited. We are indebted to Geoffrey of Monmouth not only for *Historia Regum Britanniae* but for the story of King Lear.

In summary, all the ancient sources are worth studying but need to be interpreted with caution. The Norman bias is evident in them all. Only the early chroniclers, the Nordic sagas and perhaps Orderic Vitalis are impartial in their commentary on the events of 1066.

MODERN WORKS OF SCHOLARSHIP EMPLOYED

DeVries, Kelly, *The Norwegian Invasion of England in 1066,* Boydell & Brewer. This brilliant work of scholarship provides the definitive analysis of the literary sources covering the events of 1065 and 1066.

Barlow, Frank, *The Godwins,* Pearson. An exhaustive analysis of the data that can be traced relating to the rise and fall of the house of Godwin.

Fletcher, Richard, *Bloodfeud: Murder and Revenge in Anglo-Saxon England,* Allen Lane. Richard Fletcher points out in this wonderful piece of detective work that it is only through the survival of a legal paper in which the cathedral church in Durham was concerned that we have any record of the feud that led to the deaths of the nobility of Northumbria for two generations. This illustrates that history studies what it can. If one wants to be free from this constraint then one must use inference or parallels to fill the many gaps in the ancient narrative. Such synthesis has been attempted in places.

Walker, Ian, *Mercia And the Making of England*, Sutton Publishing. A wonderful analysis of the literary sources that illustrates just how much it is possible to reconstruct of the way the kingdom of England was formed, in the two centuries before the Norman invasion, by intelligent use of the limited evidence.

Underwood, Dr Richard, *Anglo-Saxon Weapons and Warfare*, Tempus. Based on thorough research of the ancient literature, the book brings some understanding, based on re-enactment and metalwork, to how fighting took place from the departure of the Romans until the coming of the Normans.

Rex, Peter, *English Resistance, The Underground War against the Normans*, Tempus. A scholarly analysis of the literature that demonstrated the extensive resistance to the establishment of Norman rule throughout England after 'the conquest' of 1066.

Williams, Ann, *The English and the Norman Conquest*, Boydell & Brewer. Studying the survivors. This work is informative about their earlier performance.

Butler, Denis, *1066: The Story of a Year*, Anthony Blond. This is set out like a diary but is a work of scholarship that was among the first to break with the Norman version of events.

Stenton, Sir Frank, *Anglo-Saxon England* (The Oxford History of England), Oxford: Clarendon Press. A 'must-read' for any student and a good starting point for debate.

Tacitus, *On Britain and Germany*. Some well-observed comments on the Germanic peoples who would fill the vacuum left by the departing Romans.

Beowulf, especially the translation by Seamus Heaney. Provides an insight into the mind and motives of a warrior.

McLynn, Frank, *1066*, Jonathan Cape. Provides an excellent perspective on the key players and events, culminating in the battles.

A.H. Inman, *Domesday Feudal Statistics*, Kennikat. Figures can be fun. Because the available sources are remiss in providing us with the sizes of armies, Inman makes an attempt to model these, based on the economy of the time.

TIDAL CALCULATIONS

The Hydrographer to the Navy was extremely helpful at an early stage of the research with calculations of the tides of 1066. Since then, they have produced an excellent web-based tide calculator to allow everybody, for a modest fee, to work out the tide around the world for many dates in history:
http://easytide.ukho.gov.uk/easytide/EasyTide/index.aspx.

I must also thank the RNLI coxswain at Spurn Head for explaining to me how the longships might have made it to Riccall, plus the various river pilots and workers of the British Waterways who explained to me the working of the rivers Humber and Ouse.

THE INTERNET

The ability to discover or double-check dates or facts has been invaluable, especially for a student such as myself who works outside the support structure of a seat of learning.

However, it was necessary to sort out where conjecture or opinion are masquerading as fact. Using the web, it was fun to trace some errors or flights of fancy as they were embellished by other sites. It turned out to be straightforward to sort out the historians from the storytellers. Because a significant proportion of the contributions found on the web contained errors, it stimulated the need to double- or triple-check the sources. The web produces the problem but also provides the solution.

The web is packed with material and is a credit to the authors who are freely contributing their work for the benefit of others. I am immensely grateful to the hundreds of contributors I have used and especially the Scandinavian writers who write in English or have made a translation available. It was clear from the beginning that it was going to be impractical to give all of the references. This was not designed as that sort of work.

The open source Wikipedia was a valuable resource for checking facts. I was particularly impressed to find my own words extensively reported! However, this discovery reminded me of how one person's interpretation can easily become the received wisdom and I was happy to discover that the site provides the opportunity to challenge the content.

At the stage when I was double-checking this book's details, Google Books Search became available. This saved weeks of work in libraries with the attendant frustration when the book required is out on loan. Not only can Google now list the relevant references but it can also take you to the vital pages. In a matter of minutes it was possible to find several books to check a name, date, place or sequence of events within the body of scholarship that can now be searched. I adjusted the statements about the Witan and Earl Aelfgar's second period of exile to incorporate the additional information I uncovered.

FURTHER READING AND REFERENCES

Hunter Blair, Peter, *An Introduction to Anglo-Saxon England*, Cambridge University Press
Jones, Gwyn, A *History of the Vikings*, Oxford University Press
Hollister, C.W., *Anglo-Saxon Military Institutions*
East Yorkshire History Society, Collected Papers
Cameron, Kenneth, *English Place Names*, Batsford
Malmer, Brita, *King Canute's Coinage in Northern Countries*, paper, University
    College London
Abels, Richard P., *Lordship and Military Obligation in Anglo-Saxon England*
Levick, Ben, *Regia Anglorum Publications*
Crossley-Holland, Kevin, *The Anglo-Saxon World*
Attenborough, F.L., *The Laws of the Earliest English Kings*
Hyland, Ann, *The Horse in the Middle Ages,* Sutton
Lloyd, Alan, *The Year of Conquest,* Longmans, Green and Co. Ltd
Lyser, Henrietta, *A Social History of Women in England 450-1500*, Phoenix Press

PHYSICAL EVIDENCE

Ancient battlefields require a different sort of archaeology. The battle of Fulford leaves very little mark on the landscape and the recycling appears to have been very good so there are few traces to mark the event. Much work remains to be done to investigate the battlefield scientifically. The forensic investigation required on such ancient sites has yet to be undertaken. Indeed, the techniques required are still being discussed, but at last this is being done by academics and not being left to local antiquarians.

Much work has been done gathering artefacts and probing the land, to discover the surface over which the battle was fought. The landscape of 1066 revealed by all the core samples matches the one literary source that describes the site. The cyclical nature of the tides and the seasons has also helped to confirm, interpret or question the written record.

Applying a reality check to the claims made in the literature is one of the themes running through these pages. The tales about 1066 have had almost a millennium to 'develop' in the literature. The physical reality exposes some of the narrative to criticism and on a number of occasions suggests that an alternative explanation is more likely.

SUMMARY

Professor Richard Fletcher, writing in his historical investigative thriller *Bloodfeud*, writes:

> Common sense is prone to assert that 'the facts speak for themselves'. Historians know that this is just what they don't do. Facts have to be coaxed and entreated into utterance. And if they are to speak, however hesitantly, however indistinctly, however obscurely, they have to be scrutinised against a background, a setting, in a context.

The test that has been applied to all data is the 'balance of probability' rather than 'beyond reasonable doubt'. To continue with the judicial analogy, this book is a synthesis of the written as well as the physical evidence. It is designed more as court report than as a tedious transcript of the case. The credibility of some witnesses is questioned above and sometimes within the text, but ultimately it is up to the jury to decide if the case has been convincingly reported and to form their own view on these events.

The story can be told in many ways but I hope that the facts reported here are accurate. I have tried to ensure that it is always made clear when facts are replaced by opinion. When you encounter the words 'could', 'might' or 'probably', be prepared, as you are being invited to enter some speculation.

The role adopted here is one of commentator. The evidence has been assembled and assessed. Many views have been examined and tested against the latest information available. But in the end a picture is painted as clearly as possible. This must be accepted as one interpretation. Many details of this fateful day in 1066 and many of the events surrounding it will never be known for certain.

To return to my personal narrative, I recently read the diary of another army sergeant, this time from the Second World War. He was sent to find a site where his mechanical engineers could build a defensive position in the western desert. He looked at a few locations but in the end he chose the railway halt at El Alamein. Days of searching in the National Archives and studying many history books failed to reveal the name of anybody else who claimed to site this iconic defensive line. History has many loose ends, which is what makes it such fun.

List of Illustrations

Maps and Genealogical Tables

Index